# GOOD NEIGHBORS

# GOOD NEIGHBORS

## THE DEMOCRACY OF EVERYDAY LIFE
## IN AMERICA

*Nancy L. Rosenblum*

Princeton University Press

*Princeton and Oxford*

Jacket images, from the top: 1. Watercolor drawing "Indian Village of
Secoton" by John White (created 1585–1586): © The Trustees of the
British Museum. 2. New York tenements, 1900; courtesy of the
Library of Congress. 3. Aerial view of suburban housing
development, San Antonio, Texas, by David Sucsy/Getty

Jacket design by Pamela Lewis Schnitter

Library of Congress Cataloging-in-Publication Data

Names: Rosenblum, Nancy L. (Nancy Lipton), 1947–author.
Title: Good neighbors : the democracy of everyday life
in America / Nancy L. Rosenblum.
Description: Princeton, New Jersey : Princeton University Press, 2016. |
Includes bibliographical references and index.

Identifiers: LCCN 2015039738 | ISBN 9780691169439 (hardback : acid-free
paper)
Subjects: LCSH: Civil society—United States. | Democracy—Social
aspects—United States. | Neighborliness—United States. | BISAC:
PHILOSOPHY / Political. | PHILOSOPHY / Ethics & Moral Philosophy. |
POLITICAL SCIENCE / Civics & Citizenship. | POLITICAL SCIENCE /
History & Theory.

Classification: LCC JK1759 .R89 2016 | DDC 307.3/3620973—dc23 LC record
available at http://lccn.loc.gov/2015039738

British Library Cataloging-in-Publication Data is available

This book has been composed in Times Ten LT Std
and Berthold Akzidenz Grotesk

Printed on acid-free paper. ∞

Printed in the United States of America

1 3 5 7 9 10 8 6 4 2

FOR ROBERT JAY LIFTON,
LIVING SIDE BY SIDE IN WORK AND LOVE

# CONTENTS

# GOOD NEIGHBORS

# Good Neighbor Nation

### The Quality of the Day

Take good neighbor literally: people who live nearby and contribute to—or do not derange—the quality of life at home. Neighbors exhibit solicitude and hospitality but also unleash their demons on us, or in our view. Snobbery, betrayal, hypocrisy, and cruelty wreck our sleep, our nerves.[1] Relentlessly barking dogs, blaring televisions, incessant quarrels, an excess of domestic odors. Sounds that startle us at night and disturb our sleep. Bedraggled yards. Snooping and interfering. Killing time. Wounding reputation.

Myra, in Willa Cather's novel *My Mortal Enemy,* is beside herself on account of her upstairs neighbors:

> Why should I have the details of their stupid, messy existence thrust upon me all day long, and half the night? ...They tramp ... up there like cattle ... Their energy isn't worth anything so they use it up ... running about, beating my brains to jelly.[2]

Around home we are unguarded; we don't always think to arrange the face we present or to modulate our words and tone when we step out our door. Proximity creates cause and occasion for arguments, slights, acts of aggression. Family aside, we have no more constant or intimate stage for exhibiting graciousness or foul temper, or worse, than where we live.

Everyone is eager to tell a story about a neighbor and even at academic colloquia I receive unsolicited diatribes—for these are mostly accounts of adversarial encounters and good turns unreturned, costly runins and daily insults of noise or disarray, carelessness or abject social incompetence. The stories we tell reflect our bafflement, our incredulity at the misconduct or sheer obliviousness of the people next door. Even if the trouble is decades in the past and the neighbor has moved away, people narrate their stories at a high pitch—almost as if they are talking about cruelty or betrayal (as indeed they sometimes are). True, when friends sit down to report their trials we may think "how tedious." But our own neighbors are serious business.

*Of course* we tell our stories with feeling. Neighbors are not just people living nearby. Neighbors are our environment. They are the background to our private lives at home. When they give a sufficiently strong dose of themselves, they appear forcibly in our foreground. Bad neighbors diminish the quality of life materially and emotionally. That is, they diminish everyday life, everyday, where we live, at home. Hence the moral of Aesop's fable of Minerva: a house should be made movable, "by which means a bad neighborhood might be avoided."[3] Or this homely truth: "No man can live longer in peace than his Neighbour pleases."[4]

The unique power neighbors hold over our lives is explained in one word: they affect us where we live, at *home*. We have no exit. And at home we are uniquely vulnerable because of the stakes, the depth and intensity of the interests we have in quotidian private life there, and our expectation of control over our personal affairs behind the door. Not least our "sense of privacy itself . . . [as] something sacred in its own right."[5]

"Call one of the neighbors. Call the Morgans. Anyone will feed a dog if you ask them to," a wife assures her husband in Raymond Carver's story "A Small Good Thing." We value good neighbors, and the value we place on them comes from more than the grinding irritation and sometime dangerousness of bad ones. We can try to list the benefits and comforts we have in mind when we assure ourselves of "what anyone would do, here." Feed a dog. Watchful eyes over our property and children. Sweeping the building's common staircase. Closing the lid of the dumpster tightly. Knowing that in an emergency a nearby neighbor is likely to call for help or come to help. Often enough availability, not the act, is what counts.

We have a history of encounters with our neighbors and expectations that these will continue into the future. This inclines us to return good turns, even if that consists of nothing more than a wave or the standard, solicitous, but not insignificant, "How are you today?" We assess the rewards and the costs of offers and rebuffs all the time. The utility of reciprocity is certainly not lost on us, but a purely instrumental understanding of neighborliness leads us astray. Reciprocity, which provides a foothold on the difficult terrain of neighborliness, is mischaracterized if we see it as nothing more than strategic cooperation, a network of negotiated support. Instrumentalism is far from the whole of neighborly interactions. In fact, the dynamic works as often in reverse. Give and take may have little purpose except as a way of initiating and sustaining relations day to day. I am reminded of Thoreau's account of building his hut at Walden Pond:

> At length, in the beginning of May, with the help of some of my acquaintances, rather to improve so good an occasion for neighborliness than from any necessity, I set up the frame of my house.[6]

Good neighbors too are serious business. Anything is possible, from a nod of recognition to a spark of sympathy and interest, to the rare "unlooked for favor" that alters the day. We shouldn't underestimate the significance of mundane trespasses and kindnesses. The quotidian, local, and personal matter immensely.

If "the ruling passion in man ... [is] a gregarious instinct to keep together by minding each other's business,"[7] there is enormous latitude in the business neighbors have with one another. Some business is mundane, some life-changing and life-saving, but we shouldn't ignore the simple fact that our neighbors' affairs hold interest for us: "For what do we live," Mr. Bennet asked in *Pride and Prejudice*, "but to make sport for our neighbours and laugh at them in our turn?" Our interest may be to some purpose, or purely idle: "Georgie and Mother used to talk all the time. What about! ... They would talk about Georgie's neighbours, Georgie's neighbours' children, their husbands ... They never stopped. It was interesting."[8]

Together, minding our own business and minding our neighbors' are capacious enough to capture a lot about the moral psychology of dealing with people who live nearby. We might be tempted to view these poses as poles and be disposed to one or another—insistent engagement or guarded disengagement. Or, we may arrive at a satisfactory equilibrium: discrete self-distancing from our neighbor's constant company and line of vision, easy or cool familiarity, occasional practical help. Or we may achieve a more fulsome reciprocity: willingly engaging our neighbor on her terms, responding animatedly to her interests, and inviting her to appreciate ours in turn. We arrive at a sort of mutual hospitality, a selective invitation to mind one another's business. In any case, we can avoid neither; these turns of attention are in constant flux. The push and pull of minding our own business and minding our neighbors' is familiar, and the tension between them is internal to the experience of good neighbors. Both are endemic to what Lewis Mumford called the collective effort to lead a private life.

The phenomenology of everyday encounters is my starting point, then: ordinary good turns and ordinary vices, the give and take of greetings, favors, and offenses in this place whose meaning for us is different from any other. Extreme conditions and frightful degradation of everyday life at home are common enough, however, and then neighbors' responses are immensely important, life-altering. Neighbors may hold our lives in their hands.

My map of this moral minefield begins with local disorder, mayhem, and violence. Under mistrust-creating conditions neighbors become fearful and withdrawn and must struggle to sustain even rudimentary give and take.

Grimmer still, political authorities enlist neighbors as informers, instigating denunciation and betrayal. Neighbors become treacherous, unleashing on one another the viciousness endemic to the politics of the place.

Intimate violence at the hands of neighbors we thought we knew and who knew us has specific horror. The quintessential American case is lynching, and African Americans vulnerable to mutilation and murder by people they know, hoods or no, report (as survivors of other atrocities also report) on the sheer incredulity of the thing when it is *neighbors* who hold our lives in their hands.[9]

Even so, even then, some neighbors warn, protect, comfort, and rescue. We know, too, that the simplest, everyday gestures are precious under extreme conditions. When the quality of life is deranged, ordinary moments of recognition and solicitude assume extraordinary significance. "No-one during this terrible time was moved by blood, suffering and death; what surprised and shook people was kindness and love," Vasily Grossman wrote. The old teacher

> was probably the only person in the town who had not changed.... This old man seemed to be the only person left.... who still asked, "How are you feeling today?"[10]

Unable to remedy devastating reality, still, exhibitions of neighborliness provide comfort, a reminder of normalcy, and hope.

One more collision of the ordinary and extraordinary at home: a common thread in survivors' accounts of natural disasters is the assistance only neighbors—not strangers, not organized volunteers, not official rescuers—provide. Where physical upheaval obliterates the known landscape, neighbors' faces comprise the firm bits of terrain on which we reemerge. They stimulate awakening and orientation, and then they improvise rescue and aid, resisting the chaos and fury of "decivilization."

These reflections remind us that the everyday has a claim on our attention: "to affect the quality of the day, that is the highest of arts," and neighbors brighten or degrade the day, every day.[11] My argument in *Good Neighbors* is that in America this "highest of arts" is grounded in a distinct set of norms I call *the democracy of everyday life*.

## On Our Own

Neighborliness "is not an emotion but a practice, a set of hard-won, complicated habits that are used to bridge trouble, difficulty, and differences of personality, experience, and aspiration."[12] Just what good neighbor entails is elusive, however, more so, I believe, than any other significant social relation. Not because neighboring is abstract but rather because it is concrete and nothing is excluded from the wide-open domain of give and take. Reciprocity is open-ended, loose, and permissive. What counts as a fitting turn for turn? And when is a return of a favor on the calendar? It's not surprising that our calibrations are often mistaken, our footing unsure in this tentative, unchoreographed dance of give and take. Our day-to-day encounters are direct and personal, mainly discretionary, and marked by considerable spontaneity. Personal disposition plays a large part and affects whether our response to a particular neighbor is attraction, aversion, or the indifference of a clam precisely because neighbor relations fall outside of articulated social structures and purposes.

True, neighbor relations operate in the shadow of law and public policy: zoning ordinances, property law, landlord-tenant contracts, association covenants, the unlovely law of torts—nuisance above all, and criminal law as well. In many instances appeal to authorities is unavailable, however, because behavior is not a matter for the police or a civil suit, and in any event many people are ignorant of their entitlements or can't go down that costly road. The direct, personal encounters I'll explore are mostly outside or beneath the notice of these jurisdictions. We are on our own.

It is hard to think of another sustained interaction except friendship that floats so free of the institutional securities, the rules, processes, shared purposes, and agreed-on outcomes that define roles and cabin relations in other settings. No professional ethic, no articulation of "special responsibilities" of the sort moral philosophers attribute to "thick" relations of family and friends, no "associative duties" we are said to owe social groups or the nation to which we belong are suitable guides. The judgments we make of those who live close by, our responses to their good and bad turns, and our responsibilities to them (if any), don't come with scripts. Maxims abound, but hardly constitute an articulated ethic.

Except, that is, for severe Old and New Testament injunctions to "love thy neighbor as thyself." Every element of the command requires interrogation. What is this self-love that sets the measure for neighbor love? How is it possible to *will* love toward my neighbor, or anyone? And not least, who is my neighbor? In millennia of interpretation of these sacred texts, "neighbor" ranges from tribal (Leviticus's Israelites) to Christ's radical universal commandment erasing boundaries (in Soren Kierkegaard's words, "You can never confuse him with anyone else, since the neighbor . . . is all people"[13]), but not in any case simply people living nearby. "Love thy neighbor" ranges from specific prohibitions and duties set out in codes of Jewish law to nothing less than an abridgement of all the divine commandments.[14] Today, "love thy neighbor" draws its force from general morality rather than divine law but its scope and content and motivating disposition remain elusive. Mary Parker Follett, the great Progressive advocate of neighborliness as a path to participatory democracy, gave voice to this predicament:

> I am ready to say to you this minute, "I love my neighbors." But all that I mean by it is that I have a vague feeling of kindliness towards them. I have no idea how to do the actual deed. I shall offend against the law of love within the hour.[15]

Nonetheless, we can safely say *something* about what a minimal ethic of neighborliness entails: warning of danger, acting in emergencies, avoiding arrant cruelty and wanton disruption. Of course, these are matters of decency, obligations in every sphere with special application to neighbors only because living in proximity amplifies opportunity. Beyond that, a general ethic of neighborliness might be defined by friendliness and helpfulness. Something like a threshold ethic of care. These are not restricted to relations with people next door either, though, which is why the phrase "good neighbor" is frequently appropriated to refer to all sorts of volunteerism and organized beneficence.

Neighborliness has a moral aspect, plainly, but we must search for it by drawing on past experience or on stories we hear from friends and relatives, or seizing on anecdotes that circulate without attribution to illuminate how we feel (or think we should feel), and how we might respond to our neighbor's offer or offense. Small wonder that we act impulsively or erratically, are often baffled by how to react to things our neighbors do and say, or are ambivalent about engaging them at all.

All that said, our experiences and our understanding of good neighbor have ballast. The general ethic of neighborliness I described plays a part. But in the United States that ethic is overlaid by something more. What I call the democracy of everyday life gives good neighbor added value beyond basic decency, friendliness, helpfulness. It shapes expectations, disposition, demeanor, and our repertoire of daily encounters.

The scope of neighbor interactions is indeterminate, the matter unpredictable, and the temper of encounters colored by the full human spectrum of moral and social dispositions. How to contain this subject in a reasonably unreductive way, one that brings out the distinctive dynamic of neighbor relations in America? What patterns are discernible without embedding give and take in ethnography or social history? The democracy of everyday life does this work, I argue. It captures the flow of neighbors relations, which, illuminated from within, are seen to have interests, habits, and moral injunctions of their own. And the democracy of everyday life also opens out to political theory.

## Neighbors in America

First, this background. Being a good neighbor is a component of how we think about ourselves, an element of Americans' moral identity. That gives psychological as well as ethical weight to my subject. Neighborliness—with its historical roots in settler and immigrant experiences, its incarnations in popular culture, and its democratic character—is deeply engrained. For most of us (not all) much of the time (not always) "good neighbor" is a regulative ideal. We are seldom prepared to cast ourselves out of the universe of good neighbors; indeed, we may see ourselves as exemplars or enforcers. We are certainly inclined to blame and shame and speak out against bad neighbors, and we accuse them not just of selfishness, carelessness, or malice but also of a deeper failing: falling off from this ideal, which is also familiar practice.

If "neighbor" designates proximity only, neighbors are universal except in the most isolated, unsettled spots. Everywhere, people exchange good turns and bad with those living close by. Characteristically American, though, is good neighbor as a moral identity that is also a form of democratic excellence. It is a commitment to a form of goodness that entails discipline, and sometimes courage. My claim is not that the democratic ethos of good neighbor is unique to America, only that it is distinct and identifiable here.

At the same time that good neighbor is an element of personal identity, good neighbor is a common representation of national character, as proverbial as the proud self-portrait of America as a nation of volunteers who perform good works, and rivaling the representation of America as a nation of public-spirited citizens. Indeed good neighbor is prior and primary, arguably more deeply rooted as a national self-image than these. Representation of America as "good neighbor nation" has surprising force and continuity. In the face of historic changes in economy and demography, regional and social differences, enormous variation in the needs and dependencies of neighbors (contrast settlers with suburbanites), and an expanding array of residential patterns, domestic lifestyles and cultural etiquettes, the good neighbor is a steady, symbolic American.

This collective self-representation of America as "good neighbor nation" is a point of national pride that spills over into foreign affairs. President Franklin Roosevelt's "Good Neighbor Policy" was intended to resonate with standard elements of the idea of a good neighbor: benign intent, practical assistance, and respect for other states' self-determination.[16] It promised reciprocity and goodwill. It pretended rough equality and disclaimed assertions of power. Vis-à-vis nations in the hemisphere, the title of the doctrine was a mix of assurances and moral hubris. I imagine it addressed less to the government of Mexico than to ourselves.

Of course, invocations of good neighbor can be facile, sentimental, self-flattery, or wishful thinking. But when it is sober and reflective we recognize good neighbor as a significant element of personal and collective identity, and as the deep substrate of democracy in America.

I use the first person plural, "we," to emphasize that moral identity as good neighbor is commonplace among Americans and many residents here, and that "good neighbor nation" is part of our collective self-understanding. It should be abundantly clear, there is nothing uniform about neighbors' experience, quite the contrary. Contingency and sheer individuality insure that neighbor relations are variable, and so does the enforcement of "local knowledge" — "what anyone would do, here." Many of us want to live in a comparatively homogeneous home environment, most of us do in any case, as I show, but there is nothing homogenizing about neighbors' actual encounters. Still, none of us is a stranger to the tension between minding our own business and minding our neighbor's, to negotiating the terms of reciprocity, to giving and taking offense, to the impulse to withdraw and refuse to deal, or to the democratic ethos that infuses all of these. In using the pronoun "we," I mean to encourage recognition of the democracy of everyday life and to prevent myself (and readers) from disassociating from the errors of judgment and abject moral failures that corrode neighbor relations. And from sentimentality.

## The Sentimentality Trap

Settler, immigrant, and suburban narratives are the canonical materials from which both exemplary identity as a good neighbor and the collective representation of "good neighbor nation" are built. These narrative threads provide the basic content and the dominant tenors and colors of "good neighbor." They give it articulation. But many fictional narratives (think *Little House on the Prairie*) and representations of neighbors in popular culture (*Seinfeld, Mr. Rogers' Neighborhood*) come to us in a sentimental register. I pause on this point because the sentimental hold good neighbor has on moral imagination presents an obstacle to understanding.

"Neighbor" comes bathed in a certain glow. The adjective "good" is superfluous. We harbor nostalgic images and subscribe to easy nostrums. Among neighbors, we imagine, we have occasions to spontaneously exhibit solicitude and kindness. Neighbors, in this fantasy, do not give offense or drive us to distraction. Neighbors do not tax us morally. They do not require us to exercise patience or to endure slights. Or if they do, misunderstandings are quickly cleared up, offenses forgiven, conflicts amicably resolved. Things are put back in place. That is part of the satisfaction of sentimentality—to reinforce unearned, pleasurable feelings. "There is nothing in the world so good as good neighbors," Laura Ingalls Wilder wrote in *On the Banks of Plum Creek*.

Sentimental ideals differ from ideals that figure in moral and political philosophy whose purpose is to stimulate reflection on the distance between what could be and what exists, between a just society and our own. Sentimentality operates in reverse. It works by tapping previously prepared emotions and eliciting acquiescence in a flattering conventional picture. It does not provide a standard for assessment. It induces complacency. It shuts our reflective minds down. It is an impediment to absorbing social facts and to facing up to the requirements of our own and our collective well-being. What degree of attention (if any) can I tolerate from the people next door? Honestly, do I have the disposition to inquire about my neighbor's pet, to return a favor, to refrain from registering disapproval or disgust? Can I admit to discomfort where sentimentality tells me there should be easy familiarity? The peril of sentimentality is as true for neighbors as it is for friendship and love: we deliver ourselves and our neighbors up for disappointment, or worse.

Sentimentality is liable to infuse the collective characterization of America as "good neighbor nation" as well. Neighbors constitute beneficent society, on this view, *because* we offer one another company and reciprocity unfettered by rules and sanctions, untainted by contracts and commercial exchanges, unfragmented by a division of labor, without the constraints imposed by unchosen collective purposes. Like friendship, the sentimental ideal of neighborliness inverts the ways of the larger society. Our interactions are personal and expressive "all the way down." In this dream, they don't rest on entrenched social structures shaped by law or public policy, or on the constraints of "local knowledge," or on the discipline of the democracy of everyday life.

This sentimental conception of voluntary sociability among neighbors has consequences not unlike the counterpart conception of rugged individualism. Most important, it fuels a romance in which neighbors do for one another in a world of unregulated individual good turns. When government and politics disappear from view as they do, we are left with the not-so-innocuous fantasy of ungoverned reciprocity as the best and fully adequate society. Laura Ingalls Wilder portrayed settlers living outside of most jurisdictions as an idyll not a fearful Hobbesian reality. The author's daughter ("Baby Rose" in the *Little House* books) was an advocate of laissez-faire and opponent of the New Deal who refused to pay social security taxes. Sentimental accounts of "good neighbor nation" fuel antigovernment strains of American thought.

Sentimentality hinders understanding, in short. Cruelty and aggression among neighbors and the degradation of life around home are especially shocking if we start from the assumption that neighbors are marked by mutual care and concern, if we assume "thick" ties that command loyalty, if we begin from the notion that good neighbors are a spontaneous state of affairs rather than a hard-won status. We can shed sentimentality without rebounding and insisting as Freud did that my neighbor has more claim on my hostility than my love:

> He seems not to have the least trace of love for me. . . . If it will do him good he has no hesitation in injuring me. . . . Indeed, he need not even

obtain an advantage; if he can satisfy any sort of desire by it, he thinks nothing of jeering at me, insulting me, slandering me, and showing his superior power.[17]

Which is not to say that the moral identity good neighbor isn't laudable or that America as "good neighbor nation" is pious self-flattery. The sentimental ideal of neighbor is a distortion; it bends perceptions of reality. The democracy of everyday life is a sober ideal, and it is sufficiently realized to escape pure idealization.

## The Democracy of Everyday Life

"The stuff of a civilization consists largely of its substantive norms," Robert Ellickson wrote, which have "no identifiable author, no apparent date of origin, no certainty of attention from historians" and that "are among the most magnificent of cultural achievements." He went on, "The overarching substantive norm of the rural residents of Shasta County is that one should be a 'good neighbor.'"[18] But what is that? An ethnographer of "the practice of everyday life" wrote of "the murmuring of the everyday in which one can multiply the soundings indefinitely without ever locating the structures that organize it."[19] I propose that our everyday experiences around home, the meaning we attribute to them, and our identity as good neighbors have a structure called the democracy of everyday life. My task is to tease it out.

Three signature elements make up the democracy of everyday life: reciprocity among "decent folk," speaking out, and live and let live. Absent defined rules and methods of enforcement, which is the essential predicament of neighbors, reciprocity is a touchstone. We know that give and take go on everywhere among people living nearby. The specifically "democratic" in relations shaped by the democracy of everyday life is in part a matter of rough parity in the terms of reciprocity and in part a matter of who counts as my neighbor in this dance of give and take.

"Decent folk" is a common way of referring to neighbors in settler, immigrant, and suburban narratives. It is a virtual synonym for good neighbor, and I adopt the phrase. "Decent folk" gathers in the qualities—practical and moral—that figure when we size up the couple next door to decide whether we will open ourselves to or wall ourselves off from willing encounters. It reflects a modest practical assessment that these neighbors intend us no harm, will take our elementary interests into account, and are available for the rudiments of give and take. "Decent folk" designates equality in this one respect: qua neighbor. Importantly it entails disregard for our neighbors' origin, social status, and character overall, and disregard for ascriptive characteristics. It is focused on what we can expect from one another day to day. Reciprocity detached from the considerations that govern interactions in social spheres outside home is not the practice in every society. More often, neighbor encounters and the terms of reciprocity are governed by the rules of social hierarchy, rank, class, kinship, or sectarianism.

Of course, the democratizing import of "decent folk" is aspirational. It is imperfectly realized. I discuss failings, including momentous historical failings and the intersection with racial politics at length. In fact, the phrase is double-edged. The negative reverse of the capaciousness of "decent folk"—the dark mirror of its inclusive embrace as a defining element of the democracy of everyday life—is denigration and exclusion of designated "others." Then the phrase conjures categorical judgments: white judgments of African Americans, and other "out groups." Yet reciprocity among "decent folk" is a mainstay of the democracy of everyday life.

It does not stand alone. When neighbors give offense we are drawn into a familiar world of difficulties: assessing the offense and whether or not to keep our sense of injury to ourselves. And whether or not to rally with others against a neighbor's derangement of our days or nights. "Speaking out" is the second element of the democracy of everyday life. Our indignation is specific to neighbors: we are subjected to another's arbitrary and unrestrained will at home, where we are uniquely vulnerable and retreat is impossible. We can sometimes appeal to local authorities for relief but matters are not always meat for police or civil suits and we may be unhappy to find ourselves on our own. We *want* other neighbors to confirm that our indignation is justified. We recruit them to speak out in what amounts to homely resistance to a sort of despotism. In that moment of speaking out we neighbors are self-governing. We are carrying on the work of protecting ourselves from one another in the domain of daily life at home where we don't want government regulation and enforcement to be.

Among the things that make speaking out interesting as a norm of good neighbor is the countervailing value of detachment and minding our own business. Both are internal to good neighbor. Refusing to join in enforcing "what anyone would do, here" is one way in which we limit the demands neighbors may make on us and limit the demands we make on ourselves. It is a condition for fashioning our own relations around home, and for care of the self.

The injunction to live and let live is the third element of the democracy of everyday life. "Live and let live" is not at all a matter of the shrug of indifference or caution against meddling that the colloquial phrase implies. It requires close attention to our neighbors and stern self-discipline. It enjoins us to protect as we can neighbors' control over the environment of home. One characteristic expression of live and let live is reticence. Minding our neighbors' business is unavoidable, forced on us by proximity. Do we exploit this accident of proximity? Do we admonish, report, agitate? Or do we maintain the neutral ground between us created by unacknowledgment. Live and let live makes us hesitant to publicize, pronounce, and report to other neighbors or to authorities. Under repressive political conditions, we are liable to become agents in a system of surveillance, and then, whether or not we follow the injunction to live and let live can be momentous.

For the same reasons and to the same purpose, live and let live prescribes not only reticence and inaction, but also a specific sort of action—a signal and offer. In mistrust-creating situations, with a gesture or word we acknowledge one another as neighbors, regular presences. We signal that we are safe with one another and will not disturb, injure, or exploit one another. We register our mutual vulnerability. We are paying attention. We are extending ourselves. The injunction can become a casualty of hostile situations, effectively muted. But where we can proffer it, live and let live is a powerful reassurance—a quiet demonstration of our intent to protect and repair the quality of the day.

The democracy of everyday life is not only a regulative ideal, but also—and readers will recognize this—a set of implicit expectations, dispositions, and practices that actually shape our interactions as neighbors and give them meaning. Of course, the democratic ethos is not always realized and is sometimes horribly deranged. My burden is to show that as neighbors—good or bad—we inhabit a distinct domain of quotidian life. The democracy of everyday life has its own place—encounters around home. Which is to say that neighbor relations comprise just one sphere in the complex pluralism and shifting involvements among spheres that mark life in society today. The value and meaning of good neighbors, the characteristic concerns with privacy, and the sociability associated with neighbors are one part of the larger story of the moral uses of pluralism.

Often then, I emphasize discontinuities. I proceed in part by "talking against." Thus, the ethics of the democracy of everyday life are not encompassed by the usual considerations of moral philosophy. There, the subject is the particular attachments and obligations we have as citizens, or members of a family or ethnic or religious group. Or, moral philosophy focuses on our common humanity. Something is lost if the democratic ethos of good neighbor is conflated with the special responsibilities that come with family or group ties. Something is lost as well if good neighbor is conflated with universal moral decency, respect, or an ethic of care said to apply to everyone, everywhere.

The elements of the democracy of everyday life comprise a set distinct, too, from formal and informal democratic institutions and practices, from public principles of justice or fairness, from the legalism of rights, and from civic virtues. Put simply, good neighbor is not a redescription of good citizen. One is not an informal variant of the other. The democracy of everyday life is not democratic public life writ small. [20] This is not just a question of scale and scope, either. We simply do not experience neighbor relations in these terms. To represent the democracy of everyday life as if it were a matter of translating public democratic principles to fit direct personal relations among neighbors at home is a distortion. We learn more by keeping the distinct moral identity of good neighbor and the independence of the democracy of everyday life firmly in view.

Yet the democracy of everyday life does hold significance for democratic public life—just not for the reasons political theorists and civic activists might predict. I don't suggest that neighboring is a school of civic virtue, or that good neighbor is preparation or model for citizenship. Not at all. Neighbor and citizen are not coextensive. But neither are the zones rigorously separate. There are both continuities and discontinuities in the contours of our experiences as neighbor and citizen and the meaning they hold for us. I show just how nuanced interactions are between the democracy of everyday life and formal democratic principles, public spaces and institutions, and civic virtues. The important point is this: something is lost if the democracy of everyday life is overlooked or seen as valuable only insofar as it instantiates public democratic principles and practices. Good neighbor is both supplement and corrective to how we think about democracy in America.

## Biography of a Theory

Theoretical activity begins in the private world of inquirers. It works this way: something happens, and we are startled into thought. The intimate history of *Good Neighbors* began with a bully in my apartment building who tormented the family next door. The incident prompted self-reflection. Joining my neighbors in speaking out and standing up to the offender was a point of pride; I identified with this facet of being a good neighbor, which I experienced as a sort of resistance to despotism. Pretty quickly, though, I realized how challenged I was in other respects. I have only a limited capacity for friendly exchange trapped in unwelcome conversation in the hall. I harbor a frankly judgmental attitude toward neighbors' disarray. I envy the apparent ease and familiarity of less withdrawn neighbors. What sort of person am I, really, that I'm not sure I want my new neighbors to know my name? Clearly, on reflection, neighbors brought out traits I didn't know I had (or pretended not to have). Neighbors, I argue, can illuminate our reluctance to know ourselves and they can spur self-understanding. *Good Neighbors* began with my own experiences, with situations that would trouble anyone. I hope to be seen as a trustworthy narrator and theorist in part because I am present in these pages: acknowledging the awful power of ordinary anxieties and the comfort of ordinary sympathy and recognition, making larger sense of otherwise inchoate encounters with neighbors, drawing out the elements of the democracy of everyday life around home and their real shaping force in the moment.[21]

Personal experience along with stories from friends and offerings from colleagues at seminars are very much to the point. For one thing, they are direct testimony of the capacity neighbors have to brighten or degrade life at home, everyday. For another, these stories yield patterns of encounters. I'm making a more general claim, too: these stories are part of the "biography of a theoretical idea."[22] Here, the world of personal experience and my subject are connected in a simple and obvious way, but the connection is always there. It is there when theorists plunge into ideas "as if into religion or revolution"[23] as I do in appreciating "the moral uses of pluralism" and the sphere of life around home as essential to moral personality, to the quality of life, and to democracy.

Literature carried personal observation further. In three iconic representations of the United States—as a settler nation, a nation of immigrants, and as the quintessential scene of suburban life—the democratic ethos of neighboring is a constant theme. It sounds with remarkable continuity across economic and demographic changes and a host of "spatially inscribed social differences."[24] I draw out the elements of the democracy of everyday life from these narratives. I did not find my organizing concepts ready to hand in moral philosophy or democratic theory. The selections I draw from literature are not merely illustrative. I have not exploited fiction to flesh out previously existing arguments. Rather, I found there conceptual as well as material resources from which to build a political theory of the democracy of everyday life. Stories by Phillip Roth and Raymond Carver, Willa Cather's and Saul Bellow's novels, Frost's poems and Robert Hayden's and Richard Wright's do more than paint situations and encounters that make the experience of neighbors available to us, recalling us to ourselves. Beyond that, the theoretical framework of *Good Neighbors* emerged from reflecting on the truth of these narratives.

Popular culture underscores the empirical reality of the democratic ethos as well as its power as an ideal. A genre of television comedy of manners revolves around reciprocity among people living side by side. The centrality of good neighbor is evidenced too by the fact that it is a staple for children, however sentimental: *Mr. Rogers* coming home, removing his shoes and jacket, and singing "I've always wanted to have a neighbor just like you."[25] *Sesame Street* teaches preschoolers the alphabet but also the democracy of everyday life among humans and monsters on the block. These settings speak to the importance of home and place and encounters there, and to our anxiety that we might be producing "children who were never taught and would never now learn the games that had held society together."[26]

The centrality of personal experience and of literature and popular culture to the biography of the theory of the democracy of everyday life suggests that I take my bearings from "inside." Also important for my subject, then, are firsthand accounts by men and women in extreme situations of mistrust, violence, and betrayal, and accounts by survivors of neighbors who rescue. These close descriptions of the moral psychology of neighbors ward off unwarranted simplicity and abstraction. At the same time, I have had to take experiential meaning and make it less fragmentary and confused, more complete. Every move from internal experience to narration involves interpretation.[27] *Good Neighbors* embraces what we do, the language we use to think about what we do, our identity as good neighbors, and its significance for democracy in America.

Resources for my theory include empirical studies of neighbors. A large social science literature examines local government, policing and crime, racially segregated housing, group conflict, "neighborhood effects," and more. I've benefited from studies of the neighborhood as a jurisdiction and site of political participation. Studies confirm the lay of the land as I have described it: encounters carried on against the background of law and officialdom but without institutions and formal rules, often beyond appeals to any authority, with neighbors carrying on on their own. Mine is not empirical social science, but it is empirically aware.

## The Order of Good Neighbors

*Good Neighbors* is sometimes a story of neighbor relations unsettled, terribly degraded, aborted, or in eclipse. I have given this narrative the figure of an arc. The democracy of everyday life rises from the ground of day-to-day reciprocity and neighbors' responses to ordinary kindnesses and ordinary vices. We give and take favors and offense; we assist, speak out, monitor, scold and rebuke, and rally others to enforce "what anyone would do, here"; we live and let live. These situations and the dispositions and actions they evoke are the mundane stuff of life around home. The arc rises sharply to challenging terrain where mistrust is widespread and neighbors must struggle to sustain the rudiments of give and take. Insecurity can stifle even "how are you today?"—bare acknowledgment of one another as "decent folk." Neighbors' successes in maintaining or recovering the democracy of everyday life in an environment of mistrust are genuine achievements. The arc descends where the democracy of everyday life goes into eclipse, as it does when political authorities instigate or condone betrayal and murder, infusing neighbor relations with violence and fear. The light of good neighbor is visible even in the darkest times, though, present within and across racial and other lines of division. It is there, in extraordinary acts of protection and rescue that neighbors often cast as ordinary ("what anyone would do, here") and in countless moments of comfort. Even in extreme political situations, the moral domain outside of and beyond politics does not disappear.

The book traces this arc. Part I, "The Lay of the Land," is groundwork. Chapter 1 poses the foundational question, "who is my neighbor?" Proximity to home is essential, but we count as neighbors those who affect the quality of life at home, with whom we have repeated encounters. We don't confuse neighbors with strangers or with intimates and friends.

Chapter 2, "Narrative Threads," introduces accounts of good neighbor and the democracy of everyday life in American literature. Settler, immigrant, and suburban portrayals demonstrate the centrality of this regulative ideal in our moral imagination and in Americans' self-representation.

Part II, "The Democracy of Everyday Life," explores what comes from the plain fact that minding our neighbors' business is inescapable and from the fact that neighbor relations fall largely outside of formal institutions and articulated rules of conduct, are ungoverned by set obligations and established means of enforcing them. Four chapters traverse the spectrum of the elements of the democracy of everyday life that shape ordinary encounters.

Chapter 3, "Reciprocity among 'Decent Folk,'" introduces the principal defining characteristic of the democracy of everyday life: rough parity in give and take among neighbors. Reciprocity among "decent folk" fleshes out this facet of the democracy of everyday life, for "decent folk" carries a distinctive understanding of equality for the purposes of living side by side.

"Taking Offense, Speaking Out," Chapter 4, explores ordinary vices and how reciprocity works, or fails to work, when we are faced with a neighbor who gives offense. Do we withdraw? Elect detachment? Or do we speak out, rally and recruit others to the cause? What is peculiarly democratic about neighbors speaking out?

Things escalate in "What Anyone Would Do, Here," Chapter 5, where I consider neighbors as enforcers. Neighbors surveil, instruct, monitor, correct, and reproach, and become indignant when those living nearby have not learned the lay of the land, or rudely map their own way.

In mistrust-creating situations where chronic conditions of disorder, mayhem, and organized violence foul encounters among neighbors, the democracy of everyday life is tested more severely. That is the subject of Chapter 6, "Live and Let Live." Privacy—understood first and simply as protecting ourselves from intrusive authorities and from one another—is the felt necessity that makes live and let live a moral imperative. Live and let live enjoins reticence—refusing to broadcast or report what we know when revelation would have potentially disturbing, even life-altering consequences for our neighbors. Live and let live also enjoins a characteristic demeanor and form of conduct signaling recognition of our mutual vulnerability. The literal meaning of the phrase comes into play when we offer assurances that we are not threatening—that we will do no harm and will preserve as we can the quality of life around home. Live and let live is the essential, "safety net" element of the democracy of everyday life.

Part III: "Holding Our Lives in Their Hands" focuses on extreme degradation of the democracy of everyday life and on efforts to assert the rudiments of good neighbor. When political authorities exercise control by deliberately derailing life at home, encounters among neighbors are not only stressed and unsettled, they are radically politicized. At the same time, politics is personalized as neighbors turn on one another opportunistically—moved by envy, greed, unsettled disputes, an eye to advantages, or revenge. There is a distinct quality of moral breakdown when it is neighbors who betray and murder. And there is a distinct quality of moral assurance when it is neighbors who comfort and rescue. I ground these claims in detailed explorations of historical touchstones of politically instigated betrayal, killing, and rescue among neighbors in America. I study this terrain for good reason: the political apparatus of betrayal and murder is not safely in the past. And in atrocity-producing situations, the value of the democratic ethos of good neighbors remains powerfully with us. The democracy of everyday life emerges as a "saving remnant."

Chapter 7, "Betrayal," looks at neighbors turned informers. An abnormal Panoptical society, a "world without walls," replaces the ordinary boundaries and neutral ground among good neighbors. It becomes a punishable offense to see and hear yet refuse to report, and neighbors become active agents in this system of control. We associate invitations and inducements to inform on neighbors (and others) with totalist regimes, but they are hardly alien to the United States. My touchstone is the mass Japanese evacuation and internment at the start of World War II: a story of public betrayal by government and personal betrayal by white neighbors before "relocation" and again after resettlement at the end of the war. It is also a story of brittle, fractionated relations among Japanese families living side by side in the camps.

In "Killing," Chapter 8, I look into the ugly face of the democracy of everyday life aborted. Killing neighbors is the outer tail, the far reach of derangement, and the convergence of murder and home is a unique horror. Lynching is the homegrown American case of neighbors killing neighbors. Victims often knew the people who mutilated and killed them. Murderers knew their victims. Lynching was a public spectacle or in any case a public secret: these "feasts of blood" were "owned by all the town." Still, neighbors were not all implicated in the same way in this intimate violence. They may be unable to arrest terrorization and killing but they can carry on in the interstices of horror and warn, aid, comfort, protest, and protect. Strikingly, rescuers cast their extraordinary actions as ordinary—frequently invoking "good neighbor" for its homely resonance. At the same time, ordinary neighborly gestures have extraordinary force, affirming the inestimable, now-not-to-be-taken-for-granted value of quotidian life. These expressions of good neighbor are lodged deeply in the memory of survivors and witnesses.

In Chapter 9, "Disasters," I explore neighbors in emergency situations. Neighbors are always the "first responders" who do what no group of organized volunteers or government provider can. Hurricane Katrina is my set piece, and survivor narratives show that the significance of neighbors emerges in three temporal steps: recognition and witnessing, awakening, and improvised cooperation. In disasters too, rescuers often make explicit reference to being good neighbors and "what anyone would do, here." And they bring to bear as resources the elements of the democracy of everyday life.

Part IV, "Minding Our Own Business" asks just what that business is. Minding our neighbors' business and minding our own work in tandem when it comes to self-examination and transformation. We listen and observe and then compare our neighbors' lives to our own. ("I guess just watching you/Has made me lonesome too.")[28] From our vantage point as witnesses to our neighbors' lives, we gain insight into our vulnerabilities, moral resources, and the terms of our happiness. Thoreau's *Walden* is the great American reflection on the quality of life at home, in this place, with these neighbors. Good neighbors emerge in Thoreau's work as essential to self-understanding and care of the self. And Thoreau presents treating one another as neighbors as the "saving remnant" of democracy in America.

In the conclusion, I provide a systematic account of my political theory of the meaning and value of the democracy of everyday life for formal, organized democracy, as well as—what is no lesser thing—its importance for the quality of life personally and individually. I press my argument that the moral identity of good neighbor shaped by the democracy of everyday life is distinct from the political identity of good citizen. I lay out continuities as well as discontinuities between the democratic ethos among neighbors and political democracy proper, and I represent the democracy of everyday life as the hardy remainder or "saving remnant" when formal democracy seems to have lost its integrity.

Throughout, I try to make the felt experience of reciprocity, the offenses we give and take, and the circling, snaking course of our attention as we move between minding our own business and minding our neighbors' vivid. The truth to experience lies not in our perfect faithfulness to the regulative ideal but in the way it figures in our personal stories about neighbors, in our accusations against bad neighbors, in our own attempts to adhere to it. Does the democracy of everyday life capture the quality of your encounters? The meaning you attribute to them? That is, finally, the verification available. We are "the subjects for whom these meanings are."[29]

# PART I

## The Lay of the Land

# 1

# Who Is My Neighbor?

## Proximity

A greeting, a casual conversation, a request, or small act of spontaneous assistance are the start as we explore the terms and limits, the demands, costs, and rewards of encounters with neighbors. These initiate contact and normally elicit a response, however tentative or delayed. Once we address one another we have created an opening. We are no longer strangers having random encounters. In the jargon of sociology, words can act as a "relationship wedge":

> Once an individual has extended to another enough consideration to hear him out for a moment, some kind of bond of mutual obligation is established . . . once this new extended bond is granted, grudgingly or willingly, still further claims for social or material indulgence can be made.[1]

We feel out our neighbor's potential for generosity or exploitation, and our own. We anticipate ongoing interactions—proximity guarantees it. Neighbors may be more or less familiar to us, but these are not chance encounters. We are in the background (or foreground) of one another's daily lives at home.

Who is my neighbor? The answer is more elusive and more interesting than first appears. The old English roots of the word ("neah" as in near and "gebur" as in dweller) and the medieval reference to farming strips of common land ("the man who tills the next piece of ground to mine"[2]) are historical reference points. But for us personally and individually, who counts as our neighbor is not automatic with proximity. Location is not enough. We don't assign the status neighbor to everyone residing in an

officially designated neighborhood. We don't define our neighbors by police precincts, census tracts, school districts, mail carrier routes, or the historic and aesthetic contours of the place where we live. Nor is neighbor
associated in our minds with sociologists' "spatial logic" and the social
mechanisms that go by the name "neighborhood effects." For neighbor is
a matter of both location and personal knowledge, of recognition. The
people we identify as our neighbors are people we encounter regularly,
even if the only acknowledgement is a nod or its opposite—a regular,
rude display of disregard.

> My neighborhood "is a known area of social space in which, to a
> greater or lesser degree, he or she knows himself or herself to be rec-
> ognized. . . . an area of public space in general . . . in which little by lit-
> tle, a private, particularized space insinuates itself as a result of the
> practical, everyday use of this space."[3]

We assign neighbors a spot on our personal map of the lay of the land
around home. That doesn't extend to everyone living nearby, and the person residing closest to us may fall outside the domain of "actual contacts,
connections, alliances."[4] The designation is not inclusive, then. Neighbor
applies to those close to home who emerge from the background to affect
the quality of our lives. We elect the good neighbors with whom we have
willing encounters, though bad neighbors, the worst, often elect us.

Sentimental representations of neighbor emphasize the sense of belonging to this place. The stock image is a small town with neighbors of
long-standing. Harper Lee's Atticus Finch was

> Maycomb County born and bred; he knew his people, they knew
> him . . . The present generation of people who had lived side by side for
> years and years, were utterly predictable to one another: they took for
> granted attitudes, character shadings, even gestures, as having been re-
> peated in each generation and refined by time.

That was rural Alabama in the 1930s. The longevity and familiarity built
into the notion of neighbor are rare today. Within the limits of mobility
and financial means, we resist randomness in electing where to live, still,
the particular people next door fall to us without our choosing. Sorely or
gratefully, we are aware of the accident of proximity. In Frost's poem,
"Mending Wall," farmers must try to balance "the boulders that have
fallen to each," and the phrase reminds us that who our neighbors are and
the stuff of encounters is a matter of chance. There are exceptions of
course, famous ones:

"It was a strange coincidence," I said.

"But it wasn't a coincidence at all."

"Why not?"

"Gatsby bought that house so that Daisy would be just across the bay."[5]

In sum, "who is my neighbor?" emerges from personal interactions in the course of life around home, and a map of our lay of the land, were we to draw one, would reflect this vantage point. We can conjure up this home-centric perspective by thinking about the territory we inhabited as children. Scout, the nine-year-old narrator of *To Kill a Mockingbird,* can trace her boundaries: "Mrs. Henry Lafayette Dubose's house two doors to the north of us, and the Radley Place three doors to the south."[6] Place matters, the physical location of home vis-à-vis neighbors, its distance or closeness.

Commonplace references to globalization, the valorization of cosmopolitanism, universal moral norms that often seem to float high off the surface of everyday relations, media that bring us images and voices from across the world, tempt us to understate the significance of place. We become accustomed to "neighbor" as a sort of shorthand for "humanity" when speaking about events that affect everyone. Specific effects of climate change are experienced locally, for example, but we know that the forces disturbing our habitat are everywhere and have global consequences. We are metaphorical neighbors in crisis. Science and culture and morality invite us to diminish the significance of home as a personal place and our actual, unmetaphorical neighbors.

Then there are virtual neighbors. "What about them?" I'm asked. The seemingly infinite universe of online sites is unbound by earthly geography, yet networking sites propose to deliver what the term "site" implies, a physical space in which to enact virtual life—intergalactic wars, medieval fantasy games, and neighborhoods. In *Second Life,* for example, where "living, not winning" is the object of the game, "you can live anywhere." Players are invited to "Get Settled," to build and furnish a dream house, and to "meet the neighbors."[7] Scholars of Internet connectivity observe that simulated relations may be compensatory for the lack of relations in real life. For Molly, fifty-eight, a retired librarian who lives alone, her urban neighborhood "is not the kind of place people know each other.... I don't even recognize the people in the Shaw's [a local supermarket chain] ... Online I have found some good people." We speak of online neighbors only by analogy, of course. Importantly, the flaws in the analogy are also the source of the gratifications of virtual neighbors. Distance does not exist online, and portable devices allow us to carry our good neighbors with us. Online neighbors do not impose the demands of face-to-face relationships or the sheer intrusiveness of physical presence. With online connectivity we are in control. We can "move away," and we can log off. We don't have to learn to live and let live, we can just shut down. We can also change who we are. The "good people" Molly meets online are not themselves, and they too know only her avatar: the flattened profile we "create, edit, and perform." This is not to say that even though they can't help carry the groceries virtual neighbors are nothing. They may be "really something."[8] Just not neighbors.

It is tempting, then, to diminish the significance of place. But the "death of distance" needs rebutting.[9] A pair of facts—physical proximity and proximity to *home*—has a bearing on all our interactions and makes encounters among neighbors a different animal than social interactions in other settings, and certainly different than relations among friends or citizens. Proximity to home shapes the terms of reciprocity; it shapes the matters on which we give and take offense; it shapes our responsibility towards neighbors; it shapes, clearly, the delicate business of minding our own versus others' business; it gives meaning to the walls we erect and the reasons we give ourselves for building them.

## Uncertain Encounters

Easy or uneasy, neighbor relations require attention. The reasons are familiar, but an initial inventory bears setting out. For one thing, our encounters are open-ended. The stuff of give and take is virtually boundless. The commitments we find our neighbors have come to expect of us develop imperceptibly, and are liable to give rise to misunderstanding. We may unwittingly appear to be receptive to demands that in fact we find excessive, raising false expectations and appearing unreliable. Or we unwittingly signal that we are unavailable. We misjudge what counts as a fitting give and take. We find ourselves put upon or put out. Our own and our neighbor's estimates of the terms of give and take may be incongruent, jarring. With the best goodwill, we cannot always discern what our neighbor wants or assumes as her due. And we have only very dim notions of how to repair relations gone amok. Adam Smith's "thousand exceptions" to the loose rules that governed eighteenth-century personal exchange is a low count. We are aware that "the difference between his character and yours, between his circumstances and yours" sets the stage for uncertain, uneven "social exchanges."[10] The whole model of exchange has limited purchase, in fact.

The character of give and take may be lost on us if we think exclusively in terms of concrete exchange or of give and take as a tactic for managing encounters. Harper Lee makes this point about acts of kindness in *To Kill a Mockingbird*. Throughout her childhood, the nine-year-old narrator Scout was afraid of her reclusive next-door neighbor, Boo Radley. She and her brother thought of him as a malevolent phantom who dined on raw squirrels. Over time, she discovers that Boo was the secret giver who left gifts for them in the hollow of a tree: two pieces of chewing gum without their wrappers, a small box with bits of tinfoil collected from the gum wrappers, two polished Indian-head pennies, a ball of gray twine, images of Scout and her brother carved in soap, and a watch that wouldn't run on a chain with an aluminum knife. At the end of the novel Boo Radley emerges from seclusion to save her life. Scout sums up the measure of their relation as she understands it:

> Neighbors bring food with death and flowers with sickness and little things in between. Boo was our neighbor. He gave us two soap dolls, a broken watch and chain, a pair of good luck pennies, and our lives. But neighbors give in return. We never put back into the tree what we took out of it; we had given him nothing, and it made me sad.[11]

Harper Lee assigns the mistake of literalness—of thinking she had failed because she had not returned "little things"—to a child. It is immature reckoning. Scout *had* given her neighbor something; his gifts were a return for hers. Observing the children's' activities from behind drawn shades, Boo's limited, lonely world as a recluse was lit up and made interesting. Scout's father had instructed the children to mind their own business and let the Radleys mind theirs, but their curiosity was strong and their ceaseless attempts to mind Boo's business (was he alive in there? was he dangerous? could they lure him out?) was thrilling. They dared one another to run up to his porch; they left a note dangling from a fishing pole that said, "we wouldn't hurt him and we'd buy him an ice cream." Scout's regular presence was the good turn she performed for the withdrawn man. It is the irreplaceable value of neighbors, as I hope to show.

The inventory of reasons for uncertainty continues beyond the open-endedness and indeterminacy of give and take. Plainly, expectations for conduct and equally important demeanor are shaped in part by the social setting and practices of the place, which we may not fully grasp. Performance is context and act specific, linked to history, demography, and economy. Give and take is situational, calibrated to local knowledge. People "have had to agree on a certain set of rules, called etiquette and politeness, to make this frequent meeting tolerable and that we need not come to open war," Thoreau wrote.[12] The local etiquette may elude us. Besides, we have latitude to decide whether or not to conform to "what anyone would do, here."

Finally, there is the question what do we want or need? Discerning what our neighbors expect of us is hard; discerning our own desires may be hard as well. The actions and gestures we welcome, the attentions we tolerate more or less graciously, the offers we rebuff and encounters we avoid are in large part a matter of personal disposition. It is up to us whether and in what register we invite, return, refuse, stint, delay, or just stand back and mind our own business. A morning greeting—acknowledgment that we are somebody and that this is not a chance sighting—is typically taken for granted and returned. But even superficial interactions can throw us off. We suffer the infliction of conversation about the weather riding the elevator in our apartment building, and we suffer the neighbors who do not know when our conversation has terminated. Temperament or just transient moods have freer reign in private life around home than in most settings. We are more apt to display the rough edges of personality in the front yard or hallway than at work. Often enough, neighbors are less the reason than the occasion for enmity, and for exhibiting ordinary vices.

Underlying all the things that provoke us to think about what we want and need is something deeper. Neighbor relations are shaped by emotions often operating just out of conscious range. Unexplored feelings drive our behavior. They do in all our relations, true, but neighbors are uniquely lacking in constraining rules, organizational structures. So we make on-the-spot judgments, barely noticing that we do, not knowing why we do. We are heedless. Neighbors who are deliberately withdrawn, for example, can't anticipate the moment when they will welcome an overture. We don't imagine that we will be startled into awareness of the intrinsic value of neighbors: how just their presence and availability transforms the day. We surprise ourselves. If we approach the subject reflectively, we are driven to contemplate whether minding my neighbor's business might have value? And whether minding hers illuminates or diverts me from my own? Whether neighbors are obstacle, provocation, or resource? We consider more imaginatively and truly what we give and get, or could. In Part II, "The Democracy of Everyday Life," I look in detail at the actual stuff of give and take—of what we want from neighbors, at the phenomenology of these encounters, and at the shape the regulative ideal of the democracy of everyday life gives to experience. For now, I want to consider more contemplatively what we give and get, or could.

## Balancing Loaves and Balls

We have a guide: the "unpoetic neighbor"[13] has inspired poetry. "Mending Wall" is Robert Frost's rumination on neighbors. The encounter he paints is mundane, and the poet's voice is colloquial, mature, dispassionate.[14] This voice guides us past common sense, however, and introduces us to the delicacy inherent in the most practical interactions. It reveals the surprising turns minding our own business and minding our neighbors' take. The poet invokes, too, the moment we receive a rare, "unlooked for favor."

Frost's apple farmer and his neighbor agree to meet to mend the stone wall between their fields:

> And on a day we meet to walk the line
> And set the wall between us once again.
> We keep the wall between us as we go.
> To each the boulders that have fallen to each.
> And some are loaves and some so nearly balls
> We have to use a spell to make them balance:
> "Stay where you are until our backs are turned!"

The loaves and balls that have fallen to each don't balance easily, and "Mending Wall" considers the things that make equilibrium unsteady. A certain ambiguity characterizes reciprocity among neighbors—these are not formal debts or claims. The loaves and balls are not equivalent. Frost's apple farmer is alert to this: "We have to use a spell to make them balance."

The poet understands "the boulders that have fallen to each" to be their separate, divergent interests. Will the apple farmer mind his own business, which, we learn, is interrogating this business of mending wall, wondering whether it is necessary and how it can be made valuable? Or, will he turn his whole attention to his neighbor's business, which is mute physical repair? The apple farmer follows Thoreau's advice: "Perhaps it is the most generous course to permit your fellow-men to have an interest in your enterprise" and he invites his neighbor to join him in puzzling through the meaning of walling in and walling out. Lightly, uninsistently, he raises doubt about whether there is any sense in repairing *their* wall:

> There is where it is, we do not need the wall:
> He is all pine and I am apple orchard.
> My apple trees will never get across
> And eat the cones under his pines, I tell him.

The apple farmer teases his neighbor, trying to elicit a response. He proposes that "elves" keep dismantling the wall. He invites his neighbor to consider the question whether good fences make good neighbors:

> Spring is the mischief in me, and I wonder
> If I could put a notion in his head:
> "Why do they make good neighbors? . . ."

His neighbor declines the invitation to reflection. He cannot be humored or goaded into thought. The apple farmer sees that "putting a notion in his head" was fruitless, still, the encounter was valuable, providing an occasion to think the question through on his own.

Frost's neighbors name and rank the goods to be gotten by mending wall together differently, then. Still, they must find a balance of loaves and balls, as they do. The apple farmer doesn't begrudge attending to the business his neighbor finds pressing—the physical work of repair. He is willing to conform to "what anyone would do, here." He engages the task on his neighbor's terms and in the time frame imposed by the seasons. He acts for the sake of being a good neighbor according to local expectations. We learn that in the past the apple farmer had repaired the wall by himself; he could have avoided "walking the line." Indeed, Frost's apple farmer initiated this meeting: "I let my neighbor know beyond the hill." Think again of Thoreau's house-raising at Walden Pond:

> At length, in the beginning of May, with the help of some of my acquaintances, rather to improve so good an occasion for neighborliness than from any necessity, I set up the frame of my house.[15]

Like Thoreau, the apple farmer probes whether occasions for neighborliness might be improved so that it is more than "just another kind of out door game / Just one on a side" that "comes to little more." The annual repair could be imbued with the gravity of ritual, a rite nature imposes on New England by frost and thaws. Or, year after year of "walking the line" could provoke some deeper mutual appreciation. Or, as we learn, something unanticipated can come from encounters across a wall.

In the poem "Two Look at Two" lovers out on a walk halt beside a tumbled wall, thinking the day is over and that they must turn back: "This is all," they sigh. But across the wall, as near to it as they are, passes a doe, unafraid. Then a snort "bid them wait," and an antlered buck looks quizzically at them. The couple says to one another, "This, then, is all. What more is there to ask?" There is something more, though it is not something they would have thought to ask for. The sighting, they are startled to see, is mutual. The wall keeps the couple and the deer close but at a remove, just the right distance to see their attention and appreciation mirrored. They experience an unplanned, previously unimaginable moment of reciprocity:

> Two had seen two, whichever side you spoke from . . .
> A great wave from it going over them,
> As if the earth in one unlooked-for favor
> Had made them certain earth returned their love.

"Returned their love." The surprise of sympathetic recognition and response is a rare and transient but still true, unsentimental occurrence. It is the unanticipated regard, the presence that brightens and transforms the day, the "unlooked-for favor." The affinity we discover falls outside mechanical notions of give and take among neighbors. It is a surplus from ordinary encounters.

Frost's walkers could have reached out a hand to "break the spell," but they don't. Here as in "Mending Wall" neighborly reciprocity appears as something of a mystery. Difficult as it is, and still keeping the wall between them, Frost's farmers do balance "the boulders that have fallen to each." True, the apple farmer willingly engaged his neighbor on his terms, and we know that his intransigent neighbor did not return the favor:

> He will not go behind his father's saying,
> And he likes having thought of it so well
> He says again, "Good fences make good neighbors."

Yet what first looks like a one-sided, disappointing business turns out to be something more. His neighbor's thoughtlessness turns out to encourage the apple farmer's own thoughts about distance and engagement. The terms of reciprocity here were unpredictable; they remain unarticulated; they are not obvious equivalents, but finally both neighbors are well served. His neighbor gets the wall restored, and Frost's apple farmer gains insight. He gets the figure of a poem. Thoreau put it this way:

> I have frequently seen a poet withdraw, having enjoyed the most valuable part of a farm, while the crusty farmer supposed that he had got a few wild apples only. Why, the owner does not know it for many years when a poet has put his form in rhyme, the most admirable kind of invisible fence, has fairly impounded it, milked it, skimmed it, and got all the cream, and left the former only the skimmed milk.

Frost also tells us what these neighbors already know: they will have to mend the wall again and again. "Stay where you are until our backs are turned!" When their backs are turned the work comes undone. It is disturbed by natural forces and by hunters (others living nearby) who carelessly or maliciously upset the balance they achieve:

> I have come after them and made repair
> Where they have left not one stone on a stone,
> But they would have the rabbit out of hiding
> To please the yelping dogs.

Laying on the stones, Frost writes, "We wear our fingers rough with handling them." Riddling down to get give and take right is not easy, but wearing our fingers rough and trying out "a spell to make them balance" is no misfortune. Without it we miss the insights that come from assessing the boulders that have fallen to each. Without it neighbors are reduced to mute, bare utility, to gross mutual advantage.

## Imagined Geography: Four Terrains

I said that place matters: proximity to home. We count as neighbors those people who figure in our experience of life at home, who assume a role in the stories we tell. Again, the neighbors we identify make an appearance not because of location simply (our nearest neighbor may not figure) but because we assign them standing in our personal, social, or sacred geography. Nominal neighbors are strangers; we may fail to see them at all. "Thay be not neighbours, sir. Thay be near-dwellers."[16] If we were to draw a map of our lay of the land around home we might pinpoint the families on our block, say, or just a few houses or apartments, or almost a whole retirement community. Our image would show sites of connectivity and reveal expanses of blank space. Imagined geography is my term for our picture of the terrain of neighbors. The question, "who is my neighbor?"

is unanswerable, or the answer is an abstraction, unless we attend to imagined geography. It is the territory within which we mind one another's business—indeed constructing this lay of the land is part of our mutual business.

"The hood" is one illustration of imagined geography, evidence that political boundaries and school zones and census tracts are weak proxies for identifying who counts as our neighbor. The "hood" refers to a particular bit of urban territory that (typically) young males occupy and claim as their own. Their invented geography is material and fine-grained. They have surveyed it exactly. Their circumscribed daily movements trace its boundaries. The landmarks of home are mutually acknowledged, with affection. "The hood" expresses a proprietary pride. To mistake the bounds and uses of this territory is to mark oneself a stranger, a hostile intruder, or a fool. Not knowing the safe side of the street. Going to the wrong playground—the one ceded to teenagers. "The hood" is an exaggerated and acutely self-conscious example of a shared lay of the land—an imagined geography. It demonstrates the powerful hold of this place around home—in part because it is self-created; in part because it is defended against others, defined by virtual walls. For some of these young men, this geography, its concrete particulars, is identity. As it was for Hegel's Greeks: "Their grand object was their country in its living and real aspect;—this *actual* Athens, this Sparta, these Temples, these Altars, this form of social life . . . these manners and customs."[17]

Crown Heights in Brooklyn illustrates the imagined geography of neighbors divided by race and religion. Residents of Crown Heights in the 1980s and 90s included Hasidic Jews, immigrants from the Caribbean, African Americans residing there for generations, and a few Asians, black Orthodox Jews, and non-Orthodox Jews from Russia. At a time of white flight from the area, the Lubavitch Rebbe Menachem Mendel Schneerson received a revelation that God wanted them to remain. (He published this in a pamphlet, "Discourse on the Neighborhood.") His followers stayed. To them, "Crown Heights" invoked the crown of the Torah and the "crown of a good name." The neighborhood as they mapped it was called "the Rebbe's daled amos," his home. It was the headquarters of the worldwide Lubavitch movement. It was "the center of the world."[18]

*Their* Crown Heights was restricted in their minds to an area marked off by Eastern Parkway to the north, Lefferts Avenue to the south, Nostrand Avenue to the west, and Rochester Avenue to the east; for them, this portion constituted the whole of Crown Heights. We see the contours of a Hasidic woman's mental map when she asserts: "It's not really a

Black neighborhood here at all. They have nothing to do with us." It helps us grasp imagined geography to know that the Lubavitch made up only about six percent of the official Crown Heights population overall and only about twenty percent of the population of "their" designated Crown Heights, that African Americans, predominantly Caribbean immigrants, made up eighty percent, and that Crown Heights was an unusually integrated residential area. These people lived intermixed with one another; they were spatially though not socially integrated. Corrected, the woman adjusts her boundary, "Yeah but not these six blocks. Here it's really just Jewish."[19] Even there, her neighborhood was "really just Jewish" not on account of its demographic makeup or the day-to-day presence of others, the sightings and encounters, but because of the synagogue, baths, kosher grocers, and so on that tracked her life at home. The laws of religious life dictated her imagined geography. Her map of the lay of the land depended on willful unacknowledgment.[20]

Imagined geography can be a purely personal construction built from our own associations. In a beautiful, fabulous story of imagined geography, John Cheever's "Swimmer" made his way eight miles across the county by water toward his home. He saw the string of backyard swimming pools in his cartographer's eye, and the uncommon route gave him the feeling that he was a pilgrim, an explorer. He had made a contribution, in his mind, to modern geography. (There is an echo of Thoreau, another pilgrim who defamiliarized the landscape around home. When the New England ponds froze, Thoreau wrote, they afforded new and shorter routes to Concord and Lincoln, and he traveled not by road but across the string of ice.) From his watery perspective, real or in his mind's eye, Cheever's swimmer maps the lay of the land—the Grahams, the Hammers, the Lears, the Howlands, the Crosscups, the Levys, the Welchers, and the public pool in Lancaster. He narrates encounters during the course of his swim: the sociable hostess, the solicitous older couple, the patronizing man, the abusive former mistress. The swimmer may be a lost soul; we learn that his home is boarded up, his family scattered. But with the instincts of someone who once stood within this circle of neighbors, Ned assesses the particulars: the prosperous properties, the declining properties, the public pool with its pair of lifeguards abusing the swimmers through a public address system. He can calibrate his neighbors' circumstances and something of their personal lives and intimacies. He is accustomed to minding their business, even if he is beside himself when it comes to his own.

One last example of imagined geography remembered from my own childhood. A row of elderly blue-haired women sit on green wood benches in a pocket park in Washington Heights in New York City. They congregate every day after lunch, weather and health permitting, pocket-books with clasps clasped on their laps, far enough from the noisy swing set to carry on conversations about their grandchildren in the suburbs, the butcher around the corner, medical appointments, and funerals. For these immigrants from Eastern Europe, benches in the park were their community center, their synagogue. This park and its surrounding blocks were their known world. When she moved from the Bronx to Pinehurst Avenue, my grandmother, Esther Grossman, was instructed in the lay of the land by her sister, Mary. Sitting on the benches was "what anyone would do, here." Esther and Mary had a falling out (no one can recall the cause) and for a decade they did not speak. But neither one gave up regu-lar attendance at the park. They took up different places on the benches, creating a neutral ground by keeping several neighbor ladies between them. They kept up with events in one another's lives through the conver-sations they carried on separately with the company of neighbors in the park. Alienated as sisters, their posts in the park maintained their status as neighbors.

Imagined geography is, finally, the terrain on which we mind our neigh-bors' business but also our own, and constructing it is part of tending to and caring for ourselves. We elect the objects we register and regard. We take the identical route through the neighborhood on our morning walk, every day, a thousand times. We pay homage to our personal landmarks: those blue shutters, that Korean grocery, this T station, and the next. There is nothing plastic about our course; we follow our beaten track. It may be pleasing for its familiarity so that not an inch of the route spurs imagination; it is the muted backdrop that allows us to get lost in our thoughts. Or it casts the opposite spell, and not an inch of the route can be spared by the imagination.[21] Then, the things we see carry us far away: this ornate façade, this waterfront, this dark underpass make us think of foreign places and "the extent of the globe." The city blocks we circle re-mind us of earlier occupants, our neighbors across time. "East of my beanfield, across the road, lived Cato Ingraham, slave of Duncan Ingra-ham," Thoreau wrote, the past present to him.[22] As it may be for us: these streets were lined with the shacks of slaves; this suburban subdivision was a farm on the Hackensack River; before they were artist studios and cof-fee bars these buildings were home to Haitians and Chinese, and before them Italians and Jews.

## Mental Mapping

We locate home and neighbors on the terrain of imagined geography. We have latitude in designating who counts as a neighbor. For urban sociologists, "mental mapping" is both a method and a subject of study that captures attention and selection. It is a graphic representation of the lay of the land. Stanley Milgram's research asked residents to depict their experience of public geography, their spatial representations of Paris and New York. In their drawings of the city, residents chart their sense of boundaries, landmarks, and distances between places; the mental maps illustrate their zone of comfort, and their sense of status hierarchy in the city. By aggregating these drawings, Milgram could identify salient deviations from material reality that residents shared. Mental maps, he argued, are "the principal means whereby the merely geographic and physical characteristics of the city are given social meaning."[23] They demonstrate that cities are creative social constructions.[24] Mental maps of Paris or New York do not elicit the lay of the land we would plot if asked to mark our neighbors. They don't represent the perspective from home. True, neighbors encounter one another as well as strangers in public venues: church, shopping malls, and civic spaces—the likely spots on the maps of "neighborhood" that interest sociologists.[25] But "who is my neighbor?" maps a different space. Social scientists note that it would be impossible to "magically define the boundaries of each respondent's neighborhood personally" on a large scale,[26] but mental maps *could* chart "who is my neighbor" when it comes to enhancing or diminishing the quality of life at home. My examples of imagined geography make the point.

"In spatial arrangements . . . everybody is next to somebody." "Next door" matters for some things—when it comes to disturbances for example, though sound travels and there are rooms farther away that afford a view into our home. Location—degree of proximity—also proves significant when it comes to the experience of ethnic and religious division, and above all when it comes to black-white contact and integration around home, a theme to which I return. Thomas Schelling formalized the dynamic of movement in and out of racially mixed neighborhoods, demonstrating the latitude we have in designating who counts as a neighbor. Schelling built into his model findings of empirical studies that showed that individual whites who want to live in an integrated setting nonetheless feel uncomfortable when they are not an overwhelming majority. When the proportion of blacks is discomfiting to them, voluntary resegregation keeps interracial contact within tolerable levels.[27] (The desires of African Americans are similar, with the key addition that white hostility is a factor in their residential choices.) Here neither racial antipathy nor stigmatization are at work but rather something closer to "rational prejudice," meaning the discomfort that accompanies what *feels* like too much dilution of the company of one's own affinity group. Under these conditions, Schelling shows, the process of resegregation turns on who counts as a neighbor. The actual proportion of blacks and whites in an officially designated neighborhood overall turns out to be insignificant. Instead, "satisfaction depends upon how far one's 'neighborhood' extends."[28] In his initial hypothetical distribution, residents define the neighborhood as a long stretch of blocks, and everyone is satisfied with the mix. But if they limit consideration to those who live on either side of them, a quarter of whites and blacks are going to be surrounded by neighbors of the other race. This is a "tipping-point," Schelling argues, and the process of resegregation will begin, even if everyone would prefer integration. Who counts as my neighbor in my imagined geography drives the dynamic.

Frost tells us in "Mending Wall" that a habitual, senseless, unselfconsciously circumscribed lay of the land is the darkness we move in, especially when it comes to erecting walls between neighbors. It is thoughtless, that is, unless we think to ask why we map the lay of the land as we do and whether the wall gives offense. Is imagined geography amenable to critical reflection? What gives walls value for neighbors?

## "Something There Is That Does Not Love a Wall"

Walls figure prominently as metaphor and actuality in the experience of neighbors for an obvious reason. Neighbors have rooms with a view into ours. Willfully or inadvertently we learn a lot about the people next door: their health and habits, financial state, emotional distress, their children's behavior. Our neighbors have a vantage point on us, too. Walling in and walling out is a graphic representation of minding our own business versus minding our neighbors'. We understand that the people living nearby are inescapable. We have an inkling at least of our mutual vulnerability and our capacity to affect the quality of the day for good or ill. Walls, material and virtual, create some minimal "zone of privacy."

Once again the poet points the way, and I return to "Mending Wall." We know that the apple farmer's neighbor is determined to maintain the stone boundary between their orchards. He acts from primitive impulse or loyalty to what he was taught by his father as a child. Frost describes him standing with his boulder grasped firmly "like an old-stone savage armed."

> He moves in darkness as it seems to me
> Not of woods only and the shade of trees.
> He will not go behind his father's saying,
> And he likes having thought of it so well
> He says again, "Good fences make good neighbors."

The apple farmer considers questioning him more insistently. But he holds back. He is no Socrates or Thoreau, provoking and antagonizing, challenging common sense. "I'd rather he said it for himself." We readers are more susceptible to the apple farmer's prodding to "go behind" sayings and darkness, to give ourselves a fair account of our reasons for walling in and walling out and the offense we may give (or take).

> Before I built a wall I'd ask to know
> What I was walling in or walling out,
> And to whom I was like to give offense.

Some walls are intended and experienced as harsh, rude, or brutally withholding. But Frost does not take an entrenched stand against walls, not even if they sometimes give offense. Rather, aware of this "something there is that doesn't love a wall," he demands a reason for them. Their erection should be deliberate, judged necessary. The poem is an inquiry.

The poet also inquires, what is this "something" that does not love a wall? We know that nature does not love these piles of stone. Nature:

> That sends the frozen-ground-swell under it,
> And spills the upper boulders in the sun . . .

Another possibility is metaphysical: instead of his orchard bounded by a wall the apple farmer may imagine an unimpeded horizon, an open expanse: Thoreau's "my own sun and moon and stars, and a little world all to myself."[29] Or perhaps Frost means to evoke territory that is not appropriated, fenced, domestic, reclaimed from nature, but rather an American frontier as seen by Jim in Willa Cather's *My Antonia*: "There was nothing but land . . . I had the feeling that the world was left behind, that we had got over the edge of it, and were outside man's jurisdiction."[30] Or perhaps the "something" that does not love a wall is a moral intuition, and Frost shares the lament that among neighbors "the only cooperation which is commonly possible is exceedingly partial and superficial," not "true cooperation."[31] So, the apple farmer and his neighbor perform the task of mending wall but without more it is "just another kind of out door game."

The apple farmer sees no reason to restore this barrier between their two orchards ("There is where it is, we do not need the wall"). But "something there is that does not love a wall" is not categorical. The poem does not pronounce, it invites us to reflect. Again:

> Before I built a wall I'd ask to know
> What I was walling in or walling out . . .

Some walls are warranted; separation and restraint serve good purposes. "The Cow in Apple Time" roams unchecked and causes harm:

> Something inspires the only cow of late
> To make no more of a wall than an open gate . . .

She gorges on fruit.

> Her face is flecked with pomace and she drools
> A cider syrup.

She pays a price for trespass:

> She bellows on a knoll against the sky,
> Her udder shrivels and the milk goes dry.

This wall was not there to give offense. Simply, without fences we may be incapable of keeping our distance from one another. We may consume too much gossip and the "old musty cheese" of one another. We may offend more readily. We may injure ourselves by wandering and paying too little attention to our own proper business.

What Frost does not do is conjure up unmarked territory, open borders, free range. In the ideal imaginary of all fences unloved and left unmended, we would be cosmopolitans or strangers having chance encounters. Without walls, we are not neighbors greeting one another from our recognized spots ("He is all pine, I am apple orchard"), grappling with engagement and detachment, establishing neutral ground, assessing whether and how to mind our own and others' business, striving for easy reciprocity. *We keep the wall between us as we go.* The inversion of the farmer's saying is truer, for reasons I will explore in Chapter 6, "Live and Let Live": good neighbors build good fences.

## Friends and Neighbors

Neighbors who figure on the terrain of our imagined geography are not strangers. "Mending Wall" also reminds us that neighbors are not friends: "We keep the wall between us as we go." In conventional idiom the two often appear together: "friends and neighbors" but something is lost by casual pairing. Neighbors do not just fall short of friendship. Even good neighbors are not almost-friends. Neighbor relations are not weak friendships. The relation is fundamentally different. As an exercise in conceptual analysis line-drawing holds little interest unless it becomes clear that without these distinctions in place and in mind we are liable to misunderstand our experience. Without distinguishing neighbors from friends, the distinct and independent value of neighbors and, as I will show, the democracy of everyday life, is lost to view.

Certainly, pairing "friend and neighbor" is misleading if the import is to infuse love and intimacy into the modest neighbor relation. But this pairing comes easily in part because neighbors as friends is a mainstay of popular culture, an enduring genre. Choose your television neighbors: Ralph and Alice Kramden and Ed and Thelma Norton, the couples in *The Honeymooners,* or the mismatched neighbors in *The Beverly Hillbillies*, or the quirky singles in *Seinfeld* or *Friends*. The characters reveal their signature traits through interaction with their neighbors. They exhibit obsequiousness, accommodatingness, uncompromisingness. They display ordinary vices of snobbery and small betrayals. They are irritating and meddling. They dramatize giving and taking offense, suffering slights and misunderstandings. But in the fixed structure of this genre, goodwill and mutual understanding are dependably restored. The episodes have a cumulative effect as week after week these neighbors carry on their irrepressible give and take. Caught up in their back and forth, the world outside of home — work, extended family, society broadly — barely makes an appearance. Neighbors are the constant company. They have intimate knowledge of one another's troubles and aspirations. They judge and criticize but also advise and comfort. In short, popular culture underscores the thought, the hope, that neighbors are familiars. Neighbors, in these sentimental narratives, are friends.

There are other, unsentimental grounds for linking friends and neighbors. Both friend and neighbor seem to invert the ways of the larger society. Both exist outside and apart from "explicit contract, rational exchange, formal division of labor, and impersonal institutions." Both are "voluntary, unspecialized, informal, and private." Acts of friendship and neighborliness are personal and individual. They share this as well: the matters that engage friends and neighbors are open-ended. Indeterminacy and unpredictability help explain why for both friends and neighbors the simple fact of openness and availability is a great value. Both are present and respond to wants and needs, regular or unanticipated, though our friends' accessibility is not tied to physical presence. We have discretion in electing the neighbors with whom we willingly engage as we do in electing friends. We have latitude in shaping the character of our encounters. Setting them off together as a pair is significant in this respect: both friends and neighbors are an "ideal, indeed idealized, area for that highly individualized conception of personal agency central to modern notions of individual freedom."[32]

But now consider the quality of these experiences. We find particular neighbors more or less reliable counterparts in give and take. We have more or less confidence that when it comes to specifics—loaning a tool or returning a greeting—our neighbor will not misuse, exploit, or humiliate us, or make us unsafe. Neighbor relations are not all instrumental or calculating, not at all, but like Frost's farmers we laboriously balance loaves and balls and "we wear our fingers rough with handling them." This is not true of friendship. We wish to do more for friends not equivalent or as necessary. We feel free to be vulnerable and in their debt. We welcome their reliance on us. Friends want what is good for us, just for our own sake.[33] And the time frame of our commitment to friends is extended, often lifelong.

There is more to the contrast. The rough equality of give and take among neighbors, its democratic ethos, comes from the judgment that for the purposes of mundane encounters these people are "decent folk"—a moral judgment but a limited one. It is a fragmented and contingent judgment. For the most part, we know our neighbors only partially, often superficially. We are not inclined to consider them deeply, to probe their hearts or characters or their trustworthiness in every conceivable situation. We have no reason to. Our interactions are normally limited, meaning they involve neither the necessities of life nor intimacies. Neighbors are not typically given to confidences. The subjects of our conversations are bounded. Familiarity is constrained. A certain distance is preserved. Put differently, relations with neighbors rarely "proceed by way of a deepening," as friendship and love do.[34] Barring extraordinary conditions of need or peril, they remain on a plane of repeated mundane encounters.

The delicacy of neighbor relations lies precisely in the fact that deliberately or inadvertently, wanted or not, we may have bits of intimate knowledge without strong attachment, commitment, or trust.

In plain contrast, friendship is marked by the absence of barriers and abdication of a great deal of privacy. We know friends intimately and trust them implicitly. Friends are thought to reveal their authentic feelings and true self. We think of our friend holistically, as a unique, complex, and "beautiful soul," and we think of friendship as having no other constitutive feature besides mutual elective affinity. Deeply preferential, friendship is exclusive, or so we see it today. We choose our friends, though the word is inexact because it suggests deliberate selection rather than what is often the case—evolving and deepening attachment or romantic spark or the moral attraction of character. We cast a certain halo around our friends, as we should.

In philosophical accounts, a friend complements and improves us. Equality between friends lies here, in what Aristotle called "the friendship of virtue," in contrast to utility or pleasure. This is far from the rough equality of neighbors as "decent folk" for the purposes of give and take. For Aristotle, friends bring to one another wisdom, moral virtue, and goodwill. In the strong terms of classical philosophy, a friend is "another self." (Though without a certain separation, even here, friends cannot contemplate us well and goad us to goodness and improvement.[35]) Viewed in terms of the high moral purpose of friendship, a friend is "a sort of beautiful enemy," a prod to self-reflection and perfection. Thoreau and his friend Emerson were twinned in their determination to make friendship something metaphysical, not defined by emotion and removed from the mundane interactions of neighbors:

> Why insist on rash personal relations with your friend? Why go to his house, or know his mother and brother and sisters? Why be visited by him at your own? . . . Leave this touching and clawing. Let him be to me a spirit.[36]

Friends and neighbors: the conceptual difference and the divergent quality of experience might be summed up by saying that friends are irreplaceable, neighbors are not. I don't mean that any two neighbors are the same. When neighbors give a strong dose of themselves and affect life at home for good or ill, or when they profoundly alter our self-understanding or provide a rare, "unlooked-for favor," one good or bad neighbor does not substitute for another, clearly. Nonetheless, we value neighbors above all for the fact that they are "decent folk" present to us in our daily lives at home. (Not too present, we hope.) Of course, friendships may develop between neighbors and outlast moves away. For the most part, though, the "unpoetic neighbor" is not loved; she is not our friend.

The narrative threads I trace in the next chapter take us more deeply into what neighbors are and can be for one another. Settler, immigrant, and suburban narratives of neighbors play a startlingly large part in American fiction and memoir. They are a window onto the personal moral identity of good neighbor and American national identity as "good neighbor nation."

# 2

# Narrative Threads

## Settlers, Immigrants, and
## Suburban "Grotesques"

"We live in an age of unprecedented wealth, but in the realm of narrative and symbol we are deprived." Perhaps so, if like narratives of God and redeeming nation the stories we need must satisfy what Andrew Delbanco called the "unslaked craving for transcendence."[1] In the untranscendent realm of narrative indispensable to the democracy of everyday life, however, we are far from deprived. Good neighbor as a facet of moral identity and as a collective American self-representation are rich composites created from an unprecedented and ever-increasing wealth of fiction, poetry, and memoir. Three iconic representations of the United States—as a vast settler nation, a nation of immigrants, and as the quintessential scene of suburban life—have home and neighbors as a central theme. Here, I follow these threads, which fix the contours of the democracy of everyday life in our imagination and shape our encounters.

The remarkable thing is the strength and endurance of representations of good neighbor. They survive tragic episodes—really whole historical periods—of violence, prejudice, cruelty, and mistrust that wall neighbors in and out. They survive contrary personal experiences; that is, despite the ordinary and not-so-ordinary vices neighbors inflict on us, thoroughgoing cynicism and misanthropy are rare. There is just enough accuracy, coherence, and moral meaning in settler, immigrant, and suburban narratives to reinforce the regulative ideal of good neighbor and to deliver a strong sense of its democratic ethos.

The importance of these narratives to my project is perfectly plain. They make particular places and moments in time vivid. even visceral.

They endow the subject with dimension.[2] Like "thick" cultural ethnography, these narratives document what, in this place, anyone would do. Like "history," the meaning of the democracy of everyday life "is interior"[3] and through fiction and memoir we witness the accommodations of men and women as they learn, enforce, unlearn, or reject local knowledge; oscillate between minding their own business and minding their neighbor's business; puzzle out what reciprocity requires; assess when rallying together and speaking out against offenders is imperative; what it means to live and let live. Neighbors in literature as in life are driven to think about the ethics of their situation, but in fiction they think aloud. Iconic narratives deliver more than types—prairie women or suburban couples. We meet characters. Stories also bring us face-to-face with neighbors in extreme circumstances, alerting us to the special character of fear and comfort when it is *neighbors* who hold our lives in their hands.

Literature brings the abstract "neighbor" to life, then, and more: it fashions experience. "Living by Fiction" is no fiction.[4] Our thinking does not take its bearings from unmediated events. We draw on familiar narratives to assay the world. That applies to our lives, and it also applies to this study. To repeat a point I made in "Biography of a Theory," I did not find my organizing concepts—minding our own versus minding our neighbors' business and the democracy of everyday life—ready to hand in moral or political philosophy. Rather, narratives reveal patterns of experience from which I draw out these elements. So it would be a misdescription to say that the situations and quotations I offer are illustrative. I have not exploited fiction to give flesh to some previously existing understanding. Instead, I've created a political theory of the democracy of everyday life from the patterns of encounters made familiar from reading, and from popular culture, too. Settler, immigrant, and suburban narratives show unmistakably that quotidian life at home is ethically and democratically meaningful.

Frontier, immigrant, and suburban threads are distinct, of course. Anxiousness about neighbors peering into our apartment window or building fences across our property line would be incomprehensible to Willa Cather's prairie women craving company and conversation. Advice and aid among immigrants packed into New York tenements do not translate neatly into the experiences of suburbanites "gentrifying" an inner-city neighborhood. The separate threads are tangled in our imagination, though; a move to a new subdevelopment or a return to the rural South can feel like pioneering.

These threads attest to the centrality of good neighbor to American experience and its distinctive if not unique contours. It begins with the fact that separately and together these narratives expose this enduring experience: movement.

## Moving

"The red of the grass made all the great prairie the colour of wine-stains, or of certain seaweeds when they are first washed up. And there was so much motion in it; the whole country seemed, somehow, to be running."[5] Neighbors rent, sublet, buy, sell, and move away. They are our immediate, close-up measure of personal and social change. The historical time frame is wildly variable as befits settler, immigrant, and suburban narratives — from the offspring of men and women floated to America on the Mayflower and still occupying the same spot of land in Provincetown, to the "great migration" of southern blacks to the North, to the first Iraqi immigrant family in a Nebraska town, to early comers to a Florida retirement community. For romantic sensibilities, movement signifies freedom, but here it is not tied thrillingly to speed or escape or immersion in the present moment — movement for itself. It is not Kerouac's open road. Existential restlessness is one aspect of movement, and so is aimlessness: adolescents "drift[ing] from city to torn city, sloughing off both the past and the future as snakes shed their skins."[6] But in settler, immigrant, and suburban narratives moving has a destination: home.

For Cather's settlers on the move across the plains, in the perpetual forward momentum of Saul Bellow's Augie March growing up among Chicago immigrants, and for families transplanted to suburbia, moves are beginnings. Typically, the direction is "pitched relentlessly forward."[7] Arrival may come with fantasies of shining possibility: take Jay Gatsby's move to his magnificent house within sight of the green light at the end of Daisy Buchanan's dock: "He had come a long way to this blue lawn and his dream must have seemed so close that he could hardly fail to grasp it."[8] Or moving may represent some more mundane opportunity. We also know that behind all that motion may be misfortune, escape, retreat, loss, dispossession, economic fall. Empty nests, bankruptcy, aging parents, the hunt for work. Moving may be inauspicious. Moving day is not always elected, and neither is where we land.[9]

Even so, in fiction and in life, propulsion is commonplace and obdurately infused with some bit of optimism. Whether or not this initially open attitude projects a better life overall, each new move and home comes with anticipation of encounters with people living nearby and it often comes with a tentative resolve to do "what anyone would do, here." Expectancy fastens on the prospect of home in an environment of "decent folk." Perhaps especially, suburban neighbors "bear a heavy load of projection."[10] This openness is voiced by newcomers and by the neighbors who receive them. The good neighbor ideal is anticipatory, modest, and available to us—a reasonable expectation, a carrier of hopefulness.

We might predict that a whole country that "seemed, somehow, to be running" impedes neighbor relations. Certainly a history of encounters enhances the prospect of reciprocity; iteration allows us to assess and reassess neighbors as "decent folk"; it allows learning and change in how we navigate interactions. Residential churning and housing where transients predominate, where there is little question of settling for long, where newcomers are poised perilously on the social and physical periphery, and where neighbors figure temporarily on one another's lay of the land, and know it, the democracy of everyday life is truncated. Reflecting on his native mining town in the Sierra Nevada ("a place five or six years older than myself"), Josiah Royce described "a community of irresponsible strangers," "a blind and stupid and homeless generation of selfish wanderers."[11]

That is never the whole story, though. For movement does not subvert the necessity of dealing with neighbors. Think of California motels that provide week-by-week housing for migrant agricultural workers: is there reason to think that rootless people only tenuously at home in the spot where they land are oblivious to the rudimentary goods of "decent folk" next door—greeting, recognition, availability? Or that the moral identity of good neighbor has no hold on them? Studies of transience have shown that newcomers "engage in rapid and wide-ranging exploration of the possibilities."[12] The divorced man, a new resident in a temporary apartment, emerging from isolation to form a connection to an equally transient neighbor, is something of a staple of contemporary short-story writing.

> When his wife told him to get out of the house that had been hers . . .
> Valdek Moore looked in the paper and found a semi-furnished, one-
> bedroom unit at Linden Pines . . . On his first night in the single bed
> that still held the shape of its previous tenant, Valdek had felt a lift at
> having pioneered himself, at thirty years old, to a place he could never

have imagined he'd end up. But by the next morning, what was new to him was already too old, and he came to the uneasy conclusion that Linden Pines was where people lived only because they had nowhere else to go, and for now, the same was true for him.[13]

As the title of the story "Companion Animal" predicts, he finds himself making connections with neighbors at Linden Pines. For as long as they live nearby, neighbors have the prospect of ongoing interactions, exposure to one another's ordinary vices, beneficiaries of one another's benign give and take, incentives for good turns, and cautions against giving and taking offense. Until they move away (or we do), we have a glimmer of shared fate—not in some larger metaphysical or political sense but in our mutual vulnerability and the possibility of enhancing or degrading the quality of life at home.

This is not to deny the social and economic obstacles to mobility today: the reality of people who are stuck in desolate rural areas, impoverished central cities, or declining suburbs so that for them "here" just *is* all the world. Nor do I mean to ignore the fact that our personal histories have become inescapable, made indelible and accessible by the Internet and social networking. We carry more baggage than in the past. It is just to say that anticipation is indomitable.

Anticipation may be imbued with something stronger: a hint of utopianism. This shouldn't be surprising. Americans are susceptible to "the belief that it should be possible . . . to build the New Jerusalem on earth in half an hour."[14] Puritans were the fierce beginning. In John Winthrop's "Model of Christian Charity," minding our neighbors' business was "a painful search for signs of grace" that entailed relentless mutual scrutiny, instruction, and chastisement. Minding our neighbors' business was a necessity of salvation.[15] Suitably tempered and stripped of theology and close community, the idea of New Jerusalem is familiar enough. The creation myths that attended early suburban developments like Levittown still hold today. "Instant cities" crop up and attract hopeful settlers. Whole towns of elderly now exist by choice, communities as unique as counterculture communes of the 1960s. If not utopian yearning, there is at least expectancy. It is inherent in settler narratives. Lincoln Steffens wrote:

> My father, who plodded and fought or worried the whole long hard way at oxen pace, always paused when he recalled how they turned over the summit and waded down, joyously, in the amazing golden sea of sunshine—he would pause, see it again as he saw it then, and say, "I saw that this was the place to live."[16]

Before experience confirms or disappoints, like settlers and immigrants, new neighbors everywhere "have decided to love America: surely America will love them back."[17] "America" may not return their love (civil and political rights are denied; democratic participation is impossibly remote; injustice comes with a local face). But neighbors may. Good neighbor is an embodiment, finally, of democratic hope untethered to public political institutions, grounded in unpoetic quotidian life at home. [18]

## Settler Nation: Neighbors as "Decent Folk"

Good neighbor grew out of America as a settler nation with a vast territory. "Before it was a place, the New World was an idea": a place of plenitude of gold, spices, boundless level plains, abundance of teeming skies, and flashes of fishes, but also a place of emptiness, without the disappointments of the old world or, for that matter, the disappointment of coming to a promised land that was already inhabited by someone else.[19] There *were* people on this land, of course, and settlers opened new territories for themselves by violently displacing or murdering Native Americans and other claimants. ("The central drama of American history has been the struggle to force these savageries into view.")[20] The myth of emptiness "was part and parcel of settler efforts to transform themselves into 'natives' and to escape the categories of colonialism and empire and European origins"—to "assert an authentically local American ... way of life."[21] "There was nothing but land," Willa Cather's Jim Burden observes as late as the early twentieth century, "not a country at all, but the material out of which countries are made."[22] Robert Frost made the point this way: the land was "vaguely realizing westward / But still unstoried, artless, unenhanced."[23] Neighbors carried on the project of settling that would transform the "unstoried" place.

To Cather's Jim Burden arriving on the plains as a young boy it seems "that the world was left behind, that we had got over the edge of it."[24] Often outside the jurisdiction of any very visible political authority and with few organized social arrangements apart from religion, if that, settlers relied on one another to transform wilderness into society. They were not self-sufficient. Survival of crops, animals, and livelihood depended on help with plowing, harvesting, building, putting out fires, providing credit, sending messages, and receiving news. Neighbors' business *was* the news. With effort, neighbors sustained for one another the life cycle rituals of births, marriages, and burials, and the ceremonies of seasons. Reciprocity was required for getting on, and the company of neighbors was not a purely voluntary association.

Drawn from her own experience, Laura Ingalls Wilder's fictional pioneer family moves from Indian Territory, across Kansas, across Missouri, across Iowa, into Wisconsin where they lived among Swedes and Germans, and finally "a long way into Minnesota."[25] The family endures biblical plagues of locusts and an infliction unknown to the Old Testament — blizzards. They survive with the help of Mr. Nelson and other neighbors whom they assist in turn. They expect the best, ask as little of them as possible, and are rarely disappointed. Wilder's wildly popular frontier saga is a fantasy of innocence.

Willa Cather's red grass prairies and tiny towns at the "edge of the world" have a starkly different atmosphere, and her frontier neighbors exhibit a sounder moral psychology. They inhabit the vast physical space nervously, tentatively. In this landscape of the sublime, distances of ground and sky seem infinite and people infinitesimal. Mutual assistance is the slight human antidote to indifferent nature and brute luck: "Misfortune seemed to settle like an evil bird on the roof of the log house, and to flap its wings there, warning human beings away. The Russians had such bad luck that people were afraid of them and liked to put them out of mind."[26] Cather recreates the obstinacy, ingratitude, prejudice, and violence of neighbors, and the coldness and angry alienation that sometimes divided them despite the press of need. The full taste of experience is her subject.

In *My Antonia* a family from Virginia lives side by side on the Nebraska plain with immigrant settlers — Scandinavians, Russians, and Czechs. The narrator's voice belongs to Jim Burden. Orphaned, just arrived at his grandparents' on the frontier, their first conversation is about neighbors: they "talked about my journey, and about the arrival of a new Bohemian family; she said they were to be our nearest neighbors." His first foray from the house is to make their acquaintance: "We were taking them some provisions, as they had come to live on a wild place where there was no garden or chicken-house, and very little broken land."

Reciprocity is necessary for getting by, and reciprocity makes the impossibility of self-sufficiency palatable, but it is not loose and easy. For one thing, the costs of assurances and aid are steep. When a neighbor does not return a borrowed horse-collar, the Burdens go to retrieve it and find it "badly used — trampled in the dirt and gnawed by rats until the hair was sticking out of it." The borrower's surly, unapologetic attitude provokes a knock-down fight and an eruption of mistrust: "After all we went through on account of 'em last winter! I don't want to see you get too thick with any of 'em," Jim is warned. Nor can reciprocity be a sort of open-ended and rough parity, as it must, if neighbors approach give and take in an accounting frame of mind, skewed by a thumb on the scales. Neighbors like Antonia's mother are bitter, envious, complaining, grasping:

> In the kitchen she caught up an iron pot that stood on the back of the stove and said: "You got many, Shimerdas no got ... You got many things for cook. If I got all things like you, I make much better."

I pause on this novel because Grandmother Burden is the democratic ethos of neighbors incarnate. She disregards her neighbors' origin, former social status, and character overall, and concentrates on what "decent folk" can expect from one another day to day. She delivers hampers of food to the Shimerda family, offers advice about planting, presents the gift of a pot, and in all this she takes care not to injure their pride. She recognizes the family's need and persists in reaching out to them despite their ingratitude. She makes allowances and tolerates being misunderstood. For a long while she attributes the Shimerdas' dire situation to ignorance: "There's no good reason why Mrs. Shimerda couldn't have got hens from the neighbours last fall and had a hen-house going by now. I reckon she was confused and didn't know where to begin." She resists disparaging them as willfully irresponsible. She affords her neighbors latitude.

Over time, however, Grandma Burden alters her judgment. The Shimerdas are too willing to be dependent. She no longer anticipates reciprocity. Her reservoir of neighborly goodwill is drained. She does not abandon this family in need, but she now sees herself as "our brother and sister's keeper." Neighborliness is *demoted* into Christian charity. For Grandmother Burden, charity is dutifulness without piety. It is basic human decency taking the form of assistance. The inversion of moral hierarchy is striking: reciprocity among "decent folk" supersedes love. Thoreau used similar terms to criticize neighbors who appeal "not to your hospitality but to your *hospitalality*; who earnestly wish to be helped, and preface their appeal with the information that they are resolved, for one thing, never to help themselves. ... Objects of charity are not guests."[27]

When Mr. Shimerda dies and the officers of the Norwegian church refuse to extend him the hospitality of the graveyard, Grandmother Burden speaks up, and we see the democratic ethos on full display:

> If these foreigners are so clannish . . . we'll have to have an American graveyard that will be more liberal-minded. I'll get right after Josiah to start one in the spring. If anything was to happen to me, I don't want the Norwegians holding inquisitions over me to see whether I'm good enough to be laid amongst 'em.

In its way, "decent folk" is a fighting creed.

Willa Cather substitutes strong women for the standard male settler; the taste of their experience gets its due. "These women in my family would seem to have been pragmatic and in their deepest instincts clinically radical," a descendent of California settlers wrote, "given to breaking clean with everyone and everything they knew." For settlers faced not only physical danger but also the existential knowledge that their journey is

> a kind of death, involving the total abandonment of all previous life, mothers and fathers and brothers and sisters who would never again be seen, all sentiment banished, the most elementary comforts necessarily relinquished.[28]

Cather gives us the bravery of lonely women in marriages with men who barely speak. Women with few means of self-expression or lives of their own, for whom the occasional company of neighbors or just news of them is a resource for resisting despair and overcoming the paralysis of isolation. Among women, anxiety and drudgery are unceasing, and neighbors can provide emotional uplift, "unlooked for favors." There is Mrs. Harline, who

> routed lassitude and indifference wherever she came . . . Wash-day was interesting, never dreary, at the Harlings'. Preserving-time was a prolonged festival, and house-cleaning was a revolution. When Mrs. Harling made garden that spring, we could feel the stir of her undertaking through the willow hedge that separated our place from hers.

Cather's neighbors reciprocate more than labor and borrowed things, clearly; their encounters are not all utilitarian. Neighbors with the fortunate disposition of women like Mrs. Harling bring home the truth: "To affect the quality of the day, that is the highest of arts."[29]

So settler narratives evoke a time when neighbors' importance was elementary and comprehensive. Neighbors were all we had for assistance and companionship, and mainly what we had as resources for understanding, not least for having an eye on ourselves, for self-understanding.

In this narrative thread of good neighbor there is no question of minding one's own business. If they were "decent folk" neighbors could make a life side by side, created from the flawed but good enough human materials at hand.

The experience of settling did not stop with the journey and homesteading, of course. It continued as one family chose an acre on the plains and then in search of help and companionship drew other pioneers to adjacent land. It led to the growth of commerce, social institutions, and politics. Sentimental settler narratives omit this, reinforcing the idyll of neighbors on their own, outside all jurisdictions. They are skewed by denial of the policy and patronage without which the business of settling would have foundered—the railroads, federal land grants, irrigation, agricultural support benefiting those who knew even if they didn't acknowledge "that the richest claim of all lay not in the minefields but in Washington."[30] This willful omission allows the settler to be turned into a pronounced ideology of nearly unfettered individualism, excepting only the voluntary assistance of people living nearby. Sentimentality in this form has political consequences.

Rural life is no longer predominant in the United States, and in any case we are not dependent on an "economy of mutual favors," or on those living nearby for company. Social relations are rife with institutions and organizations, and embedded in markets and several layers of government.[31] Even in sparsely settled areas people have the experience of pluralism, meaning they shift involvements among spheres of life in our complex society. They work with colleagues. They belong to voluntary associations. Where they live, home, is not all the world.

Nonetheless the settler narrative remains a living thread of good neighbor and provides a "single master odyssey" of leaving a life behind, confronting material and moral challenges, meeting the uncertain and unknown in a new place.[32] So we evoke settler images often. Everywhere there are neighbors who count themselves natives and others who are tentative newcomers. When Scott Fitzgerald's Nick Carraway moves from the Midwest to West Egg on Long Island he feels like an outsider, until, a few weeks after his arrival, a stranger asks him for directions: "I told him. And as I walked on I was lonely no longer. I was a guide, a pathfinder, an original settler. He had casually conferred on me the freedom of the neighborhood."[33] The young mother in Jonathan Franzen's story "Good Neighbors" moves her family into a deteriorated urban area and begins the business of renewal. The author calls her a pioneer. The territory she enters confronts her with something like the original disappointment of a promised land that was already inhabited by someone else and the historical tragedies that ensue. She had to figure out "how to respond when a poor person of color accused you of destroying her neighborhood?" She was going to appropriate the place, and did not count "poor persons of color" as neighbors. Her task was

> to relearn certain life skills that your own parents had fled to the suburbs specifically to unlearn, like how to interest the local cops in actually doing their job, and how to protect a bike from a highly motivated thief, and when to bother rousting a drunk from your lawn furniture, and how to encourage feral cats to shit in somebody else's children's sandbox.[34]

Later arrivals on the block learn how to get along from her. She demonstrates by example and by minding her neighbors' business and instructing them in the requisite local knowledge. That is, until there are enough transplanted suburbanites to alter the terms of "what anyone would do, here." Then, the first settler's demonstrations are no longer necessary. Her pioneer status is forgotten — ancient history comes fast in changing neighborhoods. Her ministrations are unnecessary, even resented. *She* will have to learn the altered lay of the land.

"Settler" captures the risk and initial optimism of moving to a new place, of living among unfamiliar people some of whom will, for better or worse, become familiar. Immigrant and suburban narratives retell the story. Newcomers everywhere assess their neighbors' trustworthiness and absorb the rudiments of local knowledge, and everywhere new arrivals must consider whether they will make it their business to accept the terms on offer. Everywhere we are caught up in the dynamic of learning or refusing to learn "what anyone would do, here," and as important, unlearning the lay of the land left behind. Accentuated though it is in dramatic accounts of hazardous journey and social lack, the settler narrative is generalizable: the affirmation of the intrinsic good of neighbors' presence, availability, and not-at-all trivial gestures of recognition and acts of kindness that go beyond utility, and the democratic ethos of "decent folk."

## Immigrant Nation: Learning "What Anyone Would Do, Here"

Along with settler narratives there is the canonical portrait of America as a nation of immigrants. Both are infused with the aesthetic of the sublime — the sense of being a tiny speck in a fathomless space. The plains were a vast emptiness. In cities, the sublime takes the form of Whitman-esque plenitude. Instead of a sea of grass, a roiling sea of people: "bigshots and operators, commissioners, grabbers, heelers, tipsters, hoodlums, wolves, fixers, plaintiffs, flatfeet, men in Western hats and women in lizard shoes and fur coats . . ."[35] The accidental piling up of people newly arrived and their riotous movements. Men, women, and children living on top of one another, never out of one another's sight and hearing, exhibiting at close range every known act of compassion and degradation. Undiluted humanity. A half million Jews on New York's Lower East Side by 1910.

What was necessity for dispersed settlers is both necessary and physically inescapable for immigrants: there is no question of minding our own business. The promiscuous closeness of families in single room flats, shared kitchens and toilets. "Narrow streets of squeezed in stores and houses, ragged clothes, dirty bedding oozing out of windows, ash-cans and garbage-cans cluttering the side-walks." "Swarming streets" with "stinking smells of crowded poverty," in Anzia Yezierska's *Hungry Hearts*. In *Bronx Primitive*, Kate Simon domesticates the crush:

> One of the summer pleasures was to sit at the kitchen window and listen to the polyphony of courtyard noises out of twenty other kitchens . . . "Schloch [slob]! Look what you did to the dress I just ironed"; "Tie your laces so you don't fall" . . . The heavier sounds of exasperation came later with the heavier heat of the day: a crash, a slap, and "I'll break your hands if you touch that china closet again."

Reciprocity among "decent folk" was the stuff of daily life: "families in immigrant neighborhoods being inevitably interdependent, for shopping advice, for medical information, for the care of each other's children and the exchange of kitchen delicacies."[36]

The imaginative grip immigrant neighbors have on us owes in part to ongoing odysseys of arrival, disorientation, and gleaning bits of local knowledge by which to navigate the new world, often from people as fresh to the place as themselves. These neighbors knew where they stood: they understood nothing, or next to nothing. Immigrants begin as outsiders, socially disenfranchised, striving, trying to figure how to get inside this America, and what advancement meant, anyway. "Without comprehension, the immigrant would forever remain shut out—a stranger in America."[37]

The emblematic immigrant story has a familiar arc: immersion in the close world of family and neighbors, getting out and away, and as we know from every autobiography of success—looking back at the person

I was in that neighborhood of people I left behind. "Like all poor people, I lived on dreams," Yezierska wrote. Her yearning is basic: to be someone and to have a voice, and the people at hand, the first who might listen and buoy or deflate her, play a large part. "But to whom could I speak? The people in the laundry? They never understood me. They had a grudge against me because I left them when I tried to work myself up." Bitterness is the dismal reverse of anticipation, and disappointment begins often enough at home, delivered by people living nearby. Disappointment manifests physiologically: Yezierska's women clutch their throats and gasp for air: "choked," "my choked-in thoughts," "choked with hate." [38]

Neighbors figure in every immigrant narrative as background, of course, but more: as resource, measure, obstacle, and inspiration. "I was thrown for fair on the free spinning of the world," Augie March declares in Saul Bellow's bildungsroman of a child of working class immigrants in Humboldt Park. Augie takes his bearings from the people on his street. "All the influences were lined up waiting for me ... there they were to form me, which is why I tell you more of them than of myself." He is a willing receptor and neighbors oblige: Kreindle an Austro-Hungarian conscript, the undertaker Kinsman and his wife, and Lubing the social worker provide Augie lessons in "getting on." "Other people showed me their achievements, claims and patents, paradise and hell-evidence, their prospectors' samples."[39] Grandma Lausch, who lives next door, is all the evidence we need of monumental standing based on a mix of sheer force of personality and, crucially for her neighbors, the claim to be a realist. Grandma Lausch was always expressing "one more animadversion on the trustful, loving, and simple surrounded by the cunning-hearted and tough." She knew how to "use large institutions" to navigate patronage and corruption in order to claim basic social goods and services. She is "one of those Machiavellis of small street and neighborhood that my young years were full of." "She'd show us how to practice in the world."[40]

Young Augie amplifies these neighbors. He assigns their trials, deals, thoughts, schemes, and judgments the grandeur of philosophy and world history: "The resonance of great principle filled the whole kitchen." He likens them to Napoleon and Jesus. William Einhorn, the local real estate owner, evokes Caesar and Ulysses. That is, until Augie decides to compare men and men, not men and demigods: "which is just what would please Caesar among us teeming democrats." Looking back as an adult, he still sees nobility in these neighbors: "Without a special gift of vision, maybe you wouldn't have seen it in most of us." "There haven't been civilizations without cities," Saul Bellow reflects, "But what about cities without civilizations? An inhuman thing, if possible, to have so many people together who beget nothing on one another."[41] The author answers his own question in *Adventures of Augie March*: Chicago between the world wars inexorably, unwittingly, begat a democratic ethos.

Neighbors figure in immigrant narratives as resources and obstacles, and they give offense. They spurn us, hound us, depress us, treat us as invisible. They spew prejudice, exhibit contempt, practice exclusion, walling off and refusing to acknowledge us as "decent folk." The temper in which neighbors take offense and respond to it is one key to the quality of life around home. We get a taste of it in Bellow's novel. Polish boys on the street and in the poolroom call Augie a Christ-killer. Like Cather's Grandmother Burden, who exhibits a steady temper in the face of ingratitude and rebuff, Augie takes his knocks and shrugs off offenses:

> But I never had any special grief from it, or brooded, . . . and looked at it as needing no more special explanation than the stone-and-bat wars of the street gangs or the swarming on a fall evening of parish punks to rip up fences, screech and bawl at girls, and beat up strangers.[42]

Neighbors' crude offenses, the gestures of diminishment flung at us because we belong to a disparaged group (and the aggression we inflict on others), can be ignored, or sloughed off out of pride, or answered with Augie's easy spontaneity: "I was trying to refuse to lead a disappointed life." The democratic ethos of neighbors can survive hostility and prejudice given the disposition to make allowances and to refuse to magnify slights,[43] and I return to this subject in Chapter 5, "What Anyone Would Do, Here."

This is not to fault those badly stung by hate or abuse. It is simply to say that while denunciation and squashed hopes degrade neighbor relations, the democratic ethos will be fatally poisoned only if people perpetuate gnawing resentment. "I was so obsessed and consumed with my grievances I could not get away from myself and think things out in the light," Yezierska wrote. Immigrant anticipation is frayed by toxic experiences of grinding poverty, prejudice, humiliation, and corruption; it may be killed when frustration extends beyond the first into the second generation and beyond.[44] Then we find not only the individual face of failed aspiration, but also the collective face of entrenched outsider status, exclusion from the ranks of "decent folk." Outsider status itself may become an element of identity—meaning that walled out, neighbors wall themselves in, companions in disappointment, obdurately reinforcing one another's grievances.

To petition repeatedly is to be reminded repeatedly that one is not wanted, never has been, never will be ... And the snarling itself, after generations of passivity begins to feel good, and soon more than good: necessary; a thing in and of itself that is hard to give up.[45]

That said, we see in the classic narrative of immigrant neighbors and in sociological studies of immigrants over time that the eclipse of reciprocity among "decent folk" across divides does not afflict everyone and that it is episodic. New immigrant groups and new destinations shuffle the mix and rudiments of good neighbor are not entirely crushed.

Beginning in the 1980s, demographers reported unanticipated shifts in immigrants' places of origin and in the geography of settlement. From concentration in a handful of "gateway" cities, immigrants discovered the Midwest and the South, small towns and suburbs. "In 1970 a majority of foreign-born newcomers to this country were settling in cities. By 1980, more were settling in the suburbs ... Today, the numbers aren't even close."[46] Immigrant neighbors have become a genuinely national phenomenon.[47]

So, immigrants may experience the feeling of isolation more resonant of settlers on the prairie than the press of presence in the "swarming streets" of Yezierska's *Hungry Hearts*. In Jumpa Lahiri's story "Mrs. Sen's," a woman recently arrived from India with her husband lands in a suburb. Her imagined geography is all vacancy and absence. She asks the small boy for whom she babysits,

> "Eliot, if I began to scream right now at the top of my lungs, would someone come?"
> "Maybe," he shrugs.
> "At home that is all you have to do. Not everybody has a telephone. But just raise your voice a bit, or express grief or joy of any kind, and one whole neighborhood and half of another has come to share the news, to help with arrangements."[48]

Eliot's shrug is the indifference and ignorance of a child, and Mrs. Sen should not take it as confirmation that no one would come. She has made just one human connection, to this lonely boy, and she is registering anonymity, loss, and disorientation.

In other stories by Lahiri, immigrants learn and manage, engaging with Bengalis and other new arrivals and with their American neighbors. The young narrator of "The Third and Final Continent" is as modulated and discrete as Augie March is bumptious and expansive, but we see the same alertness and self-education, the same defining part neighbors play in learning the lay of the land and getting on, and the same affirmation of neighbors judging them "decent folk." Lahiri's new arrival "adjusted" to eating cornflakes and milk at the "Y"; formed a sympathetic connection to his century-old landlady Mrs. Croft; tentatively welcomed the arrival of his new bride; and assumed the role of guide to "what anyone would do, here." He then moved past "adjusting" to settling.

In the novel *A Gesture Life*, Chang-rae Lee's Doctor Hata reflects on the fact that the initial, troubling question of his status in town faded away. This Japanese immigrant has become a "known quantity" among his neighbors:

> Without even knowing it one takes on the characteristics of the local-
> ity ... their *How are you* and *Good days* ... there is a gradual and ac-
> cruing recognition of one's face, of being, as far as anyone can recall,
> from around here. There's no longer a lingering or vacant stare, and
> you can taste the small but unequaled pleasure that comes with being
> a familiar sight to the eye.[49]

In Lahiri's story, Mrs. Croft's amazement at the planting of the American flag on the moon ("splendid!") mirrors the narrator's own amazement at traveling to this continent and making it home, with a house in the suburbs and a son at Harvard, and experiencing the small but unequaled pleasure that comes with being a familiar sight to the eye.

> I know that my achievement is quite ordinary. I am not the only man
> to seek his fortune far from home, and certainly I am not the first. Still,
> there are times I am bewildered by each mile I have traveled, each
> meal I have eaten, each person I have known, each room in which I
> have slept. As ordinary as it all appears, there are times when it is be-
> yond my imagination.[50]

This narrative is fixed in Americans' experience and in national self-representation—not beyond imagination at all.

## Suburban Neighbors and Suburban "Grotesques"

In the 1920s Lewis Mumford identified three great waves of internal migration in America: settling the frontier, the move from farms to factory towns, and massive population moves from rural areas into large cities—including the unprecedented scale of black migration from the South to northern cities at the start of the century. He predicted a fourth wave: from cities to suburbs. Today, the most familiar narrative of neighbors is unmistakably suburban. Suburbs dominate statistically.[51] Most of the entities designated cities are suburbs,[52] and it is estimated that forty-five percent of the US population resides in the suburbs of large metropolitan areas.[53] Demography alone does not account for the predominance of this thread of the narrative of good neighbors, though. It owes something to the drama of its moment of origin: World War II victory, post-war economic boom, and thunderous national optimism. Cheap land, government credit, and ambitious highway construction fueled their growth.

City and suburb are one another's background and baseline. "Urban" conjures size and density, racial and ethnic mixing, wealth and squalor, political corruption, and crime. "We just wanted to get out of the city"; "the neighborhood is poor for raising children."[54] Sociologists confirm these reports, and so do first-person narratives like *Holy Land: A Suburban Memoir*.[55] For young lower-middle and working class white families as well as more affluent ones moving up meant moving outward.[56] Early suburbia is a narrative of whites only: restrictive covenants, redlining, and government-endorsed mortgage discrimination ensured racial (and initially religious and ethnic) segregation, and I turn to this aspect of suburban neighbors shortly.

Literary representations of suburban neighbors exhibit remarkable coherence because suburbs are predominantly residential. Large-scale commerce, industry, and more are absent or strictly zoned and set apart from homes. Suburban neighbors are comparatively insulated from activities apart from personal encounters, which facilitates disregard for neighbors' status in the larger society and a focus on identity *qua* neighbor and the quotidian business of give and take. The narrative of suburban neighboring is coherent, too, because reciprocity is fueled by regular interactions, and here the scale of the environment is supportive. Suburban yards and sidewalks are more amenable to encounters than apartment elevators where neighbors can't linger, and more dependable than accidental sightings. Neighbors have business outdoors: lawn care, home maintenance, supervising children at play, walking pets, jogging for exercise. They wash cars, tend gardens, hold garage sales. Neighbors interact often enough for reciprocity, and of course often enough to give and take offense.

At the same time, a suburban single-family house, which promises more comfort, space, and certainly more freedom of action than apartments permit, also provides some distance from neighbors and the prospect of keeping interactions within bounds. This deserves emphasis. In studies of the carefully designed environment of Levittown, sociologists reported that neighbors' major complaint was the lack of fences between properties. Neighbors want Frost's walls, not to give offense but to ward off unwelcome sociability and preserve privacy. Gans' report of Levittowners' expectations explains:

> They certainly did not move to "suburbia" to find the social and spiritual qualities . . . They were not looking for roots or a rural idyll, not for a social ethic or a consumption-centered life, not for civic participation or for "sense of community." They wanted the good or comfortable life for themselves and their families . . . but mainly they came for a house and not a social environment.[57]

*In the Neighborhood: The Search for Community on an American Street, One Sleepover at a Time* is anomalous. The yearning of this middle-aged man to get to know all his neighbors and to model constant, caring, minding of one another's business strikes a strange chord—well-meaning perhaps but "off," slightly perverse. He offered to spend the night in their homes as a way of initiating closer relations. Not surprisingly, some neighbors declined; they did not share his "search for community."[58] The suburbs, to repeat Lewis Mumford's characterization, are "a collective effort to live a private life."[59]

A strikingly negative set of characterizations attaches to this third narrative thread. Sherwood Anderson called his 1919 account of Winesburg, Ohio "The Book of the Grotesque," and the phrase applies to representations of suburban neighbors, sometimes quite literally. Lifting the veil on a tranquil street to expose unexpected horror is a convention in fiction and film. As dependably as a remote country road is the standard setting for the arrival of extraterrestrials, a suburban block is the standard setting for spies, serial killers, and deranged housewives masquerading as normal in the house next-door.[60] Suburban grotesques are fantastic, of course, but we should see them as entertaining exaggerations of serious moral and social criticism in which suburbia is a site of concealed pathology.

The other threads of good neighbor are not wholly benign either. Histories of settler violence against Native Americans (and one another: vigilantism, lynching) taint frontier narratives. Persistent poverty and prejudice darken immigrant narratives. But these sobering correctives do not inhibit us from invoking them as iconic images. In contrast, suburban neighbors are standing targets, and critics do more than remind us what sentimental stories leave out. They disparage the suburban thread less because it distorts reality than because they see the reality as inherently objectionable. Descriptions are moralistic, sour, and effectively tarnish the luster of "a good or comfortable life for themselves and their families" alongside neighbors who are "decent folk."

We owe the criticism that lends suburban "grotesques" a certain authority to social science. Early on in the growth of suburbs, researchers invented psychological measures to assess preferences about where to live. This information was used commercially as a key to market segmentation that characterizes developments today. Social scientists also used these assessments to support claims about the deleterious social and psychological effects of suburban living wholesale.[61]

Topping the list of indictments is the charge of mindless conformity— "in the suburbs, behavior and opinion are determined by what the neighbors do and think."[62] The external sign of inner deadness taken to a higher power in the robotic Steppford Wives is consumerism—itself doubly mindless because it is both insatiable and a product of manipulation by marketers. Suburbs bear the full weight of culture commentators' melancholic description of "this power of consumer culture to evacuate the self."[63] The list of suburban horribles continues with competitiveness; the cartoonist Arthur Ragland "Pop" Momand coined the phrase "keeping up with the Joneses" in 1913 and made it the title of a daily comic strip. (As if competitiveness were exclusive to lawn or auto envy.)

There are more indictments. Isolation and anomie, once attributed to city life among strangers, were routinely ascribed to suburbanites. Early studies predicted that commuting from work to "bedroom" communities would deter neighborly interaction. When it turned out that suburban home ownership stimulates interactions, sociability was discounted as a kind of hyperactivity, crowding out really vital social life on the one hand and personal privacy on the other.[64]

All this negativity is reinforced by aesthetic revulsion: the look of mass-produced "little boxes" or "McMansions," the off-putting stretch of blank garage faces, the lack of sidewalks and front porches, inadequate public spaces, "the ugliness of suburban sprawl."[65]

An exhaustive examination of evidence of the presumptive deleterious psychological effects of suburban living on individuals and damaging effects on social interaction concludes that the findings are "dated, overgeneralized, or not substantiated."[66] This has not inhibited repetition of the familiar charges: suburbs are "conformist, anti-intellectual, homogeneous, antifeminist, alcoholic, and shot through with anomie." None of this has deterred people from moving there when they can. On reconsideration, suburbs deliver "a neighborhood, a patch of ground, a measure of peace and security . . ." and, Nicholas Lemann adds, "dignity." Meaning that "one could be a real somebody in the life of that suburban town without having any money or outside world status."[67] I give the last word on this to novelist Richard Ford:

> The suburbs are supposedly where nothing happens, like Auden said about what poetry doesn't do; an over-inhabited faux terrain dozing in inertia, occasionally disrupted by a "Columbine" or "an Oklahoma City" or a hurricane to remind us what's really real. Though plenty happens in the suburbs—in the way that putting a drop of water under an electron microscope reveals civilizations with histories, destinies, and an overpowering experience of the present.[68]

It's been proposed that a fifth wave of internal migration is forming: the white upper middle class returning to city centers. "Gentrification" carries a critical implication of affluent whites "invading" and displacing working class and impoverished minority residents, and the alternative label on offer is "demographic inversion."[69] Celebrants of urban living boast its advantages: aesthetically rich environments; gateways for globalizing entrepreneurs; an "edgy, hip, and hypertolerant" atmosphere; public spaces that invite "encounters between people of different classes, races, ages, religions, ideologies, cultures, and stances toward life."[70] Of course this is not true of every city; many lack "urbanity" and "edginess" to say nothing of the financial wherewithal to recover from long-term physical deterioration and social decline. In any case, good neighbors are missing from catalogues of the advantages of urban living. Upscale city residents have neighbors, of course; the point is that they do not figure centrally in representations of urban life as they do in suburban, settler, and immigrant narratives.

## Resisting Randomness: "Our Localism" and Racial Segregation

Willa Cather's Jim Burden looked out of the train at the vast plains and felt as if he were outside all "jurisdictions." Jurisdictions are well marked in suburbia. Neighbors know just where the borders of their city and property lie, for good reason. "Our localism" refers to the law and politics of municipal autonomy in the United States that enable residents to build and maintain walls.[71] Local taxes, schools, zoning ordinances, building codes, transportation routes, and limits on growth are designed to control the "character of the community." Where it is economically feasible, suburbs zone out industry, large commercial establishments, multifamily residences, low-income housing, halfway houses, soup kitchens, mobile homes. They effect, in effect, something of a local immigration policy. "Local borders, once created, reinforce local identification, become a focus of sentiment and symbolism, and create a powerful legal bulwark for the preservation of local interests."[72] True enough, "with reference to any formal criteria, the neighborhood is a random association,"[73] but "one need only attend a few public hearings on controversial zoning changes in suburban areas to realize that the people consider their right to pass judgment upon their future neighbors as sacred."[74]

The true suburban "grotesque," on this view, is neighbors' selfish preoccupation with home, family, privacy, security, and preservation of wealth. [75] Residents see local autonomy as the condition for "protecting the well-being of our most important institution, the home."[76] From a censorious democratic standpoint, all this adds up to a colossal failure of civic virtue.[77] It amounts to "civic secession." The label applied to suburbs—"a very private polis"[78]—is an accusatory. "Our localism" "enables a suburb to keep its yards wide and its people few; to ensure that the children of successful families attend its schools; to keep its property tax base high and tax rate low; to keep central city problems outside its boundaries."[79]

Relatively few suburbs represent what has been called the "secession of the successful," though.[80] Suburbs vary from very affluent, to solid and prosperous, to stereotypical middle and working class, to places riddled with poverty and decay.[81] Suburban impoverishment and blight have penetrated Americans' consciousness slowly; it struck one observer only after she realized that the only chance of reversing the bad fortune of the place was to get themselves a state prison.[82] Suburbia overall is diverse, then, even if internally communities are comparatively homogenous.

In resisting randomness, assortment also proceeds by race, of course: most starkly and consequentially black/white segregation. Data confirm that levels of segregation "do not vary significantly by social class,"[83] and segregated suburbs are the counterpart of highly concentrated populations of African American poor in the inner city. "The most powerful demographic events of the past decade were the movement of African Americans out of central cities and the settlement of immigrant groups in suburbs."[84] In the years covered by the 2000 census, racial and ethnic minorities accounted for the bulk of suburban population gains, and they make up more than a quarter of suburban populations today. The pattern varies across the country,[85] but consensus has it that "melting pot suburbs" are the exception: "Ethnic Diversity Grows, Neighborhood Integration Lags."[86] Whites are a minority of the population in "ethnoburbs" where the majority is Hispanic or Asian.[87]

Although most formal and many informal barriers to suburban white/black racial integration have been challenged if not eliminated, and the earlier racialized narrative of suburban home ownership as an exclusively white American dream has lost some descriptive force, city boundaries and zoning laws continue to have separationist effects.[88] The federal Fair Housing Act is often unenforced, and mandated affordable housing continues to be built in predominantly segregated inner-city areas, reinforcing black residential isolation.[89] The result of "neighborhood effects," especially racial segregation, is well-documented black disadvantage and inequality of opportunity at every income level in everything from public services to schools to access to jobs.[90] New housing in old neighborhoods does not alter these essentials. Self-segregation is at work along with discrimination and the wealth gap. For both blacks and whites comfort and affinity play a part. As I discussed in Chapter 1, "Who Is My Neighbor?," most whites prefer to live with a majority of whites and the parallel holds for blacks—who, in addition, may feel unwelcome or unsafe in largely white neighborhoods. Here too the result is well documented: "The typical middle-income black family lives in a neighborhood with lower incomes than the typical low-income white family"; white and Asian children are much more likely to live in neighborhoods with median income similar to—or higher than—that of their own family."[91]

Emphasis on homogeneity of race, ethnicity, or class (categories drawn from the national economy and society) should not obscure assortment by life-stage and lifestyle. We are inventive when it comes to resisting randomness, and real estate developments promise to limit the risks that come with the accident of proximity. Developments are tailored to recreation, or architectural harmony, or cohousing aimed at reproducing a facsimile of small-town life; Celebration, Florida, the Disney planned community, advertises its brand sentimentally: "a community where residents strongly believe in caring for their neighbors."[92] The "suburban homestead" movement creates networks of neighbors who add edible plants, trees, and herbs "obtained primarily from local sustainable farmers" to their landscape, committing to a "fresh, green lifestyle."[93] It turns out, too, that some people prefer a "random-like" mix of age, income, and race.[94] Most significant demographically is the retirement community, where the arcs of the life cycle are made concrete in the built environment. [95] In short, elective community, with its anticipation of locating presumptively compatible neighbors, is a reality for many Americans, and here too it would be a mistake to think that they are home only to the affluent.

To complete the picture: the possibility of resisting randomness has been enhanced by the invention of private homeowner's associations, which one exuberant economist described as "the most important property right development in the United States since the creation of the modern business corporation."[96] The bylaws of homeowner associations allow for a more controlled environment than zoning or condominium and cooperative arrangements. Homeowner associations can "tax you, control your freedom of expression, limit religious expression . . . impose fines for failing to follow their rules, and tell you what color to paint your house."[97] Here, minding a great deal of one another's business is official, written into covenants so that enforcing "what anyone would do, here" becomes a legal obligation. On reflection it shouldn't be surprising that managed settings don't reduce conflict. The restrictions, mutual obligations, and onus of compulsory housekeeping formalized in covenants clash with the deep-seated expectation of private life and "our home as our castle." Minding our own business is in tension with rule-bound relations and neighbors as enforcers of these detailed regulations. Expectations of homogeneity, compatibility, and compliance cause people to trust that the environment will do a lot of the work. So ferocious conflicts afflict even the most affluent elective communities. The accidents of proximity are inescapable. There is no insurance against a bad neighbor, and it takes just one to diminish the quality of life.

We may be tempted to say that the real test of the democratic ethos arises in places marked by deep division and thoroughgoing residential segregation by race, and I take up this theme in Chapter 5, "What Anyone Would Do, Here" and Chapter 6, "Live and Let Live." From this perspective, good neighbor is buoyed in suburbia, which seems to offer some limited assurance that the people nearby are likely to share expectations for the terms of "local knowledge." Certainly, we resist randomness in choosing where to live, if we can choose. Social, economic, and racial sorting is unmistakable. Just as certainly, however, homogeneity is never complete across the conditions—personal and dispositional as well as economic and social—that make being a good neighbor a challenge everywhere. But resisting randomness should get its due.

## Good Neighbors for Children

Settler, immigrant, and suburban narrative threads provide a common store of neighbors we know well, and reinforce the hold good neighbor has on moral identity. There is no better evidence of the centrality of good neighbor as a facet of personal moral identity and collective American self-representation, however, than the fact that portrayals of neighbors is a staple for children. Popular culture reflects the democracy of everyday life as a regulatory ideal, and at the same time betrays anxiety about "children who were never taught and would never now learn the games that had held society together"[98]

The ranking antidote to that anxiety is *Sesame Street*. Launched on public television in 1969, the program targeted three- to five-year-old preschoolers with the goal of repairing the educational disadvantages of poor and minority children. With a curriculum grounded in cognitive research on child development, and imitating the rhyming qualities of jingles that make advertisements memorable, *Sesame Street* teaches the alphabet, numbers, shapes, matching categories, and concepts like over, under, around, and through. The program "became an American institution."[99]

Along with reading readiness it created indelible images of good neighbors for generations of children, and prompts stirrings of that identity. The set is an inner city block modeled on Columbus Avenue in New York City, with a brownstone tenement, a fire hydrant, and a car-lined street: no enchanted castle, no circus. The adult cast, a rainbow of diversity, enacts scripts in which "the actors would regard one another with kindness, respect, and tolerance."[100] There are no conflicts among them. No adult character takes the lead, either; their relations are cooperative and egalitarian. *Sesame Street* delivers the message: racial and gender differences, religious differences (the storekeeper Mr. Hooper was Jewish), age divides, and disabilities are normal. On *Sesame Street*, as the song goes: "They're the people that you meet/When you're walking down the street/They're the people that you meet each day."

In contrast, the monsters on the block represent the social differences and maddening personal traits that injure feelings, fuel misunderstanding, and generate conflict. *They* mirror the actual neighbors we all know well. Their terms of give and take are idiosyncratic and not always endearing. Boring Bert, the eternal but patient victim of Ernie's dominance and teasing. The obsessive Cookie Monster, whose voraciousness colors every encounter. The pessimistic Snuffleupagus, exuding anxiety. Kermit, the observer who stands above the action, on the alert for calamity. Oscar the Grouch, a genuine misanthrope—rude, antisocial, spiteful, continuously warning others away, and bullying and taunting them if they invade his turf. Some of the monsters model perfect children: Grover, who "plays well with others." Not all the monsters do. "They wrestled and bonked and body slammed and slugged and occasionally ate each other."[101] They give and take offense. With adult guidance, though, they navigate their not-so-cooperative encounters so that misunderstandings are cleared up, injuries and slights apologized for and forgiven, conflicts resolved, at least for the moment. Until, like the letters of the alphabet, offenses and conflicts and reconciliations are reiterated over and over as they are in life; their repetitiousness makes difficult personalities and uneasy dealings mundane and bearable. As with Frost's neighbors, the boulders must be put back in place day after day.

In Part I, "The Lay of the Land," I considered "who is my neighbor?" and the imagined geography of the terrain around home, and I identified the three narrative threads of good neighbor. In Part II, "The Democracy of Everyday Life," I develop the democratic elements of good neighbor—reciprocity among "decent folk," speaking out, and live and let live—as they arise in the course of concrete encounters. No arid exercise, I work from inside to make the experience of neighbors vivid. We should recognize ourselves in these accounts.

# PART II

## The Democracy of Everyday Life

# 3

# Reciprocity among "Decent Folk"

## Reciprocity and Trust

One foothold on the uncertain ground of neighborliness is reciprocity. Anthropologists propose that the norm of reciprocity, which dictates that individuals return the form of behavior that they have received from another, applies to all cultures and to all behavior within cultures.[1] Reciprocity has been categorized as a "primordial imperative" and a principal component of all value systems.[2] On these accounts, reciprocity is a fundamental principle of morality and sociability in every domain. These global claims have some force. Ancient philosophers embraced it: "There is no duty more indispensable than that of returning a kindness . . . all men detest one forgetful of a benefit."[3] It is explicit in the Golden Rule, and implicit in the biblical exhortation to "love they neighbor as thyself." Reciprocity is invoked today in reflections on international conflict and the grounds for peace: "Recognition for recognition, statehood for statehood, independence for independence, security for security. Neighborliness for neighborliness."[4] Reciprocity is at the core of one leading contemporary theory of justice: reciprocity, John Rawls explains, "a tendency to answer in kind . . . is a deep psychological fact . . . a capacity for a sense of justice built up by responses in kind would appear to be a condition of human sociability." Reciprocity cannot be reduced to the idea of mutual advantage because it has a fundamentally social and moral aspect: the shared project of a well-ordered society.[5]

Historically and in some parts of the world today, reciprocity does shape many social interactions. But social scientists characterize it as the prelude to more complex forms of coordination and developed institutions. Certainly in our pluralist society marked by a multiplicity of spheres, reciprocity does not regulate relations in every domain. The various spheres are parceled out among—indeed they are constituted by—differentiated systems of law, the organization and rules internal to groups and associations, and practices specific to particular institutions. Reciprocity may play some part in the interstices of these settings. Informal relations of give and take may develop among coworkers, for example. But workplace relations are mainly shaped by the institutional structure, roles, routines, and purposeful business of the enterprise. Reciprocity is ancillary.

Among neighbors, however, reciprocity holds sway. Perhaps uniquely, reciprocity among neighbors is not a starting point on the way to explicit rules of coordination and organized methods of monitoring interactions. On the contrary, lacking the structures and practices imposed by institutions and without standard shared purposes, the give and take of good turns and bad set the tone and terms of neighborliness. Unadorned reciprocity, direct, face-to-face, and open-ended is our foothold. It is a core element of the democracy of everyday life, the regulative ideal of good neighbor.

Another vantage point on the unique predicament of neighbors is inseparable from reciprocity: trust. If we want to be neighborly, and not everyone does, we have incentives to be trustworthy. Reciprocity depends on it, and ongoing interactions give us a degree of confidence in the trustworthiness of people who live nearby. We trust particular neighbors (or we don't) to do things from returning our greeting to bringing back a borrowed ladder to keeping an eye over children at play. We may admit to ourselves that our misgivings about a neighbor's dependability sometimes rest on irrelevant personal characteristics; his averted gaze, the hours she keeps, their visitors trigger discomfort. Mostly, though, trust and mistrust are based on experience. We build on what we learn. Some neighbors cultivate the appearance of trustworthiness but disappoint us in practice. Bad experiences have consequences, including reputational consequences. We report our neighbor's irresponsibility, deception, and dishonesty to others. (And they judge the reliability of our reports.) When neighbors are untrustworthy, they can be shunned, or we withhold reciprocity when it comes to some things but not others. The result is selective exclusion.

Trust among neighbors differs, clearly, from what is called macro-level "generalized trust"—that is, in one-time social interactions involving strangers.[6] Trust among neighbors also contrasts with "working trust" in specific contexts. In most societal settings we guard against exploitation, discrimination, abuse, humiliation, and overreaching, but trust depends less on assessments of individual character than on the reasons and incentives we have to fulfill designated roles and responsibilities. Institutional securities—rules and sanctions, transparency and accountability—do much of the work.[7] When it comes to public officials, to take the clearest example, liberal democracy provides assurances in the form of authority circumscribed by law, institutional checks, and mechanisms of accountability. At the same time, it is an article of political faith that the possibility of individual and institutional abuse of power warrants "eternal vigilance," for rarely is undiluted trust possible and nowhere except perhaps for intimate relations is it desirable. "We might desire those we interact with to be trustworthy, and that might generally be good for society, but we can make no such general claim about trust."[8] Again, trust among neighbors is personal and individual, and no institution provides regular monitoring of day-to-day encounters. We assess one another's dependability directly. We neighbors are on our own.

Returning to reciprocity, the steps are familiar. Reciprocity acts as a "starting mechanism." A greeting or small act of assistance initiates contact and typically elicits a response, however tentative or delayed. In Erving Goffman's description, "words can act as a "relationship wedge."[9] Reciprocity then keeps things going, as casual conversation, mundane offers and favors continue; iteration allows us to explore and alter the terms and limits, the demands, costs, and rewards of these encounters. We feel out our own and our neighbor's potential for generosity or exploitation. We anticipate ongoing interactions—proximity guarantees it. Neighbors may be more or less familiar to us, but these are not chance encounters. Greater scope and frequency of give and take is a possibility.

To repeat: absent defined rules and methods of enforcement, we're on our own in initiating and responding to neighbors' good and bad turns. That is the essential predicament of neighbors. Reciprocity is normally loose, voluntary, and variable. The domain of give and take is wide open and covers a virtually unlimited universe of interactions. The terms and time frame are seldom articulated: we have "time to forget, time to return, time for delayed reciprocation that is no longer a return."[10] Borrowing and timely replacement of a tool, or a turn at driving the carpool, or to-and-fro requests to lower the decibels don't always go as smoothly as we imagine they should. We misjudge what counts as a fitting give and take. We anticipate mutual benefits, though these are not always the same benefits and may, from our standpoint, be incommensurate, too much or

too little or not the right thing at all. "How many mistakes I do make, trying to do the right thing."[11] We find ourselves put upon or put out.

One complication is endemic to reciprocity among neighbors. We create expectations for give and take by our own words and past behavior.
When our encounters are regular and repeated over time, the particulars
are anticipated, relied on. These expectations take on the character of
commitments: to inquire after our children, to take turns sweeping the
hallway. And because these expectations are seldom expressly articulated, in the course of interactions our neighbors may understand them to
involve more than we thought they did. Expectations expand incrementally and without our noticing as extensions from earlier give and take. In
this sense commitments are voluntarily incurred but they are often indeterminate and riddled with ambiguity.[12]

There is this question too: what do we do about unasked for favors?
We may imagine that reciprocity has a claim on us only when we have
invited and accepted a good turn. But that principle, which has a place in
some philosophical accounts of reciprocity, does not hold in practice.[13] It
is a recipe for trouble. As is the "Pollyanna Fallacy,"[14] a bit of sentimentality that assumes offers will be gratefully received and reciprocated. So,
how to ward off unwelcome ones? How to avoid being saddled with
unmet social debt? How to avoid giving offense, which after all may cause
our neighbor to speak up and take action, embroiling us further in unwanted dealings?

As we've seen, Frost's loaves and balls fallen to each are not equivalent. They represent neighbors' separate, divergent notions of the business they have with one another. Equilibrium is uncertain and unsteady.
Reciprocity is strenuous. It requires attention. We cannot reliably depend
on convention, even when our interactions are familiar, seasonal. Frost's
farmers will have to mend the wall again and again. "We wear our fingers
rough with handling them."

A deeper personal inhibition affects reciprocity as well. Interactions
with neighbors are not all moral any more than they are wholly instrumental, and they are driven by emotions operating just out of conscious
range. We make on-the-spot judgments, barely noticing that we do. We
make them not knowing why we do. We may be unaware of what lies behind our impulse to avoidance or hospitality. So ordinary interactions can
be emotionally treacherous. They can undo us. In Raymond Carver's "A
Small, Good Thing," a couple is at the hospital bedside of their young son.
The boy has been hit by a car and by the end of the story he will die. Howard and Ann have this exchange:

"I suppose one of us should go home and check on things . . . Shag needs to be fed, for one thing."

"Call one of the neighbors," Ann said, "Call the Morgans. Anyone will feed a dog if you ask them to."[15]

Anyone would feed a dog, perhaps, but there are powerful deterrents to asking, and Howard and Ann don't. Instead they take turns going back and forth between hospital and home, each getting a brief respite from standing over their comatose son and from each other. They refuse to call the Morgans for another reason, which they don't acknowledge but readers are made to understand. They are loathe to let a neighbor into their business—not into their house and not into the dreadful event that has turned them mute, paralyzed, stunned. If they called on the Morgans they would have to submit to their neighbors' questions and expressions of concern. They would be liable to reveal their fear, their prospective grief. Their private terror would be broadcast. They would have to acknowledge it to themselves. Howard and Ann are walling off and protecting their inner lives. They need freedom to experience their emotions spontaneously and in their own psychological time. That is one thing the privacy of home, and reticence, affords. Exposure would take this space for minding their own business, caring for themselves, out of their sole hands. Still, they have enough of an eye to recognize what "anyone would do, here," and how changed they are from the people they were hours before.

## Returning Bad Turns

Reciprocity holds for bad turns as well as good. Uncertainty about proportionality and trepidation about the consequences of returning bad turns may incline us to do and say nothing at all. If the offense is a matter of irritation or minor inconvenience, we may be disposed not to acknowledge it. We keep the offense to ourselves. If we decide to respond, our initial steps are likely calm explanation or mild protest. Once we are resigned to the fact that our neighbor is not moved to acknowledge the nuisance or slight, once it is clear that no apology will be offered, and without assurance that the disturbance will stop, we fall back on our foothold: reciprocity.

Assuming we don't launch into impulsive retaliation (letting the air out of her tires, say), we are struck by the asymmetry. "Balancing loaves and balls" is different for offense and injury than for greetings and favors.

Normally we think we should respond to solicitousness — if not now, later, if not in kind than a rough equivalence. We normally think we should reciprocate good turns even if they are uninvited, even if assessing what return requires is wearing, and even if in the end we find reasons for withholding and distancing ourselves. We are less certain about returning bad turns. If we resolve to act, the disturbing difficulty of calibrating rough equivalence must be confronted. We have reason to mistrust our judgment. We may hit on a spiteful response that seems so apt and gratifying that we are pleased to imagine it is proportional.

> My neighbor forced his abutter
> to raze the warped and rotten fence
> because he didn't want to see
> the sagging wood when he sat
> on the porch in the morning
> having coffee with his wife.
> The fence was removed, replaced
> with something new, so now
> the neighbor has breakfast
> facing a row of garden gnomes,
> some naked, and a few
> of those anatomically correct.[16]

Fictional accounts of the dynamic of hostile give and take explore these uncertain attempts at returning bad turns. Thomas Berger's *Neighbors* carries us along on the fantastic ride of a mild suburban man's response to his offensive new neighbors. Harry and Ramona have taken occupancy of the only other house on Earl Keese's cul-de-sac. Learning of their arrival, Keese considers asking them to dinner. He and his wife waver: "We could probably get away with giving them no formal welcome whatever. It's scarcely a true obligation, not like giving food to a starving person."[17] Before they can make up their minds, Harry and Ramona intrude on them uninvited. Vulgar and vaguely menacing, local knowledge of acceptable suburban behavior eludes them, or, they are oblivious, or, more likely, they are nihilists of local etiquette. They don't respect personal space or possessions. They come and go from Keese's house; behave with crude familiarity towards his wife and daughter; find excuses to shower in his bathroom, put on his clothes, and drive his car. Keese feels he has lost control of his existence. The usual disapproving gestures and remonstrations have no effect. The only course open for handling the situation, he concludes, is response in kind.

Reciprocity is Keese's lifeline and the core of his identity as a good neighbor, and he tries to calculate what Harry and Ramona are owed in return for each fresh instance of derangement of his life at home. Before and again after each round of give and take, throughout this cycle of bizarre and increasingly violent offense and response, Keese tries to estimate rough equivalence. Did his traps warrant Henry's failed effort to strangle him with a garden hose? He struggles to find coherence in his "pay back," and after each evaluation of the latest give and take "he was satisfied that his version of the outcome was fair." Harry mocks Keese's effort to "think ethically." Keese never entirely abandons the aim of rough parity, though given his neighbors' radical unpredictability (and perhaps Keese's paranoia) his calculations are fantastical. Pushed over the edge, he wants things to be a bit to his advantage in the final assessment. "I've given more than I've got," he observes, and "I don't mind admitting I'm proud of myself." Still, well into this war, Keese imagines that the fallen loaves and balls can be picked up and balanced on the wall: "Everything can be put back where it belongs."[18] Berger's surreal *Neighbors* rings true because offense and response are an inescapable part of the experience of neighbors. It offers vicarious relief.

Literary accounts of taking offense dwell on neighbors' mistaken perceptions. In these stories, the initial reaction may be unprovoked but once the negative dynamic of give and take is set in motion, it is difficult to reverse. A comic account of run-away misperception is Gogol's "The Tale of How Ivan Ivanovich Quarreled with Ivan Nikiforovich." A careless word interpreted as an insult sets in motion an escalating feud between formerly friendly neighbors in the Mirogord shtetl. Each Ivan rejects attempts by the other to explain his perspective on events. They demand apologies and compensation from one another, but from the start they have made satisfaction inconceivable. One Ivan initiates a legal battle that after a decade has no conclusive outcome.[19] As one writer put it, Gogol makes us "grotesquely aware of how little we know even when we are convinced that we are 100 percent right."[20]

Unlike Gogol's Mirogord neighbors, we don't wreak havoc on goose pens, though like the two Ivans we may sue. Unlike Earl Keese, we don't cast our neighbors as maniacal, push their car into a creek, or lock them in the cellar. Nevertheless, we recognize the psychological logic that propels him. We think we accurately discern injury and offense. We are almost always innocent in our own minds of inviting bad behavior. We fear we have been naïve and allowed ourselves to be exploited or suckered. Compensating, we are prone to exaggerate and to work ourselves up.

"There is no stopping to read the riot act, no firing over the heads of the mob."[21] In the next chapter, "Taking Offense, Speaking Out," I explore this second element of the democracy of everyday life: neighbors rallying one another to identify an offense and to act together as enforcers.

## Daily Needs

Reciprocity is often difficult and uncomfortable. That said, neighbors are not ordinarily the core of our network of care and social support. This owes in large part to the differentiated spheres of social life—the circumstances of pluralism. We are nested in circles of friends and family. We are members and beneficiaries of religious and secular voluntary associations. We have work. We fall within the ambit of local government and official providers of public goods and services.[22] Today, in contrast to settlers on the plains, neighboring is not a survival tactic (it never was just that in any case). Excepting disasters and repressive political situations in which neighbors hold our lives in our hands, my subject in Part III, reciprocity is seldom a material or emotional lifeline. There are few ongoing dependencies among neighbors, our participation in the "economy of mutual favors" is voluntary, and the social costs of being a good neighbor are generally not high. So, while give and take beyond pleasantries requires a minimum of trust, and creates it in turn, the risks of mistrust and betrayal are similarly limited.

*For the most part* our interactions with neighbors are modest, that is. Under exigent circumstances, dependence on neighbors can be critical and ongoing, not discretionary and episodic. Reciprocity loses its sociable, often-casual character and becomes a way of meeting daily needs.[23] Affluence makes lending and borrowing a convenience; poverty gives it urgency. In less exigent circumstances neighbors' offers and requests can be ignored, rejected, or exploited without risk of dire consequences, and often are. We assume the give and take of reciprocity willingly or grudgingly, or we don't. For families living in poverty however, necessity drives reciprocity and doing too little or taking too long or demanding too much can make the difference in getting by:

> Sometimes I don't have a damn dime in my pocket, not a crying penny to get a box of paper diapers, milk, a loaf of bread. But you have to have help from everybody and anybody, so don't turn no one down when they come round for help.

Give and take may be performed on a daily basis: lifts to inaccessible markets or laundromats or work. Neighbors swap

> food, stamps, rent money, a TV, hats, dice, a car, a nickel here, a cigarette there, food, milk, grits, and children.... new things, treasured items, furniture, cars, goods that are perishable, and services which are exchanged for child care, residence, or shared meals.

The basics are so entwined with give and take among neighbors, there is no question of minding one's own business:

> Everyone knows who is working, when welfare checks arrive, and when additional resources are available. Members of the middle class in American can cherish privacy concerning their income and resources, but the daily intimacy created by exchange transactions in The Flats insures that any change in a poor family's resources becomes "news."

These quotations are from *All Our Kin: Strategies for Survival in a Black Community*, Carol Stack's study of poor African Americans in the neighborhood she calls "The Flats."[24] Stack identifies "the adaptive strategies, resourcefulness, and resilience of urban families under conditions of perpetual poverty."[25] We see that the value of a good is not its market value but "its retaining power over the receiver; that is, how much and over how long a time period the giver can expect return."[26] We see, too, that reciprocity involves "socially recognized kin," that is, family members and unrelated individuals who are recruited into the web of mutual assistance and over time assume reciprocal commitments.[27] Studies like *All Our Kin* map the lay of the land and "who is my neighbor?" for a particular nexus of neighbors. In The Flats, a person who eats in one household may sleep in another and contribute resources to yet another, so physical location is labile.[28] The critical factor is whether he or she is dependably at hand, available, and a willing, reliable partner in reciprocity. Objective neighborhood characteristics like bus routes and the location of stores and laundromats are significant—distance from basic services amplifies the need for assistance. But patterns of reciprocity created by women, men, and children are not as inclusive as "neighborhood" by any definition except neighbors' personal, interpersonal lay of the land.

We understand why "although there are few alternatives, and no funds to move elsewhere, many people living in The Flats say that they have chosen to live there."[29] Social scientists find that public policy aimed at "deconcentration"—efforts to disperse poor inner city residents into housing in less segregated areas—may be resisted.[30] People complain of the sacrifices and deprivations imposed by their self-created system of reciprocity among neighbors: "I'm all worn out from running from my house to her house like a pinball machine. That's the way I do." They describe themselves as practically "possessed" by the claims of mutual aid.[31] But these relations are their buffers against daily experience of insecurity and deprivation.

The critical importance of reciprocity here is a reminder, if we need one, of the subjective feeling and the effective truth that social conditions, housing, and welfare are as much beyond these neighbors' control as fire and drought for settlers on the plains. We would wish that trust and reciprocity among neighbors were not as vital as they are for needy families isolated in spots of concentrated poverty and unusually dependent on the slim resources they find there. Better put, on the resources they create through reciprocity.

## Do-Gooders: Doing Too Much

Doing too little falls outside the parameters of rough parity but so does doing too much. Neighbors fail at reciprocity in both ways. How do we understand "too much," and how do we respond to neighbors' vigorous intentions to do us good? We use negative terms to describe neighbors for whom assistance and favors is their whole business and who approach us in that spirit. "Do-gooder" is not a term of praise.

> True enough, [Miss Maudie] had an acid tongue in her head, and she did not go about the neighborhood doing good, as did Miss Stephanie Crawford. But while no one with a grain of sense trusted Miss Stephanie, Jem and I had considerable faith in Miss Maudie.[32]

Things are exacerbated if neighbors are not only benefactors but also reformers who aim at our improvement. Thoreau was an acid critic, calling self-styled do-gooders "men-harriers": "If I knew for a certainty that a man was coming to my house with the conscious design of doing me good, I should run for my life."[33] It is simply not the case that helping and improving are beyond reproach.

Consider Lady Bountiful, who exults in the donation of aid or advice, gifts of food, or taking many more than her share of turns driving the carpool. We may attribute her largesse to material advantages. Like Aristotle's magnanimous gentleman, our neighbor has leisure and the means to bestow gifts on the city. Or Lord and Lady Bountiful are gifted with superior personal capacities; they manage their own lives so much better than we do that they can spill their surplus practicality and cheer onto us. We may see this as a virtue but are as likely to experience it as an unwelcome exhibition of the ordinary vice of snobbery, and we may be right. Lady Bountiful's behavior translates as noblesse oblige. She invites us to revolve around her magnificence. For snobbery is not just a measure of relative wealth or social standing; it is a way of using these to diminish us—"the habit of making inequality hurt."[34] Quiet insults are the most common expression of snobbery: the couple next door refuses to acknowledge us; they withhold even the recognition of "how are you today?" Less remarked is snobbery that takes the form of doing too much.

Lady Bountiful's ostentatious and immoderate good turns provoke justifiable unease because her offerings offend the democratic ethos of neighbors. She likely knows that give and take on her terms is impossible for us—that is the point. Hers is a one-way street. Keep in mind that neighbors' good works are personal and direct, not at a remove. Lady Bountiful's offerings express her understanding of our relation. Beneficence, to give it a positive label, when it is not an organized effort at repairing the failings and filling in the lacunae of state provisions (to "continue and complete the work of justice") arises within relationships and these relations dictate its scope and constraints.[35] Neighbor relations rest on reciprocity, and like exploitation, excessive favors fail the test of rough equality.

It is a sign of the luster of the good neighbor ideal that some people seize on it as the route to local celebrity. We may see Lady Bountiful's magnanimity as a bid for being "the very best neighbor." Her attentions and offers are designed to be acknowledged as exemplary. We may level the charge that her ambition is cramped because her domain of action is cramped. This block is her whole world, and she has no other arena for distinction. Private life at home can be the most important part of life, of course, and being a good neighbor is a commendable element of personal identity. But neighbor relations are normally not our chief source of self-esteem.

## Remaining Aloof

The content, scope, and frequency of reciprocity are variable, then, and except for circumstances of dire need or emergency, discretionary. Something important follows: we should be careful not to confuse failing in reciprocity in the ways I've described with declining to engage in give and take. Which is to say, good neighbor is compatible with detachment. We have no grievance against the withdrawn man next door. The setting of home and the proximity of neighbors often justifies keeping our distance. This distinction is important: disengagement is not the same as failing to appreciate the terms of reciprocity, nor is detachment unsociability *simpliciter*.

Recall that expectations for reciprocity follow from repeated interactions. Our aloof neighbor has taken care to limit his encounters. He has tried not to arouse expectations by restricting give and take to a bare minimum, a nod of recognition for example, or none at all. His detachment is deliberate and consistent. We should not assume it is meant to offend. (Much less that he is secretive, staying aloof with the intent to conceal some crime.) By itself detachment does not signal hostility or deny that the people nearby are "decent folk" with whom give and take would be perfectly benign. Of course, the manner of staving off encounters can be rude, and in any case sociable neighbors may experience it as rebuff. But the domain around home is necessarily a zone of privacy where our expectation of control often extends to encounters outside our door. Privacy in this context means "to be able to live one's own life without one's neighbours voluntarily or involuntarily taking a part of it."[36]

Local etiquette plays a part. Chang-rae Lee's Doc Hata describes his neighbors' notion of decorum: according to their "ethic, if it can be called such a thing, the worst wrong is to be drawn forth and disturbed."[37] Personal circumstances and disposition influence detachment too, and this aspect of the moral psychology of neighbors is fascinatingly complex. For example, our aloof neighbor may be in emotional limbo, a psychological state that is vulnerable to upset from interaction. Recall Raymond Carver's couple: "Call one of the neighbors. Call the Morgans. Anyone will feed a dog if you ask them to," but the couple resists sharing their private terror at what they are not quite ready to admit will be their son's death. For now, they are walling off and protecting their inner lives. Another example:

> When his wife told him to get out of the house that had been hers, Valdek Moore looked in the paper and found a semi-furnished, one-bedroom unit at Linden Pines ... He hadn't meant to provoke any connection to his place. ... invisibility was like being in a deep, timeless freeze.[38]

There are additional, thoughtful reasons for detachment. Our aloof neighbor may view most encounters as killing time, as antithetical to his care of the self. He enacts, severely, it's true, Frost's caution: "We're too unseparate. And going home/From company means coming to our senses."[39] Questioned, he would declare he is minding his own business. If we think about "going home from company means coming to our senses," we detect more in minding our own business than refraining from meddling. The phrase invites reflection on the demands of inner life we are protective of at home, and I take up this theme in Chapter 10, "Thoreau's Neighbors." Privacy, the intrinsically valuable, humanly necessary thing itself, the minimal area of personal freedom, is at risk from neighbors who contract its sphere just by their presence and certainly by their claims on our attention. Detachment cannot erase neighbors' presence, but it creates an emotional wall that deflects expectations of give and take.

In sum, in this domain around home, detachment often has different reasons and purposes than disengagement or antisocial behavior in other spheres.[40] If possible, we should accept our neighbor's holding back, her resistance to the "relationship wedge" that begins reciprocity with sympathetic understanding. For the tension is internal to the idea of good neighbor. Both minding our neighbors' business—attentiveness required by reciprocity—and minding our own business have value. Both are integral to good neighbor and to the quality of life at home. Few of us are immune to the push and pull, even if we are not dispositionally or chronically aloof. We struggle to get the pose right.

## "Decent Folk"

What is specifically "democratic" in reciprocity as an element of the democracy of everyday life? In part it is a matter of rough parity. That was Keese's moral armature in his war with his neighbors, as he calculated what Harry and Ramona were owed in return for each instance of deranging his life at home. But reciprocity by itself is incomplete. Reciprocity *among "decent folk"* is my name for this element of good neighbor.

In settler, immigrant, and suburban narratives "decent folk" is a common way of referring to neighbors, and I adopt this expression.[41] The phrase gathers in the qualities—practical and moral—we use to size up the couple next door in deciding whether we will open ourselves to or wall ourselves off from willing encounters. It reflects a sensible, good enough assessment that they are trustworthy for the purposes of ordinary give and take. Which is to say, we judge that they recognize at least the utility of good turns, the rough parity of give and take, and the power we neighbors have to enhance or diminish the quality of life at home.

Looked at more closely, "decent folk" entails equality *in this one respect*: qua neighbor. The phrase designates both a valued status and a comparatively autonomous status. For "decent folk" signals disregard for our neighbor's position in the wider society. It eclipses social standing, class, work, religion, origin, ethnic identity, and aspirationally race. It is as if as neighbors we shed our social attributes and histories. It is an abstraction from a host of social categories and markers that distinguish and divide us. This is not to say that designating our neighbors "decent folk" is itself an abstraction (as the designation "citizen" almost always is). On the contrary, it is a concrete assessment of particular neighbors as they appear in this specific context and in light of our experience of encounters there. To repeat: it is a judgment of men and women personally and individually. We decline to approach them as representatives or symbols. We do this even in the face of our own prejudice, snobbery, and initial personal discomfort. Or we try. The neighbor in Robert Frost's "The Ax-Helve" puts it this way:

> I shouldn't mind his being overjoyed
> (If overjoyed he was) at having got me
> Where I must judge if what he knew about an ax
> That not everybody else knew was to count
> For nothing in the measure of a neighbor.
> Hard if, though cast away for life with Yankees
> A Frenchman couldn't get his human rating![42]

As a measure of neighbors, "decent folk" has practical import. We don't bring the particulars of categorical differences to our encounters, and drawing fine-grained class or status distinctions and taking exquisite pains to treat neighbors in the particular terms that suit their standing "outside" the domain of home is unwarranted. It is incompatible with considerations and adjustments tailored to a specific position or place, income, or other social marker. It is incongruent with refined courtesy, and can be inhibited by a too-scrupulous civility. We signal recognition as "decent folk" by demeanor, language, and conduct that are simple and consistent.

Reciprocity among "decent folk" around home doesn't require us to be color-blind or indifferent to inequalities or hierarchies everywhere and overall. It isn't a sociological observation about social structure.[43] Nothing so absurd is at issue. Again, the moral judgment entailed by "decent folk" applies to particular individuals, neighbors, and entails deliberate disregard for their position in the wider society. It entails disregard for the adversarial categories that shape our perceptions of the larger social world and that give politics its business. Plainly, viewing neighbors categorically—especially if stigmatizing ethnic or racial red lines divide our map of the lay of the land and color our encounters—violates this element of the democracy of everyday life. Manifestly so, when "decent folk" is used not as matter-of-fact inclusion in the company of neighbors with whom we give and take but as a wall. Then, the meaning and message of "decent folk" is inverted, as it is too often. We exclude neighbors from the status of "decent folk" on account of ascriptive characteristics, not personal experience. Prejudice and categorical denigration truncate the universe of "decent folk." The phrase is meanly, cruelly, restrictive. Following the poet, we are not open to inquiring what this Frenchman, our neighbor, knows about an ax. I examine this failing closely in Chapter 5, "What Anyone Would Do, Here" and in Chapter 6, "Live and Let Live." Finally, the significance of rough equality in give and take among neighbors regarded as "decent folk" "lies not only in the extent to which it actually governs behavior . . . but rather as a standard by which the quality of experience is evaluated."[44]

Now, a caveat. Reciprocity among "decent folk" does not mean that neighbors have an obligation to engage with everyone, as we are obliged to do in other social spheres—at work or in public places like stores and restaurants. In public arenas, we are required to be impartial and impersonal. Unvarying and inclusive treatment is a matter of principle and public policy, and often a matter of law.[45] Reciprocity among neighbors, in contrast, is voluntary. And we don't think to justify the compass of our everyday give and take in terms of public democratic principles of inclusiveness or nondiscrimination. Reciprocity among neighbors can be selective. It allows for elective affinity. We have latitude in how we map our lay of the land and who we count as our neighbor. But where the democratic ethos of "decent folk" shapes our encounters, our interactions are not based on entrenched categories of difference.

Reciprocity among neighbors as "decent folk" is one element of the democracy of everyday life that gives content to good neighbor here. I don't claim that its democratic ethos is unique to America (this is not a comparative study), only that it is an identifiable ideal and common practice. Give and take go on everywhere among people living nearby, of course, but give and take among neighbors is seldom expected to conform to rough parity. Nor is give and take shaped by the inclusive notion of "decent folk" in most places. Reciprocity comparatively detached from the considerations that enter into relations in social spheres away from home is neither ideal nor practice in societies where encounters are regulated by entrenched social hierarchy, rank, class, or sectarianism, kinship, clientelism, or rule by tribal elders. Or where customary forms and "symbolic exchanges" are markers of social position. In early English usage neighbor meant "to place in conjunction with something," and references were to the crown and nobility: "neighbour'd him to the Court," or "this ancient baron neighboured to a throne."[46] Even after the definition expanded to indicate residential proximity generally, "neighbor" continued to draw attention to and instantiate relative class and status. Neighboring between minor nobility and bourgeoisie—the exquisite details of class and manners, deference and superiority, pride and prejudice that are running themes in the work of Jane Austen and so many other British novelists—is antithetical to the democracy of everyday life. In *Journeys to England* (1833) Tocqueville anticipated the "irresistible march of events" that would make English sociability, too, democratic.[47] 150 years later, though, Paul Theroux wrote in his account of travels around Great Britain that every chat "meant entering a minefield of verbal and social distinctions."[48]

Peculiar to Britain (continuing with the most accessible comparison) is not the reality of the class system, one historian suggests, but "class psychology: the preoccupation with class, the belief in class, and the symbols of class in manners, dress, and language."[49] "I'm afraid I don't answer to Mr. Barrett," Zadie Smith's character in *NW* asserts, "I answer to the actual landlord—I'm a relative of the actual landlord, as in the lord of the land." Neighbors in Boston don't converse as the author's do about how "neither woman was in any sense a member of the bourgeoisie but neither did they consider themselves solidly working class either."[50] If "the appropriate discipline for studying 'class' or status differentials is not sociology but rhetoric," "decent folk" makes the democratic point.[51]

## "Decent Folk": A Fighting Creed

In canonical narratives the tenacious ideal of reciprocity among neighbors as "decent folk" appears as expectancy, as reality, as a source of pain and injury when it is willfully violated. Its significance is driven home where hierarchy, raw prejudice, and entrenched mistrust mark neighbors' encounters. In the segregated South, to take a core American example, race, class, and parentage "taunted" formal democratic claims of civil rights and civic equality,[52] and—as important—inhibited the informal democracy of everyday life among neighbors. Harper Lee's *To Kill a Mockingbird* tells two stories. One has a civic dimension: the public struggle for fairness and civil rights; its hero is Atticus Finch. The other is the tentative appearance of the democratic ethos of reciprocity among "decent folk" in the domain of personal encounters around home; its hero is his daughter, Scout. For over half a century these characters have served as moral touchstones—citizens and neighbors we all know well.

Entrenched patterns of domination and disdain scar the segregated south of Harper Lee's Macomb County, Alabama in 1935. Members of white upper society pride themselves on being products of "several generations' of gentle breeding"; they do not come "from run-of-the-mill people." Their arrogance is backed by power. African Americans are subservient, ostensibly deferential, and unsafe. They are exposed to vicious assaults and denied equal protection of law. For their part, poor whites, in this miserable society, are perpetually angry at the gentry above and at blacks below; they are simultaneously disdaining and disdained. In what amounts to a caste system, people living in close proximity withhold mutual recognition as "decent folk." Rude displays of superiority and denigration are a regular occurrence around home. A description of the Ewell's place behind the town dump, where "the plot of ground around the cabin looked like the playhouse of an insane child" is the judgment from the right side of the tracks. "Fine folk" avoid the place. Blacks do too, for other reasons: the Ewells are brutal and threatening. Individual neighbors perform personal acts of kindness across lines of class and race, as we would expect, but rough parity of reciprocity among neighbors viewed as "decent folk" is not the standard by which the quality of experience is evaluated.

Against this background, Atticus Finch is Harper Lee's exemplar of civic equality. He is a lawyer who demands fair play and equal justice, and the novel's plot is driven by his defense of a black man, Tom Robinson, maliciously accused of rape. Atticus understands that democracy requires more than nominally equal legal status: men and women thwarted in exercising their rights suffer public degradation; they are dishonored as well as powerless.[53] He is repulsed by local practices of subordination and denigration. There is no question of his rectitude or sense of obligation as a citizen to correct injustice. But this is not the same as the democracy of everyday life, and he is not its exemplar.

Here is a beginning description of where the difference lies. In a place where gradations of address—from decorous to humiliating—indicate status, Atticus exhibits unvarying courtesy toward Maycomb's gentry, dirt-poor "white trash," and blacks. His consistent language and demeanor challenge social prejudice and racism. We could label this an exhibition of public respect. Atticus's unvarying form is in part a matter of democratic principle and public civility but it is also a matter of honor with him, part of his upbringing as a southern gentleman—his "instinctive courtesy." In Atticus Finch, principled democratic treatment as an equal and gentlemanly courtesy are hard to unravel from one another.

It is not surprising that his "Mr." and "Ma'am" are received badly by people unused to the forms of civic equality or that they respond to his unvarying civility as if it were a taunt. Under questioning on the witness stand Mayella Ewell says to the judge: "Long's he keeps on callin' me ma'am an sayin' Miss Mayella. I don't hafta take his sass, I ain't called upon to take it." Judge Taylor explains: "That's just Mr. Finch's way . . . We've done business in this court for years and years, and Mr. Finch is always courteous to everybody. He's not trying to mock you, he's trying to be polite. That's just his way."[54] We understand why Atticus's demeanor is liable to be received as an expression of superiority, a taunt. In Maycomb, the forms and tenor of his address are not only alien but also effectively unavailable to most residents, and people are inhibited, even prohibited, from responding in kind. Poor whites are reluctant to seem foolish by imitating "fancy airs." (Besides, they are loath to relinquish the license they enjoy to verbally degrade blacks—their compensation for being humiliated and scorned themselves.) African Americans, in turn, would not respond in kind to Atticus's formal civility out of fear of appearing "uppity" among whites and out of the discomfort it would produce among their own: "Folks don't like to have somebody around known' more than they do. It aggravates 'em."[55] Calpurnia, the Finch's black housekeeper, makes this observation; she had command of what were in practice two languages, and censors herself in just this way.

There is a nobility to Atticus and a principled democratic commitment that is—as rights and civility require—impersonal, stringent, and unvarying. He is the same with everyone, in public and in private and in intimate encounters. Scout provides the telling adjective: "He played with us, read to us, and treated us with courteous detachment."[56] Courteous detachment. In the face of radical injustice, Atticus Finch demonstrates controlled civility; he suppresses his rage in order to get the business of justice done. He is a model of civic equality, of even-handedness and fair-dealing (mixed with southern courtesy), but an imperfect representation of the democracy of everyday life among neighbors.

Scout embodies this democratic ethos as it makes an appearance in Maycomb. Her day-to-day encounters have an open, straightforward quality that does not derive from principles of social or legal equality and are not informed by her father's code of civility or his passion for justice. Rough equality of reciprocity grows instead out of her direct personal experience with the recluse Boo Radley, the effeminate Dill, schoolmates, Calpurnia, and other neighbors. Scout cannot grasp why social standing and race should be taken into account among people around home, and she disregards them. Her brother Jem accurately observes, "Our kind of folks don't like the Cunninghams, the Cunninghams don't like the Ewells, and the Ewells hate and despise the colored folks." Scout is baffled and rejects these lines of division as arbitrary and unneighborly: "I think there's just one kind of folks. Folks."[57] She grasps the essential stakes in viewing neighbors as "decent folk" perfectly well. It is a recognition of rough equality *qua neighbors*. It invites give and take.

Scout's capacity to "stand in others' shoes" reflects the working of an especially empathic soul, and for her "just folk" is a real felt experience. It needs educating and articulation, though. In Macomb "decent folk" is a fighting creed, and Scout has to learn to resist the impulse to lash out at the haughty, defensive, and cruel members of her own family and at neighbor ladies with "frostings of sweat and sweet talcum" who measure people in terms of "trash" and "fine folk." Scout learns to control her rage. And part of her moral education is learning to articulate the wrong in failing to acknowledge neighbors as "decent folk." It is not a matter of civic injustice. Rather, living in close proximity, neighbors provide reciprocity, the comfort of recognition, availability, the minimum of "how are you feeling today?," and sometimes vital acts of kindness and rescue. "Neighbors bring food with death and flowers with sickness and little things in between."[58] Absent the disposition to acknowledge neighbors as "decent folk," the quality of life at home is sore, sad, and degraded. For those denied recognition as "decent folk," and for others who must witness it and live everyday in an atmosphere of caste and cruelty, the distinctive wrong in it is this deprivation.

The novel provides a window onto both legal equality and the democracy of everyday life. Formal democratic principles (among them fairness and civic equality on the one hand, and the democracy of everyday life beginning with reciprocity among "decent folk" on the other) are largely though not always congruent. We see in this novel and we can see in actual practice that the dynamic of interaction is fluid, back and forth. They work in tandem; Atticus and Scout are complements.

We also see that the informal democratic ethos with its moral identity of "good neighbor" has independent value. Indeed, it may do as much work as "good citizen" when it comes to enabling public institutions to effect principles of justice. Harper Lee demonstrates the efficacy of the matter-of-fact invocation of neighbor and "just folks" in Scout's dramatic confrontation with brutal neighbors threatening to lynch the accused black man. "Hey, Mr. Cunningham ... Don't you remember me ... I'm Jean Louise Finch. You brought us some hickory nuts one time, remember? ... I go to school with Walter." Then, Scout reports, he did a peculiar thing. "He squatted down and took me by both shoulders ... I'll tell him you said hey, little lady ... Let's get going, boys."[59] I return to the power of the invocation of neighbor in Chapter 6, "Live and Let Live" and Chapter 8, "Killing."

The democracy of everyday life emerges as the substrate of democracy in America. Put less insistently for now, we see that something is lost if we flatten out the distinct sphere of life around home and the distinct disposition and regulative ideal of good neighbor operating there.

# 4

# Taking Offense, Speaking Out

"Neighbor" often comes bathed in a warm glow. The term is used evaluatively; "good" is superfluous. Sentimentality is smuggled in:

> The town of Essex ... had detected the presence of newcomers and roused itself to greet us. In one week, two people knocked on the door of our rental house bearing actual welcome baskets. ... The next week we met some people our own age who had us to dinner ... the babies were laid down to sleep on the bed and the fiddles came out and the cabin filled up with music, like an episode of *Little House on the Prairie* but with beer.[1]

These idylls are not dependable, or durable. The stories we tell are more often miserable. We must deal with dissemblers, manipulators, bullies, compulsive types, emotional aggressors. Our stories reflect our bafflement, our incredulity at the misconduct or sheer obliviousness of the people next door. We become agitated again in the telling.

> A good neighbour, even in this,
> Is fatal sometimes, cuts your morning up
> To mince-meat of the very smallest talk,
> Then helps to sugar her bohea at night
> With your reputation.[2]

That our neighbor did not mean to cause trouble is not a reliable barrier to a sense of injury. That's the thing about physical proximity: inconvenience, interference, slights, and offense are virtually inevitable, and neighbors' thoughtless words and actions can seem to be aimed at us. He didn't realize that loading the dumpster with materials left over from his home repair would make it hard for me to get rid of my trash. He wasn't guilty of negligence; my trash disposal was a bit more difficult but not impossible. But that hardly registers with me. To my mind, his selfish inattention to the overloaded dumpster has made my already stressed-out life harder. In that moment, he is the last straw. We all know someone aggravated by (we might say fixated on) the neighbor who uses his yard as a shortcut or teenagers massed on the sidewalk blocking the way or pets let loose to soil the hallway. We experience bad neighbors as more than a nuisance; and a nuisance, if it persists, can diminish the quality of everyday life.[3] Neighbors have latitude to be careless and inattentive, and to unleash their demons on one another, and we have innumerable occasions to discharge our desire to get back at offenders, too. It may take enormous effort to "represse all appetite of our neighbour's hurt."[4]

## The Shadow of the Law

Neighbor relations operate in the shadow of the law, and, in some circumstances, dealing with offenses involves appealing to authorities. When we believe our neighbor has violated local ordinances, when their fence encroaches on our yard or blight fouls the area, we report to police, zoning boards, housing authorities. We appear in small claims court. We translate offenses into officially recognized misconduct and actionable grounds for complaint. We want every offense to be legally cognizable—for every wrong a remedy. We hope for enforcement and compliance and often compensation for the nuisance or emotional distress. So, neighbors file complaints and notify official agencies; they show up at the Development Review Board hearing, where just a few people voicing opposition to the design for an addition to our home (opposition that may owe to sour grapes) have influence. They invoke the General Unsightliness Ordinance. They call the police.

### Officers Remove 50 Pets From Malodorous Mich. Home

By THE ASSOCIATED PRESS

Filed at 6:55 p.m. ET August 5, 2010

REDFORD TOWNSHIP, Mich. (AP)—Police say more than three dozen dogs, a dozen cats and about six rabbits are getting veterinary treatment after being removed from a small home in a Detroit suburb. Police Lt. Eric Gillman says neighbor complaints about the smell prompted police to show up Wednesday at the home in Redford Township . . . officers described the condition of the house as "deplorable" . . . floors were "covered in dog waste, urine."

This is a standard example, a cliché.

Litigation is encouraged by the ever-growing number of legal "hooks" afforded by co-op and condominium arrangements and homeowner's associations. My homeowner's association sued and was sued in return by the wealthy buyer whose plan for new construction did not conform to limitations on square footage, roof height, and placement on the lot. When the review committee denied permission to begin construction, the owner was confident that he could have his way by out-lawyering, that is, outspending us. After a decision by a majority of homeowners, we paid our share of the legal expenses as a matter of contractual obligation. With its numerous appeals, the lawsuit dragged on for almost a decade and became famous in the state for its cost and acrimony. The District Court in Barnstable ruled in favor of Shearwater Association—the first ruling to uphold homeowner association covenants in Massachusetts.[5] It was not all legal formalism, though: the dynamic of "negative association" transformed us from stakeholders into neighbors united by a common adversary—a reliable source of solidarity. We always had something to talk about with one another.

The law is not seamless, though. Frequently the offense does not rise to the level of "extreme outrageousness" required by tort law, or the law of nuisance does not apply. All sorts of insults and injuries springing from carelessness, spite, or ordinary vices hold no interest for local authorities and do not amount to a legal harm. (Hence the wide umbrella of Britain's "Anti-Social Behavior Act," which has been described as a form of "personalized criminal law," punishing conduct that harasses, alarms, or distresses—including the case of an eighty-seven-year-old man who was sarcastic to his neighbors or the woman fined and forbidden to make excessive noise during sex anywhere in England.)[6] Often, too, the high transaction costs of appealing to officials inhibit complaints and civil suits. We can't always delegate interpretation of offenses and response to others, and when official channels fail us, we are doubly indignant.

In the multitude of cases where we neighbors are on our own, we are drawn into the difficulties I survey. We are on our own interpreting the offense. After all, anger and indignation do not come directly from perceptions but from judgments about those perceptions. And once we define our neighbor's act as an insult or injury, do we speak out or keep the matter to ourselves? Do we have a responsibility to speak out in support of aggrieved neighbors? Or can we justify minding our own business? What makes speaking out an element of the democracy of everyday life?

## Keeping Offenses to Ourselves

Sometimes we keep the offenses we suffer at our neighbor's hands to ourselves. Exercised though we are, we practice self-restraint. We pretend to ignore the nuisance or insult. We don't advise the couple across the way that because they neglect to pull down the shades we see them displaying themselves nude or arguing aggressively, and that it is upsetting to have to be exposed to these intimacies. Whether exhibitionist or just oblivious, they make the business of minding our own business harder. Still, we keep things to ourselves because we estimate that things would be worse if we spoke out. At a minimum it would create awkwardness that outlasts the offense itself. Keeping offenses to oneself is a convention of denial that operates in almost every setting. Reticence or simply "unacknowledgment" limits collisions, and cautiousness is sensible among neighbors we are unable to evade.

Most of us exercise restraint most the time. We are selectively inattentive to slamming hallway doors or to doors left ajar, to neighbors who park their car "temporarily" in our assigned spot, to the disturbances caused by unsupervised children. We don't acknowledge slights or inconveniences even if we find our neighbor's indifference maddening or detect a whiff of malice behind her excessive demands or sheer carelessness.

Besides, we often recognize these neighbors who give offense as "decent folk" for the purposes of day-to-day reciprocity and we don't want to upset our ongoing dealings. We take a warning from the neighbor who is perpetually aggrieved and agitated, who calls us out on every misstep and slight, real or imagined, who creates awkwardness and excites conflict. The premonition that our attempts to fashion a response will be fumbling and futile reinforces reticence. No wonder offenders often do their bad turns with impunity.

Calculations are not the whole story, though. There is more to keeping offenses to ourselves. A pair of reasons for reticence is rooted in self-doubt. For one, grating effects are not always known quantities that we can describe convincingly to others; indeed, we are sometimes unable to explain our reaction even to ourselves. The chemistry of proximity to certain individuals just arouses anxiety and hostility. Why do I time my comings and goings to avoid that apparently unobjectionable elderly man who sets my teeth on edge? For another, our uncertainty about whether conduct constitutes a willful offense and our hesitation to speak out may provide cover for neighbors to inflict their damage for some time before we are sufficiently miserable that we admit we have been trespassed on, exploited, misused. Then we wonder whether our weakness or misjudgment is to blame. Do I invite mistreatment? Allow myself to be bullied? Am I a patsy or a fool? We find our situation at the hands of our neighbor humiliating and we don't solicit sympathetic attention much less recruit other neighbors to our cause.

In addition to self-doubt, certain situations make us loath to have the wrongs inflicted on us known. We don't want our grievances broadcast, and we don't want to elevate the offender into a local legend. Some harms are more painful than noisy air conditioners or the stench of cats. There's personal betrayal, for example. The list of Old Testament prohibitions against coveting begins with "your neighbor's wife." Proximity provides opportunity, cover, and the *frisson* of discovery, which is why stories of infidelity frequently involve neighbors. Revelation is bound to result in maximum insult. Neighbors' gossip makes salvaging our relationship harder. And damage to our inner life comes from knowing that others know: focused on their inquiries or equally unbearable commiseration, we are diverted from our own feelings. We are distracted from minding our own business. We are grateful if neighbors don't know, or grateful for their reticence in not acknowledging what they know.

So we may keep personal betrayals and other violations of trust to ourselves. In Raymond Carver's story "Neighbors," Bill and Arlene Miller are vaguely envious of the couple across the hall. "It seemed to the Millers that the Stones lived a fuller and brighter life. The Stones were always going out for dinner, or entertaining at home, or traveling about the country somewhere in connection with Jim's work." When the Millers agree to feed Kitty and water the plants while the Stone's go out of town, they indulge their fantasies about this enviable life. The neighbors' apartment seems at one visit cooler and darker, another time the air feels heavy and sweet; it is mysterious, a foreign country. During his visits to feed the cat, Bill takes sips of Chivas Regal, pockets pills from the Stone's medicine cabinet and cigarettes from the bedside table, tries on Jim's Hawaiian shirt and Arlene's bra, uses the toilet, acts out erotically on their bed (which "seemed enormous, with a fluffy white bedspread draped to the floor"). When it's her turn to feed and water, Arlene finds pornographic pictures, and urges Bill to join her so that they can enjoy them together; they turn the Stone's apartment into a place of experiment and thrilling disorientation. One day, caught up in their play, they forget the Stones' key, locking themselves out. Kitty and plants go untended.[7] The Stones may never know the dimension of this betrayal of trust, and if they do they may be so unnerved by the indignity of the trespass and feel so queasy about their own misjudgment that they do not want anyone to know.

Then there are the painful developments in our relationships that we experience as betrayal but keep to ourselves because at heart we understand that we have not been wronged. That's true for the life cycle of neighbor relations that revolve around children, intertwining this family on the block in our daily lives. As children grow up they cease to provide the glue, interactions fall off, and we revert awkwardly to exchanging bare greetings or mundane good turns. The time frame of withdrawal is seldom the same for all parties, and cooling can feel like betrayal. Fading closeness is painful, but we don't speak out. It's not the case that our trust was misplaced; simply, walling in and walling out is ongoing and changeable, and may give offense, intended or not.

Keeping offenses to ourselves stems in part from our difficulty interpreting actions and assessing offenses and in part from not knowing how to respond: there is no established repertoire of self-defense and the consequences of speaking out are not predictable. So behind this picture of personal uncertainty and keeping offenses to ourselves is the predicament of neighbors: absence of articulated standards of behavior; absence of impartial interpreters of actions; absence of tested forms of enforcement.

## Recruiting Neighbors

We don't always keep offenses to ourselves. We don't want our bad neighbor to offend with impunity. Her behavior should have consequences, including reputational consequences. So we talk censoriously about the local delinquent. We report untrustworthiness, deception, bad attitude, nuisance, and more serious offenses to people living nearby. We know that our neighbors will judge the reliability of our reports, and we narrate her trespasses in detail so that there is no ambiguity. We want our neighbors to see things from our point of view. We want them to agree that our agitation is reasonable, that we are not thin-skinned or histrionic. It is not enough for us that they sympathetically affirm "the son-of-a-bitch should have it coming to him," though. We want our neighbors to make our business their own and to speak out. Berger's Earl Keese acted alone; we want allies. "It seems more efficient to make explicit acknowledgment function as a signal that something must be collectively dealt with."[8] We want our neighbors to mediate, confront, remonstrate, retaliate, ostracize, shame, invoke some authority, any authority. We want the matter to be "collectively dealt with."

The most damaging of ordinary vices is cruelty—maliciously degrading the quality of life at home. In my building in Cambridge, Massachusetts, one resident tormented the family next door—tormented is the right description—by locating an air conditioner on a spot on the roof that amplified motor noise and vibrations, keeping the family awake on warm nights. When several neighbors proposed pooling the cost of moving the compressor to another spot on the roof, the offender declined our offer. He insisted that he was within his rights; he hired an engineering firm to testify that the sound and vibration fell within the permissible limits set by the city; he posted the paperwork in the hallway. His willful indifference to distress, indeed his perverse pleasure in his sleepless neighbors' impotence, was apparent. The noise bully was intransigent. The victims were brought to the limits of distraction. They tried earplugs, added insulation, moved their bed to a back wall. They tried to sell (were they required to warn potential buyers of the AC racket?) but got no offers.

The noise bully's aggression is not at all trivial for my neighbors whose lives were disrupted. Moreover, his aggressive degradation of life around home shares a world with the graver, brutal forms of betrayal and violence I discuss in Part III. So do neighbors' responses, for our experience speaking out—along with other elements of the democracy of everyday life—is a resource and has special importance in extreme situations.

How do we respond to the noise bully? In innumerable situations confronted with ordinary offenses like this one, we are drawn into the storms that gather and join the circle of conversation on the stairwell. We rally round, identify the offense, voice indignation, sympathize and console, decide on collective action, and confront the offender. What does speaking out owe to our status as neighbors? And what specifically makes speaking out a defining element of the democracy of everyday life?

## Prudence, Sympathy, and Solidarity

One motivation, of course, is the sense that we are not immune from this sort of harm, perhaps from this particular bully. We know intuitively or from wretched past experience that passivity in the face of cruelty encourages the despot next door to become bolder. Passivity is debilitating too, and takes a toll on us personally and a specific toll on us *qua* neighbors. Moreover, it is easy to imagine that we will want neighbors' assistance when some noxious resident takes aim at us. Rallying to comfort the target and confront the offender is a form of insurance.

> Better to go down dignified
> With boughten friendship at your side
> Then none at all. Provide, Provide![9]

In addition, our sympathy is stirred. We observe close up the daily degradation of this family's quality of life. We are uniquely situated to recognize the deliberateness of the offense and to offer support to the noise bully's targets.

Something else is at work when we rally to confront the offender: solidarity. For the most part we relate to neighbors through particular encounters, typically one-on-one. Episodically, however, others on the hallway or on the block recruit us, invoking our standing as neighbors and asserting our solidarity. The term is resonant of unity, fellow-feeling, loyalty. The emotional resonance of solidarity adds weight to neighbors' insistence that we should take action aginst the noise bully, but it is not a constant feature of the democracy of everyday life. It piggybacks on speaking out as an element of good neighbor.

## Speaking Out

We are impelled to speak out by indignation—moral anger aroused by a neighbor exploiting the power inherent in proximity to degrade the quality of life where we live. No one should have to endure willfully imposed, purposeless distress at the hands of people living nearby. As a motivation indignation may be stronger than anticipating that we may need neighbors' support down the line and stronger than sympathy for the afflicted family down the hall. Its arises from the conviction that life at home should not be intruded on and disturbed at another's pleasure. Malice, arbitrariness, and sheer aggressiveness are, in a word, despotic. So we speak out in resistance to a homely sort of despotism.

To be clear: indignation at arrant arbitrariness derives its force from its locus at the frontier of privacy, home. It is at a pitch because in contrast to many settings, we have no exit. Neighbors are uniquely vulnerable to one another too because of the stakes, the depth and intensity of the interests we have in quotidian private life and the felt necessity of a degree of control over conditions at home. We understand that control is variable and imperfect, never what we may want. The designation "decent folk" is modest, and represents our confidence that these neighbors intend us no harm and will take our elementary interests into account. Underscore "elementary." A neighbor who casts himself outside the field of "decent folk" by arrantly, repeatedly diminishing the quality of life at home arouses indignation and moves us to join in speaking out.

Direct, personal confrontation is neighbors' way of holding the despot accountable, then. Neighbors' solid front might cause the bully to listen to reason and alter his conduct, but now we move beyond attempts at reconciliation. Our confrontation is not principally educative, either; providing lessons in the rudiments of neighborliness is not now our purpose. Our purpose is to confront cruel aggression and beat the bully back—or to be seen as resolutely trying. Aimed at capricious cruelty, speaking up, causing a fuss, running amok against the offender falls to neighbors. It is the resistance available to us. We might think of neighbors speaking out as "Lockeans" defending themselves against arbitrariness.[10] Of course, we're enforcing neither natural law (the bully has not violated life or property) nor local ordinances, but on this analogy, like Locke's resisters, we neighbors identify the offense as requiring action, and we do so after time and experience reveal the offender's deliberate intent.

By invoking resistance to despotism, I've drawn language from the political realm. The democratic feature promised by my phrase 'the democracy of everyday life' enters here. In that moment of speaking out, we neighbors are self-governing. We exercise freedom to name the offense, blame the offender, claim the support of others nearby, decide on action, and enforce our judgment. Absent known rules, authoritative interpreters, and designated enforcers, neighbors legislate the bounds of "what anyone would do, here," judge that the bully's conduct casts him outside the bounds, take the decision to act.

Economists and anthropologists study the emergence of informal norms through collective action and enforcement in the absence of formal institutions. In his classic account of cattlemen and farmers coordinating rules of liability for damage done by wandering cows, Robert Ellickson called these "adaptive norms of neighborliness that trump formal legal entitlements."[11] His case involved financial coordination (under-girding norms of neighborliness in his study were high economic stakes), and in Ellison's account of order without law, informal norms and sanctions were clearly articulated. Things are different among neighbors whose collective action is not intended as a precedent for other occasions. Nonetheless, neighbors' felt need for governing their business with one another is plain. Thoreau made the point broadly, in blistering terms: "We have had to agree on a certain set of rules, called etiquette . . . to make this frequent meeting tolerable and that we need not come to open war." [12]

Qua neighbors we must figure out how to live in relations of equality with others whom we do not choose and cannot escape, and who in the event of offense we must decide to address. In the wider society—where bullies have other titles and there are institutional checks, accountability, and formal avenues of relief and punishment—speaking out may be somebody else's business. At home, there is no one else. We are carrying on the work of protecting ourselves from one another that is often assigned to government but here in the domain of home where (crime and abuse excepted, of course) we don't want or expect government to be. The project of self-governance among neighbors precedes and extends beyond whatever formal self-government is captured by political institutions.[13]

Specifically "democratic" in speaking out, then, are the informal gatherings and considerations, the judgment of offense, rallying, and deciding to act together in response to a disruption of everyday life. In the moment of speaking out against the noise bully and the moments of congregation and decision-making preceding it, we neighbors are self-governing. The term "democratic" will appear to be misleading only if we think self-government must refer to citizen-members of a formal unit. Neighbors responding to an offense around home are not members of any organized body that takes collective decisions. They have no official jurisdiction. Moreover, only some neighbors participate; those who speak out are a self-appointed crew of sympathizers and enforcers who make no claim to be elected or representative. My use of "democratic" will appear misleading, too, if we think decision-making is democratic only where there are set rules and procedures, as there are in organized neighborhood associations, for example. Speaking out, we neighbors are not democratic in the process sense—majority decision-making is not at issue. Consensus emerges among these particular neighbors taking things into their hands. In short, neighbors rally, judge, decide, and act without the organization, assigned authority, or processes of decision-making required by formal democratic practices. Where neighbors do speak out, however, their action amounts to more than a bit of self-help. It constitutes a moment of self-government.

Neighbors don't claim authority to act in democratic terms; nothing of the sort comes to mind in this context. But if challenged, we could defend against the charge that our action was not democratic. Speaking out is democratic insofar as neighbors decide and act collectively, as equals *qua* neighbors. We cooperate to identify and effect "adaptive norms of neighborliness that trump formal legal entitlements." Note that "government without law" is not a matter of coordination among equals or self-government everywhere. Standard social science examples of the operation of informal norms include Pashtun elders or the regulations and sanctions imposed by the Mafia. Speaking out as I've described it is aptly cast as an element of the democracy of everyday life.

My description of speaking out against an offender as collective resistance to political arbitrariness and domination is evocative, but it is an analogy only. Speaking out is not a more local, intimate version of resistance to despotic political authority. It is not micro-resistance, either. It is not aimed at abuse of authority or overweening social power. The maliciously placed air conditioner is arbitrary and cruel but it is not a public injustice. It is not a violation of principles of fairness or nondiscrimination, say. The victims are not deprived of political, civil, or social rights; their standing in terms of civic equality is not at stake. Nor does it rise to the level of a violation of a basic right or fundamental well-being of the sort that grounds general moral obligations of assistance. Which is not to minimize the malice or harm; the situation has urgency for the afflicted family but it is not an emergency and there is no immediate threat of violence or destruction. Our authority for speaking out derives from our status as neighbors aware of our mutual vulnerability and indignant at this cruel exercise of the power of proximity. We are not acting as citizens or oppressed subjects. We would understand the situation differently if the disruption were officially instigated or condoned; then, speaking out *is* a form of political resistance and I turn there in Part III, "Holding Our Lives in Their Hands."

## Good Neighbors versus Good Citizens Speaking Out

The difference between speaking out against a neighbor and speaking out against arbitrariness, patent unfairness, or discrimination in public settings is at the heart of my political theory of the democracy of every-

day life. In public, standing on line in a bakery, for example, we may remonstrate in defense of a woman who is being treated unfairly, particularly if we believe she is a target of discrimination. We protest even if we
feel personally immune: we are being served in turn, and we don't belong
to her racial, ethnic, or religious group. In public contexts the victim and
perpetrator are strangers. It is precisely the force of general, impersonal
principles of fairness and nondiscrimination that excites us, and that we
affirm. On the bakery line, our protest offers public assurance to the person mistreated that she is an equal member of society, that fairness is her
due, and that we recognize that she is being mistreated.[14] Our purpose is
to see that she is served without being demeaned, and to acknowledge
the toxic public atmosphere created by patent unfairness. Our protest is
also educative. We explain our action to other customers in principled
terms—looking at them as well as the clerk directly as we insist aloud,
"that's not fair." Implicit in the background of our protest is the huge
moral achievement of civil rights: the "free speech, public assembly, protests, petitions of grievances to officials, testimony before Congress and
publicity of complaints through a free press, mobilization of supporters
and voting."[15] In confronting the bakery clerk we join this history. Principles of nondiscrimination (and others) have been legally mandated in
"public accommodations" like the bakery, and have been voluntarily in-
stitutionalized in all sorts of civil society groups. Moreover, just as we are
all owed treatment as an equal in these public arenas, we are all charged
with protecting and protesting. It does not matter who invokes these principles on line in the bakery. Democratic public culture is "an expression
of the promise of universal and equal standing,"[16] and in protesting the
clerk's arbitrariness or prejudice we affirm this.

Our action in the store has purposes that don't figure in speaking out
against the noise bully. Citizenship has something of the character of a
public office and speaking out is a civic responsibility (though it is a severe imperative we often fail to meet). Neighbor is not an office, and as a
rule neighbors don't claim to speak in their capacity as citizens. The offense we confront does not have political history behind it, and the action
we take is improvised. We don't employ the language of rights or civic
equality, justice or injustice in expressing indignation at the noise bully,
either. Rather, we judge that he has cast himself out of the bounds of "decent folk" trustworthy for purposes of mundane give and take. We grasp
these differences; it is not a matter of subtle conceptual analysis. Principles of civil equality and fairness simply don't capture our experience of
arbitrariness and cruelty at the hands of a neighbor, at home. We don't

invoke justice or equality or human rights or dignity, and if we did the appeal to these principles would strike us as grandiose.

One more difference deserves mention. Fairness applies to any single act, as the bakery line example illustrates, and our response is impersonal and does not depend on having a history of encounters with this clerk or this victim. Among neighbors, however, taking offense and speaking out is relational. In arousing our indignation and shaping our response it matters just who gives and who takes offense. Our indignation and determination to take collective action build over time, informed by knowledge of the noise bully and his victims, and the tenor and terms of speaking out are informed by experience with them too.

Home as the locus of the offense is not determinative all by itself. If the noise bully is racist, then speaking out has something of the character of a civic response to public injustice. We are alert to this; after all, disregard for neighbors' characteristics apart from whether or not they are "decent folk" is a defining characteristic of good neighbor.[17] We are generally aware when that imperative is abrogated. I'm less concerned to disavow any continuity between neighbors speaking out and the civic obligation to protest public injustice, however, than to show that the democracy of everyday life has independent meaning and value. If we conflate speaking out against the noise bully with confronting public injustice, the distinct self-governing facet of good neighbor disappears from view.

We know too that good neighbor and good citizen can pull apart. Speaking out against the noise bully may signify little or nothing about our commitment to principles of civic equality, much less our disposition to protest unfairness or discrimination. The reverse is also true: men and women dedicated to public democratic principles may fail to speak out as neighbors in defense of the quality of life at home.

## Detachment: Whose Responsibility?

Everyone is charged with being a guarantor of public principles like fairness in the spheres of government and civil society; although silence in the face of injustice is not a legal offense, it is derogation of an obligation of citizenship. This alerts us to a further reason for distinguishing good neighbor from good citizen. Put simply, neighbors have latitude when it comes to whether or not to join in speaking out against offenders. Not all neighbors participate in collective action to enforce the "etiquette" that prevents open war. How should we think about the woman down the hall who holds back from adding her voice to the chorus of protest against the noise bully? Is minding her own business justifiable?

Her aim may simply be to avoid unpleasantness. Or she may have a myopic view of reciprocity and discounts her own potential need for assistance. Or she may have a crystallized assessment of the situation and is satisfied that the offender is within his rights or that confrontation is misguided. If she has no history of encounters with the noise bully or with his target, she may be immune to the furious goings-on, invulnerable to the surge of indignation felt by those in the thick of things.

In any case, detachment from the action need not indicate selfishness or indifference or obliviousness. For there is tension between self-governing neighbors speaking out on the one hand and minding our own business on the other. Minding our own business, a catchword for reticence and withdrawal, is part of being a good neighbor, which is just what makes disengagement interesting. Consider: this neighbor may recognize full well that the bully deserves moral blame. In terms of the basic "ground relationship" of neighbors he failed to do the minimum—desist from willfully degrading the quality of life of those around, and beyond that he is aggressively intransigent. He has removed himself from the company of "decent folk." If she has interacted with the bully in the past, his conduct will alter her attitude toward him; their relationship is impaired. T. M. Scanlon explains: "Blame is not mere evaluation but a revised understanding of our relations with a person, given what he or she has done." Her judgment does not necessarily lead to speaking out, though; the intention to challenge or to demand justification or apology "need not be present in every instance of blaming."[18]

Why not? For one thing, the terms of neighborliness are indeterminate and no set list of constitutive acts or presumptive responsibilities to or for people living nearby defines good neighbor. True, some acts and failures to act serve as a "bright line" test: arrant cruelty, refusing to warn of danger or to respond in an emergency. These constitute a general if not universal ethic of neighborliness that is thinner than the contextually articulated elements of the democracy of everyday life. The woman down the hall who refuses to speak out against the noise bully has not violated this barebones ethic of neighborliness. But has she violated the democratic ethos of neighbor by refusing to speak out?

Indignant engaged neighbors are likely to insist on her responsibility to support the victims and join the resistance. And she may have this responsibility, if not inherently *qua* neighbor then because of her own past actions. Recall my earlier discussion of how we regularly take commit-

ments on ourselves.[19] Our give and take generates expectations that create reliance on us, to sweep the hallway, say. Moreover, expectations
evolve incrementally as a result of repeated encounters. Because reliance
flows from relations over time in this way, our commitments are voluntarily incurred yet at the same time vulnerable to divergent understand-
ings. With this in mind, let's say the neighbor who refuses to join the collective action engages in a modicum of give and take day to day. Her
refusal to speak out does not denote wholesale indifference; she does not
erect an impenetrable wall. But she has taken some care to delimit the
terms of relations to a set of modest gestures of give and take, to insulate
herself from expectations she is likely to disappoint and from expanding
commitments, perhaps especially when it comes to collective action.

This neighbor has one particularly strong justification for remaining
aloof: the countervailing value of minding her own business as a condition for her quality of life at home. In the most general terms "minding
our own business" owes to acknowledgment of our separateness and our
need for privacy and control. I'll quote Frost again: "We're too unseparate. And going home / From company means coming to our senses."[20]
The woman down the hall assumes a detached pose out of jealous regard
for control of her life at home and for care of the self. Reticence and reluctance—minding her own business—is an especially strong personal
need or disposition in her case. We may wish she would mind her neighbors' business in this matter of speaking out. We may disagree with her
judgment about the priority of protecting herself, at least in this case. But
we understand the necessity and indisputable value of both minding our
own business and minding our neighbors'. She won't earn any accolades,
indeed she is likely to figure as a secondary villain in her engaged neighbors' tales. But it would be a mistake to call her a "bad neighbor" or in
violation of the latitudinous terms of "decent folk." Besides, minding our
own business is an armature we are justified in putting on for another
reason: when it comes to collective action, it protects against our own and
others' bad impulses.

## Neighbors as Enforcers

Resistance to the petty despotism of neighbors is a signature element of
the democracy of everyday life. The importance of speaking out against
the noise bully unfolds as I consider graver, even appalling examples of
neighbors' aggression and betrayal in Part III. But even under ordinary
conditions, activist neighbors may not stop with remonstrance against a

neighbor's cruel arbitrariness. Their aims may be expansive, imperial. The accident of proximity gives them, they imagine, presumptive authority, which they are keen to exercise. They magnify the importance of what they know and with that magnify their own.. They ward off a host of possible offenses proactively by surveillance and cautions, warning neighbors who are errant in any of a hundred different ways. Moved by fear of social disorder or zeal for improvement they censure, correct, and confront. Confident in their judgment and buoyed by a sense of efficacy they may slip over from speaking out against this noise bully to acting as general monitors and enforcers, my subject in the next chapter.

Neighbors as enforcers are not self-governing in the provisional and improvisational way I described in response to the noise bully's offense. When neighbors move from spontaneous mutual support to organized activism, when they form associations and assume the role of compliance officers, they make claims on us that extend beyond ordinary reciprocity and speaking out. They condemn both violators and neighbors who do not join in collective action. From their standpoint, just keeping up the old greetings and considerations will not suffice.

Take suburban neighbors who organize in favor of passing a leaf-blower ban in their town. They write to local papers, create websites, convene meetings, design strategies, arrange for invited experts to gather at a "No Blow" barbecue. They pronounce to everyone living nearby that it is their responsibility to take action, and failure to participate provokes the charge of complacency. "Somehow the blower issue became a referendum on what it means to be a neighbor: whether neighbors constitute a community or are just nuisances and Nosey Parkers."[21] Reluctant, reticent neighbors who fail to join in are castigated by the activists next door. Indeed, disengagement is represented as a civic as well as personal failing. Neighbors are no longer viewed in the simple guise of "decent folk." Bad neighbor is fused with bad citizen. Neighbors in Jonathan Frazen's story fire these accusations at the woman on the block who runs errands and bakes cookies for the neighborhood children but:

> There was *no* larger consciousness, *no* solidarity, *no* political substance, *no* fungible structure, *no* true communitarianism in Patty Berglund's supposed neighborliness. It was all just regressive housewifely bullshit ... it was obvious that the only things that mattered to her were her children and her house—*not* her neighbors, not the poor, *not* her country.[22]

The author intends us to read this characterization as histrionic. The conflation of good neighbor and good citizen amounts to piling on.

Of course, neighbors *do* organize and take civic and political action. The dynamic leading from the perception of common problems to casting the domain around home as a site of protest, to agitating, forming neighborhood associations, appearing before local officials and supporting candidates for office is common enough. Studies of neighborhood groups, voter turnout, and local politics examine the circumstances that produce recruitment and collective civic action by neighbors. Other studies identify negative "neighborhood effects"—the diffuse atmosphere of fear and passivity that inhibit even informal cooperation and speaking out, as I show in Chapter 6, "Live and Let Live." My point is that for reforming neighbors, my refusal to join in, speak out, or form associations represents a civic failing, as indeed it may be, but they are liable to take my refusal for something it is not: derogation from the ideal of good neighbor.

# 5

# What Anyone Would Do, Here

We assess neighbors all the time, not just in relation to ourselves but also for local fit. Neighbors carry on around home in ways that seem to our minds to deviate disturbingly from "what anyone would do, here." They seem to subscribe to "the rules of behavior associated with amusement parks," or barrooms, or bedrooms.[1] We aim at enforcing local etiquette. We monitor and reproach. Our tone is censorious. We don't always trouble to conceal our contempt. In the most disturbing cases, our judgment is colored by prejudice, and we characterize our neighbors' conduct in a way that is overtly stigmatizing.

Neighbors enforcing familiar, comfortable ways of doing things here differs from speaking out in response to a singular offense. The noise bully upsets his neighbor's quality of life but we would not accuse him of upsetting the "character of the community" wholesale. That is my subject here, neighbors who harbor a broad set of expectations for appropriate conduct, and who judge that those who do not conform require correction or exclusion. They do not belong. I explore the moral psychology of neighbors incensed (and fearful) because people living nearby seem not to have learned the lay of the land, or rudely map their own way. I identify two moral taproots of the warrant for minding one another's business in the spirit of reproach and with the aim of repair. Of course, collective benefits flow from watchful neighbors prepared to take collective action against delinquency, but my main purpose is to examine the dark side of neighbors speaking out. I outline "local knowledge traps" that give us unfounded confidence in our authority to assess "what anyone would do, here." I look at prejudice coloring the actions of neighbors who go beyond monitoring and correcting to hostile exclusion, building walls. The democracy of everyday life, with its disposition to regard neighbors as "decent folk," shapes both how we censure and how we ourselves receive and respond to reproach, or should.

In Chapter 4, "Taking Offense, Speaking Out," I observed that we are sometimes reticent. We keep slights or insults, carelessness or intrusiveness to ourselves. We skirt neighbors who give offense and avoid confrontation. We don't appreciate the neighbor who is always agitated, registering complaints; we don't want to be like her. Restraint may not be difficult when the offense is discrete and the consequences bearable, but reticence is difficult when the offense is perceived as broader—nothing less than our neighbors' discomfiting disregard for local knowledge.

We resist randomness as far as possible and make our home where we expect to find agreeable neighbors whose behavior is familiar. In Chapter 2, "Narrative Threads," I pointed to the residential sorting that goes on today; in a vivid analogy "mobility enables the sociological equivalent of assortive mating."[2] Wherever possible people consider not only social and demographic characteristics of neighborhoods but also "life-style" and "communities of interest."[3] In one microscopic example, people reported that they realized that they were living in a community where they didn't belong when they saw neighbors using lawn chemicals.[4]

But few of us can select into a self-regulating environment. No matter the extent to which a particular neighborhood is statistically homogenous, there is no eliminating social, cultural, and aesthetic differences in conduct around home. Apart from religious and secular perfectionist enclaves, few places are closed pockets with a signature set of accepted conventions and sanctions for violating them. Even in segregated areas or gated communities, neighbors detect and call out deviation. In short, few places are homogeneous when looked at from the point of view of the quotidian experience of people next door or down the block. It takes only a few outliers to produce the sense that because of these neighbors the environment around home is disrupted, and to spur some neighbors to assume the role of compliance officers. So speaking out in defense of "what anyone would do, here" and reproaching the family whose behavior deviates from expectations is common. Neighbors mind one another's business and act as enforcers even under conditions often described as anomic. An urban commonplace has it that interactions are negligible: "Guys, guys, guys this is New York City! You don't get close to the neighbors. You nod at them politely in the hall. You call the cops if you haven't seen them in a while and you smell something funny, and that is it."[5] This exaggerates; the desire for compliance prevails there too.

We shouldn't underestimate how closely tied our sense of well-being is to adherence to "local knowledge." A study of immigrant incorporation in the United States reports that whether or not immigrants are good neighbors is Americans' chief concern. Of course, we have opinions about immigration policy based on concerns about jobs, the cost of public services, ideology, or prejudice. In practice, though, acceptance of *these particular* men, women, and children living nearby turns not on documentation but on mundane encounters around home. Adhering to the rudiments of good neighbor in the local idiom turns out to be more important for immigrants' acceptance than earning, paying taxes, or legal status.[6] We are reassured of their desire to do what anyone would do, here; put strongly, their desire that "the holy nation had henceforward to be understood as including them."[7]

## Neighbors as Enforcers

Confidence in our concrete grasp of what, where we live, "anyone would do" helps explain our propensity to moralism, the poor cousin of moral judgment. Pronouncing local orthodoxies can be effective all by itself. We don't always experience ourselves as bowing to pressure to conform, either, but elect to make the effort to fit in. We obey Hobbes's law of complaisance: "That every man strive to accommodate himself to the rest." Clearing our yard may be worth the trouble if neighbors are monitoring, if local standards are clear, if others generally adhere to them, and if the loss of standing for refusal is credible. Assuming, that is, that we want to avoid being the object of a concerted campaign of correction or outright hostility. Doc Hata in Chung-rae Lee's novel explains: "Once I decided to remain in this country . . . the question of my status mostly faded away . . . this must have been beneficial to me over the years, to have so troubling an issue removed from the daily turns of my life." It was removed from the daily turns of life because he had scrupulously reassured neighbors that as an interloper he was able to "immediately recognize and so heed the rules of their houses."[8]

What about neighbors who offer no such assurances? Confident in our grasp of local etiquette, we mind our neighbors' business. We admonish deviations and instruct didactically, directly, bluntly. Few lessons are delivered with thoughtful delicacy. "They didn't look the part, and it was our duty to make them aware of it."[9] The commission to impart and enforce local knowledge amounts to permission, we imagine, to surveil, intrude, instruct, admonish, condemn, broadcast, and interfere in ways that we recognize public officials should not and distant strangers generally do not, but neighbors do, and many are adamant should. The familiar sequence is this: we start off taking our neighbor's measure privately, berating them in our minds and to our family, and we go on to share our assessment of their unacceptability with others nearby. Then we may serve up reproach. Our instruction and correction is not all defensive, either; we aim unselfishly, we think, at our neighbors' improvement and the common good.

The usual preoccupations hardly bear mention. They are conventions. Our confrontations are like "a tribal ceremony, a morality play, a ritual encounter."[10] In Jhumpa Lahiri's story, "The fathers complained that Mr. Dixit did not fertilize his lawn properly, did not rake his leaves on time, and agreed that the Dixit's house, the only one with vinyl siding, detracted from the neighborhood's charm."[11] That neighbor with the derelict cars in the yard is degrading the value of our homes. "For the eleven months leading up to this day. . . . the neighborhood adults had muttered similar sentiments with the same folding of arms and tsk-tsks in their appraisals . . . they didn't appreciate having a squalid unkempt wreck of a home framed in their picture windows."[12] Disapproval can fasten on anything. In Eudora Welty's "A Curtain of Green" a young widow works day and night in her garden but she fails to thin or tie back the flowers and bushes to keep them from "multiplying out of all reason." She is "without any regard for the ideas that her neighbors promote as to what constituted an appropriate vista, or an effect of restfulness, or even harmony of color." The garden is proof of her unneighborliness: "It was impossible to enjoy looking at such a place."[13]

Illustrations from suburbia come readily to mind, but neighbors there have no monopoly on speaking out in defense of "what anyone would do, here." That's clear from the fact that few things arouse us more strenuously than the behavior of other people's children. As a correlate of interaction, children take precedence over income, education, ethnicity, religion, and race.[14] (Pets come in second as a point of contact and conflict.) Audible and visible, children are lubricant and friction. They put adults in one another's company and their activities, illnesses, bedtimes, friends and "enemies," achievements, and troubles fuel conversation, comparison, competition, and criticism among neighbors. Children visit one another's homes, places their parents never set foot in, and may become unwitting spies, grilled for meat for gossip. Most feuds and estrangements among Levittowners, Gans reported, were generated over children.[15] This provocation to judgment is amplified by the fact that child-rearing is a great American ideological divide. We hold closely to favored tenets and pronounce our neighbors' parenting correct or errant, rarely "good enough." People who would never wish a child ill, do so indirectly—their son's problems confirm our predictions. Encounters over children produce the most sanctimonious judgments, our interventions are the least welcome, and the temptation is strong to believe that our corrections are meant to be improving.

Above all, we take the measure of neighbors' children to see whether they have been taught "what anyone would do, here." We assume that their attitudes and behavior reflect their parents' or caretakers' adherence to local knowledge. David Drury's neighbors in "Things We Knew When the House Caught Fire" level this condemnation: "Apparently the Bainer parents . . . attended no church, they gave to none of the local charities, they didn't frequent the local businesses. They seemed fine with letting their children wreak unsupervised havoc in public view."[16] They have not taught their children well.

## Collective Benefits / Deficits

Monitoring and enforcement gather force from the conviction that neighbors' conduct has cumulative beneficial effects. Social science documents the advantages of neighbors on the lookout, keeping track, speaking out. Property left unwatched is a magnet for vandalism in affluent as well as in run-down areas.[17] More generally, neighbor relations produce diffuse but measurable "social capital"—cycles of interaction that generate trust and enable cooperation to produce public goods from which we cannot be excluded. Robert Putnam, a scholar of "social capital," confesses that he never attended a barbecue in his Cambridge neighborhood; still, he points out, "I benefit from those social networks," which have "powerful externalities." He can travel abroad "confident that my home is being protected by all that social capital."[18] Putnam is a free rider. He does not intend to exploit his neighbors; like many of us, he takes the conditions created by their attentiveness to the environment around home for granted.

A vicious cycle of disorder and dispirited withdrawal from encounters is the reverse of accumulating social capital. Petty destruction and the presence of "disreputable or obstreperous or unpredictable people" (panhandlers, drunks, addicts, rowdy teenagers, prostitutes, loiterers, the mentally disturbed) have a cumulative effect too. Disorderliness and incivility cause neighbors to stay home, walk hurriedly, avert their gaze.

They inhibit interactions and dampen neighbors' sense of control over the habitat of home. "Broken windows" policing policy is a response. It calls for officers to attend to minor offenses as well as crime, by informal means as well as by arrest, and by enlisting neighbors to look out for, confront, and report those who violate the "appropriate level of public order." [19] The policy has been criticized as a license for police to harass residents for minor actions, and for acting out racial bias.[20] Where it has been successful, "real crime" rates do not go down but advocates conclude that neighbors are more apt to see themselves as effective guardians of local expectations for "what anyone would do, here." [21]

In related research, sociologists studying inner-city areas speak of "neighborhood effects." The absence of social capital cannot be adequately explained by the attributes of individuals who choose to live in these areas or by general conditions such as poverty or ethnic and racial make-up. A more holistic, "neighborhood-based" explanation has it that persistent perceptions of disorder and neighbors' comparative lack of interaction are self-reinforcing. They impede a sense of collective efficacy defined as "social cohesion combined with shared expectations for social control."[22] Importantly, social scientists' concern about negative "neighborhood effects" does not lead them to call for a return to traditional community loosely defined by solidarity, loyalty, and "thick" personal relations. On the contrary, strong ties are "excessively personalistic and parochial"; they are obstacles to social capital because they isolate neighbors "from larger associations and public resources and role models in 'mains stream culture.'" "Weak ties" based on infrequent interactions are the critical resource:[23] Community organizations where neighbors develop the capacity for collective action are key. This is a close cousin to the long-standing theme in democratic theory that casts neighborhoods as the basis for political participation and reform, but in the literature on "neighborhood effects" the theme is muted. The hoped-for outcome is less civic spirit and political engagement than rudimentary cooperation in countering people who flaunt reasonable expectations for "what anyone would do, here."

## Local Knowledge Traps

Focused on poor urban areas, social scientists explore the conditions that inhibit "shared expectations of social control." They don't attend to the reverse—the moral psychology of neighbors as enforcers speaking out to exert social control. Nor do they focus on how judgments of "what anyone would do, here" are skewed by common errors. The terms of what is expected need interpreting, after all, and confidence in our grasp of local knowledge and our perceptions of deviance is seldom entirely warranted. I call these distortions "local knowledge traps." Here are three.

First, where neighbors are homeowners, there is the propensity to translate immediate complaints into larger ones, arguing that our neighbor's negligence or disregard for the aesthetics of the place is diminishing property values. As in Lahiri's story, we invoke large economic stakes and blame the Dixit's in advance for our hypothetical losses. Property value is fertile ground for misperception and self-deception.

It allows us to represent ourselves as hardheaded rather than intolerant or intrusive—even though invoking property values may be an automatic reflex, divorced from facts. In fact, it may mask prejudice, aggressive insistence on conformity, or just an occasion for aggression.

A second local knowledge trap is not restricted to homeowners: we view our neighbors' behavior through the lens of "decline of community." The "ideology of lament"[24] about the erosion of community "is longstanding and finds vigor in every historical period," one scholar observed.[25] The trap involves magnification and projection—generalizing from our experience of "unsupervised havoc" down the hall and anticipating more and worse.

The "decline of neighbourliness" is "one of the longest established interpretative themes in the social history of early modern England" and early New England townships.[26] Historians of the sixteenth and seventeenth century measure the "rise of the spirit of individualism" and with it the unraveling of webs of cooperative, religiously oriented neighbors. They draw on evidence from parish records and documented disputes over money, status competition (the right to occupy a particular prestigious pew in church), and litigation over defamatory words. Clearly, the baseline of "community" from which we measure decline ranges widely, from the sixteenth century to just a few decades ago, but the consistent indicators are impersonal and transitory social ties said to produce "social disorganization."[27] The jeremiad is repeated by uncomfortable, fearful neighbors everywhere. "American community is undergoing a transformation at its very core," affecting "everything from our propensity to innovate to our capacity to care for one another,"[28] according to one recent book. Social historians of decline represent it as a linear, irreversible process and identify the dynamics of change but from the standpoint of people distressed by neighbors who deviate from comfortable ways of doing things, decline is not a large-scale social process viewed in retrospect, and we don't rely on empirical research to raise the alarm. We just point to incidents of "unsupervised havoc" down the hall.

"Declinism" accompanies just about any social or demographic change where we live. An "invasion" of newcomers, for example, even if the numbers are small, will do. "The trouble with these new people" is a common refrain. The baseline is some point, any point, in time when things were as we expected, after which things changed. The status of having lived here the longest is the democratic substitute for descent (the two may be intertwined: the Mayflower floated our family to America and "our people" settled Wellfleet), and newcomers may be indifferent to or challenge our social standing. Joan Didion observes in *Where I Was From*: "I grew up in a California family that derived, from the single circumstance of having been what Ira Ewing's mother called 'born here for generations,' considerable pride, much of it, it seemed to me later, strikingly unearned."[29] The native/newcomer divide may go back to the Dust Bowl or just a few years to the first wave of arrivals in a new subdivision or retirement community. This errant neighbor is taken as proof of a larger trend, a sign of coming disharmony.

The local knowledge trap at work here is plain: magnification and projection.

> The center was not holding. It was a country of bankruptcy notices and public-auction announcements and commonplace reports of casual killings and misplaced children and abandoned homes and vandals who misspelled even the four-letter words they scrawled. . . . Adolescents drifted from city to torn city, sloughing off both the past and the future as snakes shed their skins, children who were never taught and would never now learn the games that had held society together.[30]

Projections of disintegration underscore felt experience, and contribute to shaping it.

Finally, a third local knowledge trap: our assured perception of "what anyone would do, here" is skewed. This mistake is cognitive: perceptual bias. Certain that the terms of interaction among neighbors are transparent and static, we are incapable of seeing that there are actually different ways of doing things here. America is a culture of subcultures and when neighbors rudely reject our understanding of local knowledge, or are indifferent to it, or live by their own variant, we don't acknowledge that they are establishing and enacting other accepted practices. Again, Thoreau advised that "we have had to agree on a certain set of rules, called etiquette and politeness, to make this frequent meeting tolerable and that we need not come to open war."[31] But plural sets of rules (which are never rules in any case) spur condemnation and strenuous efforts to enforce compliance with our view of "what anyone would do, here." I'm reminded of Roger Williams, America's great advocate of religious toleration and a latitudinarian when it came to modes of civility, who nonetheless abhorred "Quaker innovations in salutations that replaced the practice of kissing hello with an 'uncouth, strange, and Immodest way' of 'feeling and grabling'—i.e., shaking hands."[32] True we don't parade deviants in the town square. But censorious neighbors don't accommodate unfamiliar ways without resistance and reproach.

## Love Thy Neighbor: "A Model of Christian Charity"

We offer these standard justifications for monitoring, instructing, and correcting our neighbors but we are largely unattuned to the deep taproots of the warrant for minding our neighbors' business with a view to enforcement. One taproot is the sacred command to mind one another's business in order to assist one another in sustaining a godly life. The other is secular and progressive: personal and social improvement require us to concern ourselves with one other's "well-doing or well-being." These taproots are the source of the pitched arguments we give for enforcing "what anyone would do, here." They infuse and color the moral psychology of minding our neighbors' business. We don't turn to these foundational texts in the ordinary course of justifying censorious judgments and speaking out against nonconformers. I'm not saying that they operate as authorities. They work in a subterranean fashion, outside our ken. We echo them without knowing we do, but once alerted it is not hard to recognize their force.

The original scripture for America is John Winthrop's "A Model of Christian Charity," composed on the ship Arbella in 1630. He addressed the passengers as a congregation of brothers in Christ, and invoked the command "love thy neighbor as thyself."[33] Biblical texts and the use to which they are put are revealing, and not just to those for whom America is "Godland." "The whole destiny of America is contained in the first Puritan who landed on these shores," Tocqueville advised. Winthrop's exhortation "love thy neighbor" is foundational.

A standard reading of the New Testament injunction to "love thy neighbor" is universalist. In the King James Bible, there are no distinctions, no drawing of lines. "Thou shalt love thy neighbor" recognizes no particularities or dissimilarities, no preference or selection or exception.

There is no need to interrogate who is my neighbor: "You can never confuse him with anyone else, since the neighbor . . . is all people."[34] With this, religious commentators and ethicists disconnect the command from actual physical neighbors and from specific acts of love as well. The New Testament command is open-ended, in contrast to the legalism and concrete specificity of Jewish laws.

We know, however, that "love thy neighbor" is always spoken in context; its compass is specific. The admonishment (for that is what it is) is necessary when people fail to regard one another in the proper spirit. So it is with Winthrop's Puritans. As he explained, the love required of the Puritans owed to their being "in some special service for the church." [35] They were tasked with being "A Model of Christian Charity." Like the Biblical Jews, they had a sacred commission. Consider the original Old Testament text, Leviticus chapter 19, where "love thy neighbor" comes in the middle of an array of prohibitions and imperatives[36] ("thou shall not steal; neither shall ye deal falsely, nor lie one to another"; "thou shall not oppress thy neighbor, nor rob him.") Each command in Leviticus is followed by an explanation of the extraordinary surplus meaning for the Jews: for "I am the Lord your God, who brought you out of the land of Egypt." My point is this: in the Hebrew Bible and for the Puritans, the acts commanded by "love thy neighbor" are performed in relationship to God. "Ye shall be holy; for I the Lord your God am holy." "To be out of charity placed the individual concerned and by extension the whole community in spiritual jeopardy."[37]

Winthrop's message addresses bearers of a sacred commission who are entering "a community of perils." The exigent conditions of the New World demanded that they "strengthen, defend, preserve, and comfort one another."[38] The ferocity of "Model of Christian Charity" owed to the fact that nothing guarantees the "shining city." This was not a promised land, only a radical possibility, which explains the Puritans' anguish, fear, and guilt.[39] Winthrop was clear: righteousness depends on "strict performance." The city rests on a foundation of stricture, criticism, and self-criticism. It demands transparency and public accountability. Neighbors must be inquisitorial, and errors must be exposed. "Terrified at their own weaknesses and suspicious of their neighbors' lapses" they had to muster fortitude in monitoring, judging, reproaching, and sanctioning one another. Naturally, transgressions understood as offenses against God heighten the fervor and the stakes of minding our neighbors' business, and the Puritans excelled at spiritual aggression.[40] Minding their neighbors' business could be persecutory. In short, their commission linked love and punitive enforcement. Better put, correction *is* an act of love: "And now, neighbor, take this my admonition in love."[41]

Centuries later, Winthrop's "shining city on a hill" has become a national charm. Invoked by presidents, it casts the nation as exceptional, an "anointed land" blessed by God.[42] When it is not unadulterated self-flattery or hubris linked to power, "shining city" is a sort of rhetorical encouragement to live up to American aspirations variously understood, only today it is uttered in a spirit of confidence, unhaunted by the Puritans' ferocious self-doubt. When it comes to actual neighbors, the moral psychology of severe mutual instruction and correction found in "Model of Christian Charity" has life today in elective communities whose members see their domain as exemplary, a New Jerusalem. Americans ceaselessly erect religious and secular utopias (a book on twentieth-century communities is titled "Cities on a Hill"[43]). For most of us proximity is accidental, but these neighbors elect to join a bounded community of the whole. The whole life, the whole person, is committed in what amounts to a rejection of pluralism. Surveillance and discipline are endemic to perfectionist communities; only exit ends the monitoring and punitive love.

Winthrop's "model" with its currents of stricture and censure has general resonance for us beyond utopian experiments. It is the taproot of the local knowledge trap that sees deviation as a "decline of neighborliness" and sees decline as a prophecy of social and moral disintegration. We all know neighbors who have a pious attitude toward local knowledge, who speak out to unmask deviation, and who warn of the dangers if errant neighbors are allowed to carry on unreproached and unsanctioned. We know the censorious type; we may have had the urge to sermonize and expose ourselves. We recognize the self-righteousness and the urgency. Concern for lapses is directed at neighbors who seem not to recognize that we live in what has become a "community of perils."

Outside of New Jerusalem, however, neighbors should not be objects of love, meaning improving zeal. Good neighbor needs rescuing from moralism and reforming energy, from sacred roots and special commissions. It needs protection against the local knowledge trap of magnification and projection. That is the work of the democracy of everyday life, which acknowledges neighbors as "decent folk," good enough for the purposes of mundane give and take. We take neighbors pretty much as they come and don't think of our encounters as steps towards righteousness. Nor, except for natural and political disasters, do we think of neighbors as protection against the wilderness. If neighbors are delinquent we limit our encounters, withdraw, or respond in ways I come to shortly. The temper of reproach matters, and speaking out in defense of "what anyone would do, here" is constrained by a democratic ethos, as I will show. But first consider a second warrant for neighbors as monitors, instructors, and enforcers.

## "It is a right, and it may be our duty, to caution others against him . . ."

No single secular taproot of minding our neighbors' business has the authority of Winthrop's "city on a hill." My candidate for canonical text is J. S. Mill's *On Liberty*, which applies to the terrain of neighbor relations as well as society generally, and resonates strongly today. For in clear terms Mill locates the tension between personal liberty and minding our own business on the one hand, and censoriously minding our neighbors' business on the other. Readers typically focus on Mill's arguments for *limiting* interference with others' behavior, overlooking his brief for censure and intervention. This is understandable. *On Liberty* is a foundational treatise on the value of individual liberty and the dangers posed not only by coercive laws but also by "the tyranny of the prevailing opinion and feeling." The scope of liberty Mill commends is expansive: the inward domain of consciousness; absolute freedom of opinion on all subjects; liberty of expressing and publishing opinions; and, closest to my theme, "experiments in living" — "'framing the plan of our life to suit our own character."[44]

At the same time, Mill is a philosopher of personal development and historical progress. Here is where the essay takes a turn. Mill famously defends paternalism for "barbarians" if it aims at civilizing improvement. Less famously, he insists that personal liberty unfettered by law and illiberal social control does not translate into a prescription to mind our own business. "There is a need of a great increase of disinterested exertion to promote the good of others," he enjoins, and condemns "selfish indifference, which pretends that human beings have no business with each other's conduct in life and that they should not concern themselves about the well-doing or well-being of one another."[45] I'll highlight key passages: Men and women rightly incur loss of consideration by a "defect of prudence or of personal dignity." Folly, lowness and depravation of taste, rashness, obstinacy, self-conceit, engaging in hurtful indulgences, intemperance, extravagance, being a nuisance, and much more warrant making someone an object of distaste or contempt. We are right to judge him a fool, or "a being of an inferior order." "We have a right . . . in various ways, to act upon our unfavourable opinion of any one," and Mill goes on to canvass a surprising range of measures. Some are tutelary and congruent

with the liberal tenor of *On Liberty*: "remonstrating with him or reasoning with him, or persuading him, or entreating him." That's not all, though.
We have "a right, and it may be our duty, to caution others against him, if
we think his example or conversation likely to have a pernicious effect."
We may give others preference over him in "optional good offices." We
are not bound to seek his society; we can "leave him to himself" on the
understanding that this is not indifference but a signal of reproach. Plainly,
nothing deters strong expressions of indignation or, to borrow the Puritan phrase, "constant admonishing of them [in their] unclean walking."[46]

We give ourselves these justifications today when we monitor and instruct neighbors in "what anyone would do, here." We tell ourselves that
we are minding their business disinterestedly, for their own good and for
social improvement, though we are liable to lack Mill's countervailing
preoccupation with personal liberty and our own fallibility. *On Liberty*
prescribes minding others' business and at the same time acknowledges
the trap of failing to entertain doubt about the rightness and reliability of
our perception of "what anyone would do, here."

Both "Model of Christian Charity" and Mill's progressive improvement predict that our efforts will typically be self-righteous. We don't con-
cede that "our manners are corrupted by communication with the saints,"
though we should.[47] We bolster our actions with moralistic intentions:
attending to our neighbors' "well-doing and well-being" is a demonstration of "civic friendship." Both warrants are potential instruments of aggression. At the extreme, neighbors as enforcers are vulnerable to the
charge of fanaticism, if we define a fanatic as "a great altruist":

> He wants to save your soul, he wants to redeem you, he wants to liber-
> ate you from sin, from error, from smoking, from your faith or from
> your faithlessness. . . . He is always either falling on your neck because
> he truly loves you or else he is at your throat in case you prove to be
> unredeemable.[48]

Looked at more closely, however, both justifications for minding our
neighbors' business and speaking out in defense of "what anyone would
do, here" come with cautions and constraints.

## The Temper of Reproach

The cautions have to do with inner disposition—the frame of mind and
sensibility we should bring to monitoring and correcting neighbors. True,
"Model of Christian Charity" and "On Liberty" are imperfect windows

onto the disposition of good neighbors as shaped by the democracy of everyday life, and I'll draw contrasts in a moment. But the temper of reproach in these taproots of minding our neighbors' business sets the stage.

When despite his preoccupation with personal liberty and the adverse effects of social conformity, Mill insists "there is a need of a great increase of disinterested exertion to promote the good of others," it's evident that he sees silence as an impediment to improvement. It's clear, too, that both external treatment and disposition separate permissible from impermissible ways of minding one another's business. Mill allows more than reasoning and persuading, and recognizes that disagreeable consequences naturally flow from judging, correcting, shaming. At the same time he attempts to set parameters. Put simply, he argues that we should not imagine that we have a right to control others. "We have a right . . . in various ways, to act upon our unfavourable opinion of any one," but not to control, coerce, or compel them. We should not think that we are justified in prohibiting another from "framing the plan of life to suit her own character." This line between correction and control, disapproval and punishment is famously ambiguous. Coercion is not defined solely by threats and violence, though. It includes compelling change by eliminating possibilities so that our neighbors cannot conduct their lives around home as they see fit. It includes paternalism—altering their conduct in ways of which they may be unaware and do not understand.[49] The limits Mill sets can be said to turn on the temper of reproach. Our frame of mind is not aggressive and we are not hateful. We "shall not treat him like an enemy of society." We give miscreants consideration we would not give an enemy, and confront and correct in a manner and temper that cannot be confused with coercion and control.

We find the same attention to disposition in the biblical "love thy neighbor." Immediately preceding the Leviticus command is another: "You shall not hate your brother in your heart; you shall surely reproach your neighbor, and you shall bear no sin because of him."[50] Confronting and correcting are required ("you shall surely reproach"). But what is this imperative not to hate our neighbor "in our hearts"? By concealing our anger we are deceitful or despairing of correction, and we are exhorted to externalize the feelings neighbors arouse. (On this reading, the passage goes: "You shall not hate your brother in your heart, *but instead* you shall surely reproach your neighbor, and you shall *thus* bear no sin because of him.")[51] That said, reproach is fenced in by constraints. We reproach insistently but not in a way that is threatening or so overzealous as to make settling with her impossible. We "deal frankly and lovingly."[52] Disposition matters. We begin to get a sense of how demanding the biblical exhortation is. It requires us to call up certain emotions and forbids others. Thou *shall not hate* thy neighbor (at all, not just in our hearts). Thou *shall love* thy neighbor. Love is not spontaneous but a rigorous duty. Reproach in the right spirit is a renunciation of actual feeling. And the same demanding requirement applies to us as targets of reproach; "And now, neighbor, take this my admonition in love."

Sigmund Freud observed that if we were hearing the command "love thy neighbor" for the first time we would be utterly bewildered. To will love is inconceivable. Freud called it the "grandiose commandment" and rejected it as psychologically impossible on the terms of his theory, which gave central place to a fundamental inclination to aggression. Freud also renounced the ethic of "love thy neighbor." We always have a particular neighbor in view, after all, and there must be something in relation to him to make this neighbor deserve my love. Yet, again, my neighbor "seems not to have the least trace of love for me and shows me not the slightest consideration . . . if he can satisfy any sort of desire by it, he thinks nothing of jeering at me, insulting me, slandering me, and showing his superior power."[53] Freud rejected the command on all counts. But even those who are not dismissive acknowledge the enormity of "love thy neighbor." Kierkegaard wrote, "Let us not . . . forget its originality—that it did not arise in any human being's heart."[54]

## The Democracy of Everyday Life
## and the Temper of Reproach

Cautions about the temper of reproach are built into both warrants for monitoring and correction, for minding our neighbors' business. The democracy of everyday life is our counterpart. It too commends a certain temper and frame of mind when we reproach neighbors for deviating from "what anyone would do, here." The disposition is less demanding than either "love thy neighbor" or Mill's unselfish concern for others' "well-being and well-doing." Neither righteousness nor "a great increase of disinterested exertion to promote the good of others" is required of us. Instead, the temper of reproach is modulated by the disposition to bring to our encounters the modest practical assessment that these neighbors are "decent folk," trustworthy (or not) for the purposes of mundane give and take. Our judgment does not rest on our neighbor's exhibition of virtue or faith or civic spirit. We don't seek knowledge of our neighbor's true inner self or character overall. "Decent folk" is unromantic, and wholly profane. It requires a certain frame of mind to see neighbors in this morally significant but limited light, which cabins hate and love and has no place for the company of saints.

This democratic disposition shapes and constrains neighbors as enforcers. We often attend to things that loosely correspond to Mill's list: folly, lowness and depravation of taste, rashness, obstinacy, self-conceit, engaging in hurtful indulgences, intemperance, extravagance, being a nuisance. We are not required to be silent or hide our indignation, not at all, but in speaking out we do not threaten, wrong, or coerce. We do not react to ordinary offenses as dominating enforcers. The importance of this disposition emerges clearly when our disapproval is roused by what we perceive to be deviation from "what anyone would do, here." The Dixit's "squalid unkempt wreck of a home framed in their picture windows" may arouse disapproval and move us to censure and correct. But openings to ordinary reciprocity are not cut off. Neighbors who deviate in familiar ways from local knowledge are nonetheless "decent folk," or so the democracy of everyday life commends.

Just as targets of Puritan reproach were enjoined to receive it in the spirit of love, a certain frame of mind holds for us as targets of our neighbors' disapproval as well. We may be helpless to avoid our neighbors' interventions and harangues. We may have to resign ourselves to hearing them out repeatedly for the sake of a modicum of peace. If we aren't being coerced or controlled, we may have the good sense to draw on reserves of patience. We can retain a sense of proportion and our pride.[55] Neighbors can usually tolerate disagreement about "what anyone would do, here" as long as we don't experience reproach as demeaning. As long as we are not being singled out prejudicially on account of race, religion, ethnicity, or sexual orientation. As long as reproach at the hands of neighbors enforcing "what anyone would do, here" is not performed in a temper that effaces our status as neighbors and "decent folk."

## Prejudice

We fall off from the democracy of everyday life when we direct criticism and zealous correction not at an individual—at Mr. Dixit or our local equivalent of Winthrop's transgressor or Mill's fool—but at neighbors as members of a group that to our mind does not belong here. We fail, manifestly, when speaking out to enforce "what anyone would do, here" is laced with prejudice. Then, we don't see our neighbors for themselves but as representative. The basic pattern is this: we view these neighbors categorically. We ascribe offending behavior to them by virtue of ascriptive characteristics. In some cases we see their deviation from "what anyone would do, here" as a manifestation of inherent traits. *These people* just are disorderly, uncivil, and let their children wreak unsupervised havoc in the hall. Their differences appear to us to be normatively significant, turning stereotyping into stigmatization. Studies of the psychological mechanisms of prejudice advise us to distinguish unconscious bias from conscious derogatory attributions and from ideological racism,[56] but every type of prejudice is capable of taking over perceptions and dominating our responses.

So our repertoire of reproach and enforcement is likely to alter when we see neighbors' rejection of local etiquette as an ascriptive, perhaps inherent, failing. We give ourselves license to drive home lessons in local knowledge in ways that involve humiliation. Our correction is demeaning, and we know it. (*You people* ...) A recent study suggests that today political polarization is such that a deeply conservative neighbor in a progressive community "was not someone to be argued against ... he needed to be isolated, sealed off, and expelled."[57] As a description of partisanship among neighbors this is surely hyperbole. The dynamic of sealing off is real enough, though, and especially disturbing when group relations involve a history of entrenched advantage and disadvantage, domination and subordination as they do, enduringly, between whites and African Americans.

We don't need to rehearse the lessons of philosophy and psychology to remind ourselves of the unjust distribution of opportunities and other harms stigmatization entails. Nor do we have to remind ourselves that attributing attitudes and conduct to people by virtue of the group to which they belong goes on in every domain of social life. Stereotyping and discrimination by race, gender, sexual orientation, and more is present in workplaces. It is the raison d'etre of many exclusionary voluntary associations. It operates in politics: "It impedes the formation of intergroup political coalitions, facilitates divisive political appeals, and enables officeholders to make decisions that disadvantage segregated communities without being accountable to them."[58] Antidiscrimination and antiharassment law check prejudicial treatment in official arenas, "public accommodations," employment, and much of civil society; social interactions in most settings are regulated by mechanisms for reporting unfair and demeaning treatment and processes for holding perpetrators as well as those responsible for enforcing regulations accountable.

What about neighbors? Because prejudice is not idiosyncratic but grows out of a history of inequality, it always has a political face. The instability of the personal and political in the context of neighbor relations is undeniable, and part of its interest. Still, without pressing the distinction too far, prejudice among neighbors has its own qualities. Among neighbors, interactions are unstructured, with few institutional checks. No one is charged with monitoring and reporting hostile or demeaning encounters at home, and absent violence or repeated harassment appeals to authorities are futile. It is less amenable to any kind of organized pushback. We will miss the significance of this facet of the moral psychology of neighbors if we collapse prejudice there into public acts of discrimination. It is at once more personal, close, and inescapable than in other spheres of life, penetrating the zone of comparative privacy and fouling the quality of life at home.

One or a few hostile neighbors can create a toxic atmosphere that spills over from particular encounters to effect others living nearby, creating conditions that enable or even invite passive acquiescence. Some of us are uncomfortable with our neighbors' aggressive way of confronting and correcting deviation but we prefer to fade into the background, neither condoning nor objecting. Or, we understand—we feel—the particular evil of stigmatization and don't want to live in this environment day-to-day, but we acquiesce for fear of being charged with betrayal by neighbors "like us" if we insist on regarding the people next door as "decent folk."

Something else about prejudice among neighbors is worth noting. With exceptions, we have no grievance against the neighbor who spurns encounters. It is not always easy to separate detachment from hostility, and it is not hard to assign reasons for avoidance that are unrelated to race or other identity markers. Our aloof neighbor could disavow that her behavior springs from prejudice. So, in addition to the direct harms prejudice inflicts, it can cause maddening doubt and self-doubt. Particularly when the form prejudice takes is not overt, aggressive reproach but building walls.

## Building Walls

Social scientists puzzle over the microfoundations of prejudice, particularly when it comes to residential segregation. Does prejudice cause segregation? Or is the process reversed, and segregation is motivated by comfort with our own affinity group and way of doing things? (The term is "homophily," "or the tendency of people to interact, associate, and live near others like themselves.") [59] From this perspective, we believe that particular neighbors "genuinely encapsulate [our] interests"[60] and share our local values, and we hold the corresponding belief that neighbors who deviate from "what anyone would do, here"—Muslims, or gay families, for example, do not. "Discrimination in contact" describes the choice of people with whom we associate and those with whom we refuse to deal.[61] Where physical segregation is impossible and neighbors live intermixed in buildings and on blocks, we may build virtual walls.

These take the form of avoidance. Not the sort of avoidance that is a sound technique for escaping conflict or preserving privacy but rather avoidance that is communicative and delivers a signal that these neighbors do not belong. We assume a menacing or blank demeanor. We pretend neighbors are invisible, beneath notice. The "contact hypothesis," which proposes that the experience of integration has beneficial long-term effects on behavior and attitudes, is aborted. There is no learning. No accommodation. No appreciation of shared reality. No imagination or empathy. No willing opportunities to "practice interaction on terms of equality" *qua* neighbors, as "decent folk."[62] Recall Frost's poem:

> Before I built a wall I'd ask to know
> What I was walling in or walling out,
> And to whom I was like to give offence.

Neighbors on either side of the virtual wall understand to whom offense is given and the social meaning of walling in and walling out.

Of course, good neighbor in the terms set by the democracy of everyday life has none of this. To review: Although give and take is seldom inclusive and proximity is no assurance of interaction—so that only some neighbors figure on our map of the lay of the land—reciprocity is not exclusive, either. We regard our neighbors personally and individually, not as representatives or symbols. When we monitor and correct, as we may, we view our neighbors out of uniform, wearing only the light moral garb of "decent folk." We don't tailor our interactions to perceived status or class, race or religion. Drawing fine-grained distinctions, scrupulously addressing and interacting with neighbors on terms set by the nuances of social standing or racial or religious markers is inconsistent with the democratic ethos of "decent folk." We act in a way that neighbors could recognize as consistent.

When we do, though, there is no assurance that we won't run head on into a wall. That's the rub. We expect our disposition to regard neighbors as "decent folk" to be reciprocated, or at least to be received as benign. An ounce of sensitivity should warn us not to be complacent. Treating people "identically and with easy familiarity" is not always taken in the spirit intended. Our neighbors may have definite notions of the form of address and level of interaction acceptable according to their particular notion of local etiquette. Interaction on their terms is a matter of pride, and anything else is presumptuous. Neighbors mistake our regard for nothing except the rudiments of "decent folk" as an offense.

An example is the "code of the streets" that operates among poor, young, urban African American men. As Elijah Anderson explains it, demeanor and conduct are geared to identifying and preserving a particular position in a precarious social hierarchy of deference and respect. Every nuance of dress and comportment, from sneakers to swagger, is choreographed to signal and aggressively defend one's status.[63] This subculture sets the terms of interaction within the group, and it sets the group apart. The aptly named "code" is no guide for encounters with people living nearby generally. It is impenetrable. Unfamiliarity with how to tailor interactions marks us as effective strangers.

All this is to say that the frame of mind to treat people with rough equality as "decent folk" may require self-discipline. We have to ward off resentment at having been rebuffed and misunderstood. We may become hesitant, uncertain whether further encounters will lead to more rebuff. So we must be slow to take offense. We must cultivate the disposition to make allowances and resist the impulse to magnify slights.[64] We also have to face up to the limits of our understanding. We try to see this other way of doing things here as adaptive, perhaps a response to historic conditions of prejudice and exclusion. In any case it is not aimed at us personally. Adhering to the democratic ethos requires resilience, willingness to try to understand these encounters, competence to do so, and an iota of confidence that walls are penetrable, if not with this neighbor then with another. We hope that encounters repeated over time produce the minimal reciprocity—a nod of recognition; "How are you today?" I return to this surprisingly complex dynamic—the third element of the democracy of everyday life along with reciprocity among "decent folk" and speaking out—in the next chapter, "Live and Let Live."

## "Eli the Fanatic": Neighbors in History and Anti-History

Stereotyping fastens on neighbors' social identity or ascriptive characteristics, provokes aggressive correction and enforcement of "what anyone would do, here," and builds walls. This is not restricted to neighbors who view one another across the divide of race or some other entrenched social categorization. Something similar goes on among neighbors identified with (and identified as) members of the same ethnic or religious group. For people striving to be accepted, desperate to secure a foothold in some just-achieved spot on the lay of the land, a mindset of eager compliance with local etiquette is common enough. Social insecurity motivates not only exertions to fit in but also embarrassed disassociation from neighbors who are unassimilated, stuck in the old ways. The yearning to move up and to belong converts "what anyone would do, here" into an instrument of aggressive normalcy. There is a particular meanness to this fierce adherence to "what anyone would do, here" aimed against familiars; it is a sort of betrayal.

Philip Roth tells this story in "Eli, the Fanatic," a beautiful, sorrowful conclusion to my theme of neighbors as enforcers. A small group of orthodox Jewish immigrants, including eighteen children displaced by the Holocaust and one Hasidic survivor of a death camp, have bought a house in suburban Woodenton, New York. They are using the home as a yeshiva—a violation of the town's zoning regulations. The self-styled "modern community" of Jews in Woodenton is embarrassed by the appearance of a Hasidic Jew on Coach House Road:

> The gentleman in the black hat, suit, etc. . . . This is after all the twentieth century, and we do not think it too much to ask that the members of our community dress in a manner appropriate to the time and place.

Neighbors commission Eli Peck to advise the refugees that either the Hasid gets a new suit, sheds his black hat, and appears on the street as a modern American or they will enforce the zoning ordinance and have them evicted.

Their motivation is plain: their standing in this progressive Protestant suburb feels provisional ("It is only since the war that Jews have been able to buy property here.") Any misstep, they fear, and they will fall from the good graces of their gentile neighbors. As a neighbor on Eli's block puts it: "If I want to live in Brownsville, Eli, I'll live in Brownsville" (a poor Jewish immigrant area of Brooklyn). He means that the "modern Jews" are Americans, and here come newcomers transporting the old world to this suburb, inviting the old insults and injuries. These European remnants "have all these superstitions . . . because they can't face the world, because they can't take their place in society." (Roth wrote of his father and those like him: they were "the best citizens. Europe stopped with him.")[65] So the neighbors put up stiff resistance: "I refuse to sit by and watch it happening on my own front lawn."

Eli agrees to serve as emissary to the newcomers, the survivors. He agrees to make it his business to reproach the yeshiva's owner, Tzuref, and demand compliance. He adopts his neighbors' moral logic: the Orthodox have called this trouble down on themselves. "If a man chose to be stubborn then he couldn't expect to survive." (The terrible implicit message: if European Jews had abandoned their "extreme practices," they might have been safe from persecution.) Eli writes an official letter to Tzuref: the Jews and Gentiles of Woodenton "alike have had to give up some of their extreme practices in order not to threaten or offend the other." "This is the 20th century," Eli tells him.

Tzuref's response to Eli's threat of eviction is: "Stop with the law! You have the word suffer." Death was palpable in that house on the hill with its "dark tomb of a corridor." The Hasid with the offending suit stands "in a deep hollow of blackness." When Eli introduces himself, casually mentioning his fatigue after a long day at work, the old survivor asks, "it's the commuting that's killing?" When the children run from him in fear and he says to Tzuref: "I didn't do anything," Tzuref shrugs and "the little movement seemed to Eli strong as an accusation." The moment comes when Eli absorbs the fact that the black-suited Holocaust survivor has lost everything. "The suit the gentleman wears is all he's got," Tzuref explains to Eli. Meaning not that it is his only suit but that he has nothing else. "A mother and a father? . . . No. A wife? No. A baby? A little ten-month-old baby? No! A village full of friends? A synagogue where you knew the feel of every seat under your pants? That leaves nothing, Mr. Peck. Absolutely nothing!" "I misunderstood," Eli says.

What is it he now understands? He hears the Hasid's moan, "it could raise hair, stop hearts, water eyes," and he understands the moral obtuseness of his Woodenton neighbors' repeated mantra "this is the 20th century." It is a stamp of American presentism: the imperious here and now, the single-minded pursuit of domestic happiness.[66] It is not just the Hasid's "crazy hat" that eats at them but the way the survivors are "making a big thing out of suffering," when everyone knows there "will be no pogroms in Woodenton." Eli's "modern" neighbors do not see themselves as agents in this tragedy of the twentieth century. They wall it out along with their refugee neighbors.

Who is the fanatic in the title of Roth's story? The background is the Nazi Holocaust—genocidal fanaticism. In the eyes of Woodenton Jews, who do not want to make a big thing out of suffering, the Orthodox are the extremists—unwilling to fit in and complying, as they eventually do, only out of sheer exhaustion and nowhere else to go. ("We stay," Tzuref tells Eli. "We are tired.") These "modern Jews" are the fanatics if we allow for fanatical moderation, extreme normalcy, compulsive adherence to "what anyone would do, here." The Woodenton Jews fall on Tzuref's throat to wrench that bit of compliance, their normalcy, out of him. Only the Orthodox are exonerated of the charge of fanaticism. They do not ask anyone to change. They do not want to improve their neighbors, mend them, engineer them, or straighten them up rather than let them be. They live and let live. That is the third element of the democracy of everyday life.

# 6

# Live and Let Live

Mundane offenses and ordinary vices were my subject in Chapter 4, "Taking Offense, Speaking Out." Offenses are sometimes more than mere nuisances; they can make existence miserable, and indignant neighbors are impelled to rally against cruel and arbitrary derangement of quotidian life. I looked at speaking out in another tenor, neighbors taking on the role of enforcers, in Chapter 5, "What Anyone Would Do, Here," and I probed the warrants, benefits, traps, and moral dangers of minding our neighbors' business with a view to compliance. There, the temper of reproach was central—whether neighbors exhibit the disposition entailed by the democracy of everyday life. Now I take on grimmer distortions of relations around home: mayhem, intimidation, and violence that generate mistrust and escalate the risks of misplaced trust. The terrain is treacherous, and neighbors' behavior can have life-altering consequences. The third element of the democracy of everyday life—which I call live and let live—comes into play here.

Colloquially, live and let live implies minding one's own business, often with a shrug of indifference. As an element of good neighbor, however, it is far from washing our hands of the people next door. Like reciprocity and speaking out, it is deliberate, constructive, attentive, and signals recognition of neighbors as "decent folk." We live and let live when we pull back from acting on knowledge that, if broadcast, would disrupt our neighbors' lives, perhaps radically. In declining to advertise their affairs, we protect as we can their control over the environment of home. Reticence is rooted in appreciation of the value, the essential human necessity, and the fragility of privacy. Privacy is disturbed by neighbors knowing what we do not intend for them to know; it is deranged by neighbors telling what they know. Our identity as good neighbor gives disclosing, publicizing, and reporting something of the feel of betrayal. We also live and let live when we signal to neighbors by word or gesture that we recognize our mutual vulnerability in an environment of mistrust; that we intend no harm; that we acknowledge them, just as they are, as "decent folk."

Both facets of live and let live—reticence and signaling acknowledgement of neighbors as "decent folk"—serve the value implicit in the commonsense understanding of live and let live: acting in a way that does not diminish our neighbors' control over life at home. We are not heedless or insulated from our neighbors' situation and the sources of their misery, and we are aware of what we do to exacerbate it and could do to relieve it. Leaving one another alone is an inadequate summary of live and let live. For a colloquialism, the imperative is surprisingly complex.

## Mistrust-Creating Situations

Although every dimension of neighbors' give and take requires a minimum of trust (and creates it in turn), the risks of misplaced trust are normally limited. That's not the case under disorderly and unsafe conditions. We can name the conditions of chronic mistrust—vandalism and arson, intimidation, verbal harassment, theft and muggings, random mayhem, and organized violence. Government irresponsibility, discrimination, lack of resources, or lack of political will are often implicated. At its worst, "in reality, many inner-city Americans live without enforceable rights because, having been effectively abandoned by their government, they are virtually stateless."[1] A neighborhood run amok is not a state of nature, but it is uncertain enough. Neighbors suffer "the inescapable knowledge that the environment [they] must endure . . . is uncontrolled and uncontrollable, and that anyone can invade it to do whatever damage and mischief the mind suggests."[2]

Physical destruction is concrete evidence impossible to ignore that the environment around home is uncontrolled. Philip Roth describes the literal dismantling of Newark, where he grew up:

> All over Newark, the oldest buildings were missing ornamental stone cornices—cornices from as high up as four stories plucked off in broad daylight with a cherrypicker . . . The big Negro churches (Bethany Baptist) closed down, boarded up, looted, bulldozed . . . Gutters, leaders, drainpipes—stolen . . . Everything stolen by gangs in cars, stolen by the men who roam the city with shopping carts, stolen by thieves

working alone . . . They'd dug up the cobblestones . . . and carted them away.[3]

Damage creates desolation.

Random mayhem may be the most stressful obstacle to ordinary encounters among neighbors. It is helter-skelter to the many gentle people living among others who "are not on the field of play," who are "out of bounds." Perhaps there are safe havens—a local church or school—but life on the street, at the bus stop, in the apartment hallway, the front yard, the living room whose windows face the street is perilous. People are hostages in their homes. When they go out they hurry to their destinations. When lines of conflict are drawn by organized gangs or members of mutually hostile ethnic or racial groups, mental maps of the lay of the land chart a divided society with neighbors (that is, some, never all neighbors) like rival nations. Residents know that most people living nearby are not dangerous, but local knowledge does not allay simmering anxiety or enable trustworthy neighbors to carry on ordinary business with one another undisturbed.

Certain individuals may be favored by the agents of fear and receive special consideration, like Ida Mae Gladney, 83, living in a second-floor apartment in Chicago:

> A man is selling drugs out of a trash can. She can see, plain as day, where he puts them and how he gets them out of the trash can for the white customers in their SUVs with suburban license plates. Another hides his stash in his mouth. And when customers come up, he pulls a piece of inventory from his tongue.

These drug-dealing neighbors call Ida Mae "Grandma," Isabel Wilkerson writes: "They warn her when not to come out 'because we don't know what time we gon' start shootin.'"[4] This particle of protectiveness reflects the arrogance of power to wreak havoc. The anecdote is maddening proof of willingness to act recklessly, knowing that violence spills over onto vulnerable neighbors. Chaos is created deliberately even if not every outcome is intended, like the "accidental" shooting of children caught in the cross fire. Quite literally, brutal neighbors do not live and let live.

Mistrust suppresses regular interactions. It dampens reciprocity. It induces "universal irritability, servility, perpetual defensiveness, backbiting, nervousness, and an ever smoldering compensatory contentiousness."[5] A common outcome is social isolation. The added damage mistrust inflicts is knowing that the agents of destruction are living among us, willing to harm us and to ravage the quality of their own lives at home. How do neighbors experience this and respond? Live and let live is one of several patterns of response, and I give them all their due. The character of live and let live as an element of the democracy of everyday life emerges in contrast.

## Neighbors Policing and Neighbors Frozen in Place

In an environment of chronic mistrust ordinary encounters are fraught, and at the same time neighbors are more than usually dependent on one another for watchfulness, warnings, and solicitousness of one another's well-being. Reliance is a staple of any account of good neighbor. But it is not a dependable feature of daily life among neighbors inhibited from monitoring common spaces, reporting damage, confronting delinquents, intervening on behalf of one another, providing an element of mutual support, and enlisting authorities to ensure safety and keep the peace. Some people do manage to carry on under exigent circumstances, but other patterns of response are common. Consider two poles: self-deputization on the one hand and numbness on the other. Live and let live stands in contrast to both.

When Rosa Parks was mugged in Detroit, "her neighbors found the culprits and subjected them to harsh punishment."[6] Under peaceful conditions we count on a division of labor between authorities and the rest of us. Only under extraordinary national circumstances (like the block patrols that looked out for air attacks during World War II) do we represent self-deputization as a duty, and then our identity as "citizen" eclipses "neighbor." That said, where mistrust prevails, some residents voluntarily join a neighborhood watch or are enlisted by local officials to assist in ordering the environment. At best, this is participatory democratic action, with an organizational apparatus, committed leadership, and resources. But mobilization may be the provocative pose of enforcers marking their lay of the land and defending it against deviation, exhibiting the local knowledge trap of distorted perceptions of social disintegration and danger. It may consist of menacing behavior that exacerbates fear and mistrust. The slide from vigilance into vigilantism should make us wary of these protectors. Groups patrolling and punishing to effect local justice are a perverse version of the touted "capacity for collective action."

At the other pole of response to arrant disorder is retreat. Life at home is directed at staying out of sightlines and out of trouble. Neighbors risk retaliation if they speak out and challenge delinquents directly, much less if they "snitch" and cooperate with authorities. The offenders are not bullying owners of a noisy air conditioner, after all.

Mistrust-creating situations produce lack of confidence in one's own agency, and docility. Fear inhibits what we can call practical reasoning. It eliminates as felt possibilities the responses that under other conditions are considered standard defenses of the quality of life at home. [7] Habits of observing, rallying, and speaking out seem to belong to another place. There is no reasoning forward. Neighbors are numbed, frozen in place. Psychological reality tracks conditions around home: an erratic, closed in, closed down terrain. But this psychological structure of immobilization is not perfectly rigid and can be altered and opened out, perhaps by a neighbor's persistent solicitousness and repeated assurances. As with so much democratic conduct—from voting to the informal business of the democracy of everyday life—"somebody asked" matters. That invitation, I will show, is proffered by live and let live as a signal of trust.

## Minding Our Own Business Owing to Injustice

First, though, another pattern of response to mistrust-creating situations arises where authorities themselves are the cause. People naturally have little confidence in public provisions of security where disorder reigns, but a deeper mistrust of authorities is sometimes at work as well, and neighbors mind their own business and keep what they know to themselves for reasons rooted in their sense of injustice. Local government's failure to provide protection, fairly, does not mean that coercive authority is absent from the streets around home; police surveillance, stops, questioning, and arrests are daily events. "Acquaintance with the state as a disciplinary force comes early,"[8] directed at young black men especially "with crushing force." "The police in the United States are excessively armed: they have too much testosterone. They do not like to be questioned, criticized or challenged. They definitely do not like to be filmed. And when it's black people who are doing any of those constitutionally protected activities, forget about it. The police will show those folks who the real boss is."[9]

Beyond policing, African Americans especially see a legal system disfigured by "racial profiling, stiff penalties for minor parole violations, felon disenfranchisement laws, and general harassment of young urban blacks."[10] Being "virtually stateless" and vulnerable to errant neighbors is intolerable, but so is cooperating with what is experienced as official discrimination. If events support the belief that conditions "exceed the limits of tolerable injustice,"[11] neighbors may not actively protect the drug-dealer next door but they may be loath to deliver him up to a cycle of arrest, imprisonment, unemployment, and reincarceration. Added to mistrust of police and the institutions of criminal justice is the belief among residents of the "dark ghetto" that they live within a larger political system that works to "contain, exploit, and under-develop the black urban poor, to deny them equal civic standing and punish them when they refuse to accommodate themselves to injustice."[12]

We may not agree with a global assessment of discriminatory enforcement or institutional injustice; and even if we do, we don't have to think that it relieves neighbors of responsibility to report certain crimes, certainly violent crimes, and to cooperate with authorities. Even so, we can grasp the painful situation of people doubly betrayed by destructive neighbors and by government that fails in its elementary tasks of safety and fairness. This variant of response to mistrust, minding our own business rooted in a sense of injustice, differs from docility, numbness, and retreat. Here the response is alert, self-conscious, self-protective, and meaningful. Neighbors retain some sense of agency and control over their interactions, if not the environment. In its way, this pattern of response is an antidote to isolation and despair. It has something of the temper of political resistance. These neighbors are not frozen in place, though the field of possibility is limited. Their sole resource seems to be expressive disengagement, noncooperation. There are no positive prescriptions here. Minding our own business does not anticipate systemic change and is unlikely to produce even local improvement. Moreover, the terms are set by others—by delinquent neighbors and mistrusted authorities.

## Live and Let Live: Signaling Neighbors

Neighbors deputize themselves and police the block, or they are numbed and frozen in place, or they keep what they know to themselves in response to perceived injustice.[13] The injunction live and let live is another pattern of response to mistrust-creating situations, and it applies with particular urgency among neighbors with a history of conflict. It consists of a guarded invitation to interaction. In a ritual gesture or word (direct eye contact, a nod, "nice day") or small act of assistance we acknowledge that we are neighbors, regular benign presences. Neighbors maintain cautious distance and at the same time send the message: I recognize you as neighbor and "decent folk." Like Vasily Grossman's old teacher who under conditions of atrocity still asked, "How are you feeling today?," neighbors mitigate mistrust. [14] Live and let live is an assertion of normalcy—modest, limited, and requiring a certain discipline.

A concrete illustration of live and let live is the well-studied case of Brooklyn's Crown Heights. A racially mixed area, Hasidic Jews and African Americans lived interspersed on blocks and in buildings. After an episode of violence wracked the neighborhood in 1991, officials planned meetings and organized demonstrations of civic spirit. Most Crown Heights residents did not attend these supervised events designed to encourage contact and engender mutual respect. They did not participate in efforts to construct dialogue, instruct in the terms of civility, and avow commitment to the principle of toleration. But individually and spontaneously neighbors did act to contain and interrupt the cycle of violence and mistrust. They called upon this element of the democracy of everyday life: live and let live.

The context is this: a young black boy, Gavin Cato, was struck and killed by a car in the motorcade of the Lubavitch Rebbe. Hours later, apparently in retaliation, Yankel Rosenbaum was fatally stabbed by a black teenager. Three days of riots followed before police effectively stepped in. The events roiled New York City politics and provided a stage for opportunistic political leaders. Throughout the country the violence became a Rorschach for pundits who activated every stereotype and cast the 'other' in the role of their historic oppressors. The boy Gavin Cato was called a martyr in the struggle for racial justice, and the Reverend Al Sharpton linked "diamond merchants" in Crown Heights and Tel Aviv to the apartheid regime in South Africa. (In fact, the Lubavitch were a relatively poor orthodox community and their African American neighbors were on the whole at least as affluent.)[15] For their part, some Jewish commentators described Rosenbaum's murder as an anti-Semitic hate crime, and represented the violence as a brutal pogrom—a "Kristallnacht."[16]

So it's notable that most Crown Heights neighbors resisted vilification and stigmatization. Rosenbaum's brother called the killers "criminals" not anti-Semites. Residents described the mayhem as the work of outside agitators.[17] A Hasidic woman put it this way:

> Do you know that the Blacks who came here to riot were not my neighbors? . . . the people in this community want exactly what I want out of life. They want to live in nice homes. They all go to work. . . . They want to send their kids to college. They wanna live a nice quiet

life ... The people who came here to riot were brought here by this famous Reverend Al Sharpton ... My Black neighbors? I mean, I spoke with them. *They were hiding in their houses just like I was.*[18]

Her words reflect a thoughtful calibration of "who is my neighbor?" We know from my discussion of imagined geography in Chapter 1 that Hasidic Jews and African Americans mapped the area of Crown Heights differently. Lubavitcher residents imagined "our neighborhood" as a separate domain. ("It's not really a Black neighborhood here at all. They have nothing to do with us.")[19] But the woman quoted here refers to "my black neighbors." She avows a connection. They are not on the map of synogues and kosher butcher shops that guides her day-to-day movements, but "my black neighbors" acknowledges their shared vulnerability to those who, like Frost's hunters, would upset the balance of things:

I have come after them and made repair
Where they have left not one stone on a stone,
But they would have the rabbit out of hiding
To please the yelping dogs.

For this Hasidic woman, regular encounters with "my black neighbors" made her confident of commonalities beyond the desire for safety. They share a reality. They share a point of view. ("They want to live in nice homes. ... They wanna live a nice quiet life.") She may not know many of her African American neighbors personally (we "don't mingle socially") but she acknowledges their rough equality qua neighbors as "decent folk."

Consider in contrast the disposition to build walls. Hearing that black residents "often complain that their Hasidic neighbors aren't so neighborly, that they rush around unconcerned with others, without making eye contact or saying hello," one woman responds, disingenuously, that "we're just as rude to each other." She goes on:

Sachris [the morning prayer] has a time-frame. Micha [the afternoon prayer] has a time-frame, Maariv [the evening prayer] has a time-frame, Shabbos has a time-frame ... And that's why Jews are always rushing ... the fallout is that people wonder, they consider us insular, they consider us snotty ... but that's just ignorance.[20]

"That's just ignorance" reveals reluctance to avoid giving offense and indifference to being misunderstood. Aware of mismatched expectations and misread conduct, she is complacent. She is disposed to wash her hands of these neighbors.

Live and let live exhibits a different disposition and delivers a different message. Neighbors grasp the damage that vicious back-and-forth charges, visible aversiveness, and menacing demeanor on the street and in the hallway wreak on quotidian life. The Hasidic woman who avows that the rioters were not her neighbors knows what to do: in the poet's words, "I have come after them and made repair." In encounters in buildings and on the street, in a gesture or word, neighbors acknowledge one another. They communicate that they are safe with one another. That they intend no harm. That they will not humiliate or threaten one another. We proffer this bit of give and take. We decline to erect walls, to efface neighbors, to refuse to deal. A few words and gestures acknowledge mutual vulnerability and deliver a dose of empathy along with reassurance. Crown Heights neighbors, many of them, received and returned this offering. All this requires a certain discipline. Cautious overtures open us to rebuff, after all, which is why live and let live—the offer and response—demands willingness to expose our personal need.

There is more. Crown Heights neighbors indicate that they will live and let live just as they are. However alien and discomfiting, Lubavitch and African-Americans accept coexistence alongside this otherness.

> I don't love my neighbors. *I don't know my Black neighbors.* There's one lady on President Street—Claire—I adore her. She's my girl-friend's next-door-neighbor. I've had a manicure done in her house, and we sit and kibbutz and stuff. But I don't know them. I told you we don't mingle socially because of the difference of food and religion and what have you here.[21]

"We don't mingle socially" is a coherent stance, compatible with encounters that fall short of social integration. In seeing things from our neighbors' perspective we do not pretend to know her thoughts, feelings, or reactions with certainty; her history is not ours. "I don't know my black neighbors." Still, "recognition that others have experiences and ideas similar to ours is already a significant moral achievement."[22]

Apparently minimal, live and let live is demanding. It carries a load of meaning. It is fully attentive and communicative. "How are you today?," the quick assist climbing a stair or navigating a curb, says that I am not oblivious to how you are. We are paying attention. We are extending ourselves. To moral philosophers committed to more demanding expressions of mutual respect or principled toleration, live and let live falls short. To disparage it is a mistake, however. For neighbors faced with similar strains, who would give and receive a signal that they are safe among "decent folk," it may seem positively aspirational. The obverse of hostility and mistrust is not love but peaceable, guarded, quotidian encounters. The opposite of war is life.[23]

Live and let live is our best and practicable response to fearful, mistrust-creating situations. It is a residual of normalcy, an assurance. Its practical significance is to enable neighbors to "exist within open-ended situations."[24] I think of it as the safety net of the democracy of everyday life. The disposition to live and let live may not mitigate the damage of mistrust. The injunction can become a casualty of hostile situations, effectively muted. Mistrust may be so diffuse and run so deep, hostility and danger may be so apparent, and ignorance or misreading of one another's intentions so thorough that neighbors' capacity to communicate the intent to live and let live is stunted. They turn to self-deputization or they are frozen in place. Where neighbors do signal live and let live to mitigate as we can degradation of this uniquely important domain, we should recognize it as an achievement.

Live and let live has specific meaning among neighbors. Once again we see the significance of differentiated spheres of life and the fact that we are fully capable of embracing pluralism in this sense. The injunction differs from the prescription to "engage a stranger in conversation as a political friend," for example.[25] On this view, learning to talk to perfect strangers in public spaces is practice in citizenship. Both are expressions of democratic disposition, but their meaning and value are different and they apply in different spheres. The democracy of everyday life has its place among neighbors not strangers and is not preparation for citizenship. The democratic ethos of live and let live consists of reticence, assurances, and regard for neighbors as "decent folk."

## Reticence or Reporting Misdeeds?

Live and let live is a complex injunction. The second facet of live and let live, reticence, keeping what we know to ourselves, is as important as assurances. The positive gesture is active: an offer, a communication of safety. The other, seemingly inactive face of live and let live is solicitous too, but quietly, anonymously.

Strictly speaking, minding our own business is often impossible. Whether we are passive even unwilling recipients of information or eager receptors, we learn things about the goings-on next door—neighbors' habits, events, emotional and physical states, and intimacies. We have what philosophers call "epistemic opportunity." We have opportunity to observe their garbage, hear their children's incautious conversations. We know details of their lives that don't necessarily count as intimate or the stuff of confidences, but things they don't expect to be exposed to view much less become a matter for collective attention. The question here is less what we know than what we do with what we know, or think we know. Do we exploit the accident of proximity? Do we broadcast our neighbor's exhibitionistic displays of nudity or noxious disarray? Or do we take no overt notice? Live and let live demands selective unacknowledgment.

Declining to gossip about a neighbor's domestic disorder is one thing, but harder cases bring live and let live into its own. It comes into play around misconduct that in other spheres and under other circumstances disclosing what we know is "what anyone would do, here," and, some would argue, should do. Certainly, there should be no hesitance when it comes to reporting serious offenses and violence.[26] But when a neighbor has perpetrated some misdeed or violated some regulation, live and let live is a potential counterweight to disclosure. Here's how it works.

A colleague tells this story about his experience with next-door neighbors, people he did not know well.[27] He was aware that the husband and wife were sex workers whose business provided strippers for private parties. My colleague suspected that they also engaged in prostitution and produced pornographic videos in their home. When these neighbors asked him to water their plants while they were away, he found equipment and photographs in plain view. He could not be certain how systematically they crossed the line into illegal activity, but his suspicions were confirmed. He said nothing to the neighbors when they returned, and he did not report what he had learned to local authorities. Why?

In part his reticence was dictated by prudence. It is not always possible to report anonymously. His neighbors might retaliate in some fashion. To some degree this calculation applies in any setting; it can make us hesitant to report a coworker, for example,[28] though exposure to hostility is enhanced where we live. In part, too, my colleague judged that these were victimless crimes (some feminists might dispute this characterization). Plainly, this reasoning has no particular footing in the fact that the pornographers were his neighbors either. Nor does the general squeamishness we might feel to "rat" on others.

These considerations operated in the background, but my colleague expressly attributed his reluctance to report to something else: his identity as a good neighbor and his belief that neighbors should live and let live. His thinking went this way. He owed what he knew to the fact that he lived next door; he had private knowledge that comes with proximity. True, this can cut in both directions. Knowledge unavailable to anyone else can be said to increase responsibility to report, which is where his estimate of prostitution as a victimless crime enters. That said, my colleague was reluctant to exploit private knowledge that would unsettle his neighbors' lives. His reticence rested on appreciation of the necessity of privacy, a degree of control over life at home, and what comes with it—control over what is revealed. We might come to a different decision, but we too would probably feel some hesitance to report. In short, among neighbors, assessment of the gravity of the offense and of the presumptive civic obligation to report have to contend with the injunction live and let live.

When it comes to signaling assurances under conditions of mistrust, we saw that live and let live requires determination—we are vulnerable to being rebuffed, or worse. When it comes to reticence live and let live requires discipline too because by its nature this neighborly act of solicitude and protection will go unacknowledged. The couple down the hall may never learn that we have performed the good turn of refusing to broadcast or report. We relinquish recognition as a good neighbor.

## Reticence or Reporting Undocumented Immigrants Next Door

We see both the burden of private knowledge and the felt moral force of live and let live in the timely case of reporting the undocumented immigrants next door. Few disruptions are as profound as detention and deportation; the harm is immediate and irreversible. Institutional roles assign some people specific obligations to report (employers or certain government officials) and prohibit reporting by others (teachers, health care providers), but once again, we neighbors are on our own.

Turning in undocumented neighbors is not a far-fetched hypothetical. The expanding number of receiving communities across every state means that many people have first or second generation immigrants as neighbors.[29] Moreover, the apparatus of reporting to immigration authorities is publicized and accessible. ICE (Immigration and Customs Enforcement) advertises its 2008 "Secure Communities Strategy" for identifying, detaining, and removing undocumented immigrants, and websites instruct "How to Report Illegal Immigrants."[30]

In addition, the way immigration is officially framed in the United States gives reporting the color of a civic act. ICE employs the term "criminal aliens" and advocates of deportation play on its ambiguity. The term refers to immigrants who enter the country without authorization and to the many who overstay visas,[31] and at the same time it refers to noncitizens regardless of immigration status who commit deportable offenses ranging from petty infractions long in the past to serious felonies. Since 9/11 undocumented immigration has also been linked politically and institutionally to national security; in 2002 the Immigration and Naturalization Service was rolled into the Department of Homeland Security, structuring immigration along security lines.[32]

On the other side stand general reasons for reluctance to report undocumented immigrants.[33] For those who consider closed borders an unjust violation of the human right to freedom of movement or an obstacle to correcting global inequality, for those who think deporting those who have put down roots violates "human decency," these moral considerations are overriding. Americans have specific reason to mistrust the process of immigration enforcement as well. In most settings the fairness of legal proceedings is assumed (though by no means guaranteed) but immigration law treats foreign nationals differently from citizens, and arbitrariness and discrimination on the basis of alienage is "generally permissible."[34] These considerations can explain reluctance to report regardless of whether or not we are a neighbor.

Against this background, the independent force of live and let live operates among neighbors. If we suspect the family next door is undocumented (or that legal immigrant neighbors have committed some nonviolent but deportable civil or criminal offense) why do we keep this information to ourselves, if we do? Live and let live is rooted in quotidian experience, and our neighbors' lives are a reality for us. We have families in view—elderly relatives and children, and private knowledge that these neighbors are "decent folk" not "criminal aliens." So we keep what we know to ourselves. Live and let live does not extend to an active "duty to protect" these neighbors. Churches and humanitarian groups preach "love thy immigrant neighbor," provide material aid, and declare themselves sanctuaries. As the religious resonance of sanctuary suggests, extended protection is understood as an exhibition of kindness and love, a universal moral imperative. From that perspective, live and let live is deficient. It owes to our accidental status as neighbor.

If live and let live permits partiality toward neighbors and prescribes reticence even in situations that might otherwise call for publicizing and reporting what we know, what justifies it? Can reticence be justified, that is, apart from the refusal to be complicit in some injustice?[35] Justified, that is, in the terms of good neighbor?

## Can Moral Philosophy Help?

Moral philosophers pose the question: are there "agent-relative" considerations that have weight when determining actions we should take or not take? That is, do we have special responsibilities toward some people? Is partiality justified? Perhaps neighbors' reticence can be understood as just this sort of "special responsibility." In this literature, "special responsibilities" attach to family and friends, and neighbor is not a standard item on lists of relations that warrant partiality. When it does make an appearance (e.g., "we have special duties to a person, we may say, because she is our sister, or our friend, or our neighbor"[36]) neighbor appears to be an unexplored add-on, implying an intrinsically valued relationship like friendship or strong attachment like the one we have to our sister. But neighbors don't correspond to these relations—not even if our interactions are fulsome, much less if they are thin, weak, and clearly bounded.

Nor do neighbors fall into the category of "associative duties" that arise from what Avishai Margalit calls "thick relations" of belonging on the model of family and blood ties.[37] National, racial, ethnic, and religious groups claim us as their own and impose duties of loyalty. Perhaps neighbors segregated by religion, or race, or immigrants from the same town of origin are strongly identified with one another in this way, in which case associative duties arise from ties that neighbor status may amplify but does not create.

So what might explain including neighbors in the statement: "We have special duties to . . . our sister, or our friend, or our neighbor"? An account of the abstract, formal structure of special responsibility may help: Samuel Scheffler's notion of "intrinsically valued relationships." "It seems that whenever people value an interpersonal relationship they are apt to see it as a source of special duties or obligation," he argues. To see a relationship as valuable "just is, in part, to see that person's needs, interests, and desires as providing one with reasons for action."[38] So neighbors might be encompassed by the claim "I cannot value my relationships (noninstrumentally) without seeing them as sources of special responsibilities."[39] The dynamic by which we come to see our neighbor as a valued relationship has also been stated in general terms. They are built up out of repeated interactions. Constancy and duration matter. And shared adversity or mutual dependence may enhance connections.[40]

The general structure of valued relationship and special responsibility can be plausibly extended from friends and family to neighbors with whom we have a history over time and valued relations shaped by reciprocity, then, but its scope is limited to those who have a central spot on the terrain of our imagined geography, our lay of the land. What if we do not have a history of reciprocity? What if we are only passing acquaintances, familiar only in the sense of recognizable? What if these neighbors have given or taken offense? Live and let live induces hesitance and often reticence quite apart from whether a particular neighbor is a "valued relation." Insofar as we are sensitive to our mutual vulnerability and the particular harm of deranging private life at home, we likely feel some reluctance to disclose what our neighbor did not mean for us to know or tell, even if we did not "mislead, seduce, deceive" by giving her reason to think that she has a claim on our loyalty.[41]

Live and let live entails minding our neighbor's business, plainly. We are not detached. We actively imagine the life-altering consequences of publicizing and reporting. And there is something moving us beyond figuring the effects of telling what we know. Live and let live rests on our capacity to grasp and keep in view the significance for this neighbor, as for us all, of the zone of privacy at home. Live and let live is creative because it opens the field of possibility. That is, we find in ourselves another way of responding to what we know as a result of the accident of proximity besides disclosing and reporting on the one hand and sheer passivity on the other. Live and let live entails an internal adjustment. We find new meaning in live and let live, which now, we appreciate, contains a notion of excellence—an element of good neighbor.

## Privacy and Private Knowledge: Rooms with a View

It is worth considering opportunity and special knowledge more closely. Some neighbors are exhibitionists who provoke us by making it difficult to mind our own business. Of course, opportunities are enhanced by prying—peering into windows, rummaging through trash, or as with Raymond Carver's Bill and Arlene, seizing the occasion of their neighbors' trip away to do more than water the plants and feed the cat.

Neighbors have private knowledge quite apart from exhibitionism and prying, of course. Affluence and architectural design make privacy a possibility today where—given shared outhouses and routes through rooms to get to rooms—it once was "neither a practical possibility, nor, one imagines, even a theoretical aspiration."[42] Few of us are invulnerable; care and cautious self-distancing are uncertain protections against the things neighbors witness or overhear or smell. Balzac's meditation on apartment living can be generalized: "They make each apartment simultaneously function as an observatory, theater, and mirror in which the residents of one apartment spy on those of another, provide unwitting spectacles for each other, and see their own lives reflected or inverted in their neighbors."[43]

If "the central part of 'privacy' is limited *cognitive* access,"[44] neighbors often lack it. The architect Walter Segal reflected that privacy was "to be able to live one's own life without one's neighbours voluntarily or involuntarily taking a part of it,"[45] and the point of live and let live is to refrain from "taking a part." By reporting, disclosing, bringing to the attention of others, the zone of privacy is contracted or erased. It would be odd to propose the psychologically illogical "duty to ignore," but we *can* keep things to ourselves. We can allow our neighbors the "as if" they control what to reveal and are able to determine the face they present to the world.

The consequences of intrusion on privacy go beyond disclosures that set other neighbors or officials (immigration authorities, building inspectors) in motion. Some effects are internal. The possibility that things we keep to ourselves will be made public is enough to cause upset, contortion, suspiciousness. We become excruciatingly self-conscious. We concentrate on protecting ourselves from neighbors' ears and eyes, distorting everyday functions and relations. We transform privacy into concealment. We have "limited and sometimes fragile powers of attention,"[46] and emotional energy is exhausted explaining or covering up. [47]

The coincidence of information we think we should be able to control and keep to ourselves and the physical space we think of as especially protected makes revealing what we know about neighbors *feel* different from reporting on the basis of other sources of private knowledge in other settings. It heightens the burden of reticence. Live and let live is linked, then, to our appreciation of the need for some domain, not too narrow, of privacy and personal control—the domain of home. In Isaiah Berlin's formulation: "The sense of privacy itself, of the area of personal relationships [is] something sacred in its own right."[48] Privacy, the intrinsically valuable, humanly necessary thing itself, the minimal area of personal freedom, is at risk from neighbors. Not least, in this respect: the privacy of home affords freedom to experience emotions, tend to thoughts, and arrive at self-understanding spontaneously and in our own psychological time. We are not well insulated from our neighbors' situation, and we require a certain distance that is more than physical. "Individuals, like nations, must have suitable broad and natural boundaries, even a considerable neutral ground, between them,"[49] Thoreau wrote. We create and observe neutral ground when we live and let live.

## Live and Let Live and the Lightness of (Liberal) Democracy[50]

Arrant violation of privacy is a signature of antiliberal, antidemocratic authoritarianism, totalitarianism, and revolutionary excess. Governments with totalistic ambitions involve neighbors in the business of informing on one another, and I take up this grim material in the next chapter, "Betrayal." Privacy is a foundational liberal-democratic value; reasons for valuing privacy are articulated[51] and limits to the scope of the public interest are set out. Privacy is one reason for limited government, designated rights, rules of trespass, warrants for searches, limits on surveillance. Strictures rightly apply to government first of all, but mechanisms for protecting privacy have a firm place in civil law. Louis Brandeis's classic "right to privacy" is famous for embracing a host of interests and protections, including "non-publicization" as well as rules against access to private places and "cognitive access."[52] The lightness of democracy (liberal democracy that is) is one of its chief claims to allegiance: commitment to minimize trespass on private lives and private spaces.[53]

The lightness of democracy also turns on hospitableness to noncivic relations and the responsibilities they entail. Conflicts of loyalty and obligation arising from actions mandated by government are deeply disturbing. Hence efforts to reconcile obligations of citizenship and demands of faith through legal accommodation of religious practices, for example, and the spousal exemption from testifying against one another in court, which protects us from having to make what may qualify as a tragic choice. In the same way, though obviously less intensely and only informally, a presumptive civic obligation to report undocumented immigrants to authorities, say, can be said to cut against the promise to relax conflicts between the obligations of citizenship and the demands of good neighbor. Limited government, limited tests of loyalty, and limited challenges to personal and social attachments are intertwined and commend live and let live.

There is more to live and let live operating as it does at the level of the democracy of everyday life at home. We shouldn't underestimate the capacity of government to disrupt our not blameless but good enough, ordinarily law-abiding life as a reason to keep what we know to ourselves. Justice Jackson explained: government "stands a fair chance of finding at least a technical violation of some act on the part of almost anyone."[54] We are all selectively law-abiding: we dispose of trash improperly, don't report cash income, our car couldn't pass inspection, a rental apartment in our three-decker is not up to code, we hire yard-workers who we suspect are undocumented immigrants. The list is long. Journalist Hugh Massingham leased a room masquerading as a rent collector. Neighbors became suspicious, he reported, and each one's fear was a projection of what he or she had to conceal: "An overcrowded family thought he was a sanitary inspector. A prostitute thought he was collecting information against her. Each neighbor recognized the position of power that a person with knowledge of their secrets might have."[55] We are all guilty of something, and one neighbor or another, one official or another, is ready to monitor and hold us to account. We have to make an appearance before the development review board. We have to meet with tax assessors, registry workers, building inspectors. Often enough "the process is the punishment"—the distraction, distress, energy, and, expense of having to account for or refute even minor violations. We may not be technically guilty of "three felonies a day," but three reportable violations of some kind is no exaggeration. So reticence is recognition of our mutual vulnerability and an informal, quotidian check on sometimes officious and arbitrary authorities who enjoy discretion to investigate, call us in, demand an account. Reticence is also, importantly, a bar to the politicization of neighbor relations themselves. Exploiting proximity, telling what we know or threatening to tell—even at the level of gossip—can be an exercise of power, coercive and often enough motivated by malice or revenge, personal animosity, or prejudice.

The two faces of live and let live—reticence and signaling assurance—come into their own under mistrust-creating conditions and assume the same essential stance. Our neighbor's affairs have become our business. They have our attention. We are not insulated from our neighbors' situation or the essential social facts. We are not indifferent to their well-being.

In Part III, "Holding Our Lives in Their Hands," I take on catastrophic conditions: neighbors who betray and murder, and authorities who enlist them to turn on one another in frightful ways. I also look at disasters and at rescue by people next door. These situations are not part of our regular personal experience; when it comes to mundane reciprocity and the noise bully's offense we recognize ourselves, but not here. To make "holding our lives in their hands" vivid, I explore touchstone episodes of betrayal and murder by neighbors in American history. But we should not assume that atrocity-producing situations that radically degrade the quality of life at home are relegated to history. It is important, just now, to study both the eclipse of the democracy of everyday life and to reflect on its resilience. On why ordinary acts of neighborliness have special significance under extreme conditions. Put simply, the more deranged the environment, the more valuable stubborn assertions of the democracy of everyday life and neighbors' recognition of one another as "decent folk." They are bulwarks against the worst, and marks of hope.

# PART III

## Holding Our Lives
## in Their Hands

# 7

# Betrayal

Good neighbor relations depend on trustworthiness, and the stakes of misplaced trust range from trivial to vital. We may feel foolish when the woman next door rebuffs our greeting. A small matter. Or, the confidence we place in our neighbors' reticence is mistaken, and we suffer the gossip of the neighborhood. A painful matter. Ordinary vices produce more disturbing personal betrayals—infidelity or inexplicable cruelty. I explored larger-scale conditions in Chapter 6 "Live and Let Live": chronic disorder, vandalism, theft create a diffuse atmosphere of mistrust and escalate the risks of misplaced trust. In some places prejudice undergirds mistrust. And in some place neighbors' mistrust extends to authorities themselves.

The possibility of sustaining the democracy of everyday life diminishes further, drastically when government officials actively derange life around home by politicizing encounters, using offers and intimidation to get neighbors to turn on one another in frightful ways. Driven by the insatiable desire for information, authoritarian regimes—and democracies at war or in search of internal enemies—create vast systems of surveillance and informing. Denunciation is encouraged. Betrayal is made easy. When authorities exploit neighbors' proximity and private knowledge as an instrument of political control, the atmosphere around home is suffused with suspicion. The convention of reticence that preserves privacy and commends us to live and let live is assaulted as government converts what we know about our neighbors into a burden and threat. Where officials exercise their power to confiscate, relocate, imprison, or deport, we come to see our neighbors as a source of danger, and we pose a potential danger to them in turn. It is the effective criminalization of minding our own business.

Neighbors' motives for betrayal arise as well from the history of their personal encounters. Once the structures of reporting are erected, inhibitions on acting out of envy, greed, unsettled disputes, and grudges are weakened. Politicized neighbor relations are also personalized, in short, as neighbors exploit official opportunities for betrayal. "While political actors 'use' civilians to collect information . . . it is also the case that civilians 'use' political actors to settle their own private conflicts." Officials who administer systems of informing and invite denunciations know that they are likely to be overwhelmed by innuendo and false charges. Betrayal and even violence "is often a reflection rather than a transgression of neighborliness," "though a perverse one."[1]

Under these conditions all the elements of the democracy of everyday life are stressed and distorted. Live and let live most clearly: we put ourselves at risk if we refuse to cooperate with official demands to listen in and report on the activities of the people next door. The favor or disfavor in which authorities hold the offensive woman down the hall trims our conduct in other respects too, so that rallying neighbors to speak out against her troublesome behavior loses its spontaneous self-governing character and takes on the color of complicity with or opposition to official policy. A latitudinous embrace of neighbors as "decent folk" is bound to be blunted if neighbors are under suspicion of disloyalty or are targets of officially condoned discrimination. We are unable to personally fashion relations, or only with exceptional mutual effort and at some risk.

Americans' self-understanding as good neighbors and the regulative ideals of the democracy of everyday life are hardy but not invulnerable. My purpose in surveying this grim territory is in part to ward off complacency. Typically, we associate the apparatus of betrayal that subverts neighborliness with totalitarian regimes, but deliberate derangement of neighbor relations has a place in American history and in the present.

Neighbors hold our lives in their hands. Sometimes, inspiringly, they come to our rescue. The impulse neighbors muster to assist or to do no harm might be characterized as simple human decency. As indeed it is. It might seem that a steady moral compass has little to do with identification as a good neighbor specifically. The near-total eclipse of the democracy of everyday life that is my subject here is worth considering even so, if only because it helps us see what has been lost. But not only for that reason. I say "near-total eclipse" because the disappearance of the democratic ethos of good neighbor is not total. Vestiges of reciprocity, speaking out, and live and let live survive even extreme conditions. Quotidian encounters shaped by the democratic ethos are deeply engrained and answer a deep need, it seems. The story of derangement and recovery demands a close look, and I explore a touchstone case of betrayal in some detail: the evacuation, internment, and resettlement of Japanese citizens and residents during the Second World War.

## World without Walls

Minding our neighbors' business can be converted into a technique in the exercise of power. It is a regular part of the functioning of abnormal Panoptical society, where a "world without walls" is the political ideal. It's useful to start by outlining the essence of political derangement of the lives of people living side by side. The formidable Soviet program of mandated communal housing, which lasted until the 1980s, was utopian communist design made concrete. Residential arrangements were organized to facilitate monitoring by housing committees, block leaders, janitors, and neighbors.[2] Communal housing was "an institution of social control, and the breeding ground of police informants."[3] Svetlana Boym's metaphor for Soviet Russia casts "the whole country as a gigantic communal apartment."[4] In a similar spirit and to a similar purpose, East Germany initiated "Operational Person Control." The system cultivated informers and rewarded denunciations, relying on "unofficial collaborators"—a "vast army of surveillance, intimidation, and repression"[5] embedded in homely settings. Neighbors reported to authorities, delivering up information, rumors, suspicions, and lies in this system based on "*whisperers.*"[6]

A political environment of this kind makes informing on neighbors something almost anyone would do. Willing participants are motivated by ideology; coercion and incentives do the rest—blackmail and bribery, visas to travel, jobs and promotions. Informers profit by taking over the shabby room or not-so-shabby apartment of the neighbor they betrayed:

> In due course some Party enthusiast might inform on the "bourgeois class origins" of the former owner of the apartment; he might be sent to a camp and his room might be appropriated by ideologically correct neighbors, who would ... acquire new prestige in the communal hierarchy.[7]

The personalization of politics is unexceptional, and agencies charged with collecting information note that "the supply of denunciation never seems to fail to satisfy the demand."[8] Greed, jealousy, disputes over rent, the chance to finally avenge a neighbor's offense produce information and malicious misinformation, false charges leveled with impunity. "Spite informers" captures it. Jan Gross called this "the institutionalization of resentment" and observed that the business of coercion "was franchised, as it were, to local individuals, who used their power to pursue their private interests and settle scores."[9]

A prevailing motivation, of course, is fear of being charged with disloyalty or subversion oneself. "One tried to disarm any suspicion, to show how cooperative one was, by chatting away," giving out what might seem to be "harmless detail."[10] This is a desperate wish because the political objective is not solely to ferret out dissident activity but also to keep everyone intimidated and off-balance. We know the result. Mistrust suffuses the atmosphere. The sounds we make, people who visit, our children's friends, our comings and goings, even our jokes, can be insinuating, potential evidence of political disloyalty, or infraction of some rule, or just a bad attitude. "When a guest comes to the apartment it is everyone's business, a mini-event, a source of gossip and argument."[11] Neighbors may make themselves blind and mute; like residents in violent inner cities, they are "frozen in place." The whole of life is directed to staying out of trouble. But this strategy is no guarantee. In one *Stasi* report, intelligence was gathered about a resident who had been singled out for suspicion precisely because she was "very quiet and withdrawn," without "any friendly contacts with her neighbors . . . and only engage[d] with them when spoken to, and then . . . only with great economy and superficiality."[12]

The structure of betrayal produces betrayers, still, it is experienced as personal, how not? It is betrayal if confidences were incautiously exchanged and we trusted our neighbor to keep her knowledge to herself. It is betrayal if neighbors were deceitful and invited our trust. Neighbors who later denied the charge of collaboration because they gave out what they thought were benign snippets of information have been accused of indulging our "infinite capacity" for self-denial.[13] Perhaps, but in a world in which there is no way to act blamelessly, betrayal is morally opaque. The term "betrayal" denotes pure condemnation, but every bit of writing worth attention on the subject is nuanced and tentative. Not everyone is willing to excuse much less forgive betrayal, though. "No one is born an informer; you forge your fate daily at the price of your life," Adam Michnik wrote.[14] And some people cannot excuse themselves: "Most terrible of all . . . were the humiliations to the soul."[15] In Canto 32 of *The Inferno,* Dante relegates "the bottom of all the universe" for spectacular betrayals: Judas, Brutus, Cassius. There are no more gruesome stanzas than the ones describing betrayers of loyalty and trust as neighbors in hell, writhing in pain and gnawing on one another's skulls and brains.

If the actions neighbors take are not amenable to simple moral judgment, political degradation of life at home is. Of the many aspects of repression and fear produced by totalist regimes and by democracies in the grip of campaigns to uncover disloyalty, the wreckage fouls the ground of life at home and afflicts everyone. In Vasily Grossman's words:

> Hearts were being infected by callousness, pride, and indifference. Cowards, fearing for their own lives, were thinking how to save themselves by denouncing a neighbor. And so it was in every town—large and small ... Murk rose up from the beds of lakes and rivers; toads swamp up to the surface; thistles sprang up where wheat had been planted.[16]

Measured by consequences, betrayal by neighbors may be the functional equivalent of informing by a coworker or fellow member of an artistic circle, but the experience has a distinct tenor. We have the testimony of memoirs in which victims italicize *"neighbor,"* indicating their incredulity, underscoring their pain. The defining characteristic of betrayal by neighbors is, again, place: home. It is not surprising that East Germans romanticized home as "a place of trust," a "counterworld" to the public, official one. Nor is it surprising that we don't seem to let up the effort to create the "as if" of a protected private space. In internment camps during the Second World War, Japanese Americans tried to create a facsimile with blankets as curtains or flimsy plywood barriers.

Everywhere in contemporary life the frontier of privacy is shifting. The moral and legal barriers against observation and publicization are redrawn for reasons of public policy, technological innovation, and cultural changes that contract or expand our tolerance for revealing things about ourselves and having them revealed by others. The Internet and appetite for virtual "life on the screen" make publicizing details about our lives, thoughts, and associations seem normal, smoothing accommodation to omnipresent surveillance cameras, geographical tracking, and more.

But a physical domain of privacy cannot be pulled back beyond the front door, kitchen, or bedroom without devastating effects. Mistrust of the family nearby creates personal havoc. We contort our affairs, our inner and outer lives, in the effort. Our energy is expended cringing, keeping our head down. There is little surplus. Nervousness is wearing. Absence of privacy ultimately affects our sense of self—losing control over our thoughts and intimate conduct. Isaiah Berlin felt compelled to characterize minimal privacy in absolute terms, as "inviolable" and "human." The commandments to preserve some frontier "are grounded so deeply in the actual nature of men as they have developed through history, as to be, by now, an essential part of what we mean by being a normal human being," he wrote.[17] The language is telling: "normal," "human." Violation induces a shudder of revulsion.

## American Informers

"By the early 1950s the place and defense of privacy became a common ideological yardstick with which to measure the differences between the 'free West' and the 'totalitarian East.'"[18] Liberal democracy takes totalitarianism or more broadly totalism as its *summum malum*, as it should, but invitations and inducements to inform on neighbors (and others) to authorities are hardly alien to the United States. The standard justification for officially requiring or inducing ordinary people to mind one anothers' business is to uncover disloyalty during wartime and its extensions—the Cold War and the "war on terror." Creating and mobilizing informants may indeed be requisite for national security, but on a massive scale and involving everyday affairs at home it is bound to elicit innuendos and lies, to damage relations among neighbors (and others, of course), to fill the atmosphere with poisonous distrust, and to suppress vigilance against government overreaching and abuse of power. Invariably civilians are called on to trust official claims that threshold-trespassing, privacy-destroying, rights-violating policies are necessary for security. The need for information is represented as a decisive moral counterweight to minding our own business and live and let live.

Fear of disloyalty, sabotage, and subversion is particularly acute in liberal democracies where openness and freedom of movement and association seem to provide cover for hidden enemies and fifth columns, spies and terrorists who reside among us. In this vein, Walter Lippmann wrote in a syndicated column after Pearl Harbor that the absence of any actual case of sabotage proved that Japanese Americans were only waiting until they could strike with greatest effect.[19] This defies logic, but it conforms to psychological logic: subversion is surreptitious, it takes advantage of trust, and it follows that suspicion is rightly aroused by the appearance of normalcy and professions of loyalty. The "enemy next-door" is a familiar trope in popular culture—spies camouflaged as ordinary neighbors.

The hunt for communists in the McCarthy era is the best-known episode of domestic informing.[20] The House Un-American Activities Committee hearings and the Hollywood connection made for dramatic spectacles.[21] More systematic, however, was the "loyalty-security" apparatus carried on out of public view, which filtered down to local-level schools and nongovernmental settings, producing four million investigations, 12,000 hearings,[22] and demanding widespread participation by ordinary people. Coworkers and neighbors were interviewed and told what they knew or thought they knew—mostly "trivial allegations, rumor, and gossip."[23]

Neither the political atmosphere of mistrust nor the institutional apparatus for informing is safely in the past. Since the 9/11 attacks, Muslim citizens and residents in the United States have become targets of security profiling. Groups are infiltrated; individuals' activities and contacts are monitored; agents cultivate informers, encouraging neighbors along with coworkers and coreligionists to report suspicious behavior, suspicious associations, suspicious talk. A virulent atmosphere of mistrust is most easily produced when those suspected of disloyalty share a distinct ancestry or religion,[24] and Japanese Americans who experienced wholesale charges of disloyalty during World War II recognize the parallel: "I get very upset because the same kind of thing is happening to Middle Easterners today. Maybe not on the same scale, but it's happening to them. . . . How many are innocent?"[25]

## Japanese Internment and the Loyalty Frame

As revealed in memoirs and reports, novels and histories, the mass Japanese evacuation and internment during the Second World War is the American touchstone for personal and political betrayal. Japanese Americans were betrayed by their government: "You hurt. You give up everything that you worked for that far . . . You have to throw everything away. You feel you were betrayed."[26] This public betrayal instigated betrayal by white neighbors before what was euphemistically called "relocation" and again after "resettlement." It produced brittle, mistrustful relations among Japanese families living side by side in the camps as well. Japanese were forced by circumstances to consider its meaning. "How to determine one's loyalty, when loyalty exists not only to one's country but to one's family, friends, personal values, conscience . . . betrayal leads inexorably to one individual's betrayal of another, until everyone is a traitor and everyone is betrayed."[27]

My focus on this episode of betrayal by neighbors and the near-total eclipse of the democracy of everyday life necessarily begins with its official public face—for without institutional structures and rapid socialization, attitudes and actions that would have been unthinkable before were justified and widely performed. The basic outlines are well known. The day after Pearl Harbor, imprisonment began for those deemed dangerous "enemy aliens"—people who had already been brought to the attention of the FBI. They were summarily arrested and became prisoners of war, detained without charges.[28] A short time later, Executive Order 9066 mandated mass evacuation from "exclusion zones" and forcibly moved roughly 110,000 Japanese—American citizens of Japanese ancestry and noncitizen Japanese residents living on the West Coast: "orphans, foster children in white homes, Japanese married to Caucasians, the offspring of such marriages, persons who were unaware of their Japanese ancestry, and American citizens with as little as one-sixteenth Japanese blood."[29] In 1942 that population was moved inland, first to assembly centers (pigpens and the infamous horse stalls at fairgrounds and racetracks in California, Oregon, and Washington) and then to tarpaper barracks partitioned into four or five rooms, one for each family, in ten desolate camps. The US government became their jailer. A large military and civilian structure was created to administer the evacuation and years-long internment, which proceeded "with a drill sergeant's thoroughness and lack of sentimentality."[30] It included an exhaustive record keeping apparatus supplemented by the War Relocation Authority's decision to install "trained social scientists with no other duties" in each camp to observe and evaluate the effects of incarceration.[31]

The rationale for removal was the military's anticipation that Japan would bomb or invade the West Coast, and that Japanese fishermen loyal to the Emperor would assist in the attack using shore-to-shore radios to signal to enemy submarines.[32] Something beyond national security concerns enabled mass exclusion, detention, and the system of informing that extended to life at home. The normal restraints—the disposition to see Japanese as citizens and neighbors as "decent folk"—must be weakened. Brutal treatment is invariably accompanied by dehumanizing, humiliating, dignity-denying language.[33] Here, latent racial prejudice escalated into unadulterated racism. Subhuman or nonhuman characterizations of Japanese (as reptiles, apes, yellow monkeys, swarming ants) were commonplace. Gomer Pyle reflected: "In Europe we felt that our enemies horrible and deadly as they were, were still people . . . But out here I soon gathered that the Japanese were looked upon as something subhuman and repulsive; the way some people feel about cockroaches or mice."[34] "Yellow peril" elided the difference between ethnicity and nationality, foreign enemy and US citizen: "A Jap's a Jap."[35] West Coast military commander General John DeWitt asserted, "the Japs we will be worried about all the time until they are wiped off the face of the map," and warned that "over 112,000 potential enemies, of Japanese extraction, are at large today."[36]

The Congressional Commission charged in the 1980s with investigating internment struggled to find the right terminology. They rejected "concentration camp" (the phrase actually used in government documents and by President Franklin Roosevelt at the time) because it "summons up images and ideas which are inaccurate and unfair."[37] Conditions in the internment camps were harsh and calculated to be humiliating. Detainees lived under the gun, with constant threats, often abuse, always arbitrariness. But these were not death camps. It was a company of stunned Japanese American soldiers who liberated Dachau in 1945. After the war when facts about the concentration camps in Europe became widely known, Japanese detainees felt compelled to report that their own internment "wasn't that bad."[38] Many declined to describe themselves as prisoners. Few called themselves "survivors." But there is this singular similarity between concentration camp and internment camp victims: comprehensive lifelong silence. Prisoners spoke never, or rarely, or only obliquely and evasively, about their experiences.

Racism underpinned the pervasive atmosphere of fear and mistrust that enveloped Japanese in the United States, then, but the official frame was loyalty. None of the loyalty bureaucracy's several agencies managed to settle on a coherent definition; selling secrets, sabotage, material support to the enemy, and plots to overthrow the government are distinct from personal associations, from the content of beliefs, from feelings and attitudes that are easily misread. Yoshito Wayne Osaki describes her family disposing of anything that the FBI in its searches of households might consider reason to designate them "enemy aliens": pictures of the emperor, flags, photographs of the children in school uniforms that looked too militaristic, above all the *tanto*, or sword, a family gift.[39] When disloyalty is amorphous and suspicion diffuse we can expect scrutiny of the tea leaves of small actions and expressions. A novelist puts these agitated thoughts in the mind of an ordinary Japanese American:

So go ahead and lock me up. Take my children. Take my wife. Freeze
my assets. Seize my crops. Search my office. Ransack my house. Cancel
my insurance. Auction off my business. Hand over my lease. Assign me
a number. Inform me of my crime. Too short, too dark, too ugly, too
proud. Put it down in writing—is nervous in conversation, always
laughs loudly at the wrong time, never laughs at all—and I'll sign on
the dotted line.[40]

We can understand why the loyalty frame was adopted by Japanese
Americans themselves. Insofar as the political category loyalty replaced
or was ostensibly severed from racism, it could be contested. Loyalty
oaths administered in the camps pushed in the direction of discriminating
among individual cases, evoking if not affording an iota of due process.
The loyalty frame played a part in enabling Japanese Americans to return
after release from the camps confident of their blamelessness, and created, as racism could not, openings for acceptance as "decent folk." For
men who joined the 442 Regimental Combat Team, "We proved our loyalty to the USA and so doing have made life better for all of us."[41]

But the loyalty frame was also an invitation to betrayal. From the start,
some second-generation Japanese Americans were intent on cooperating
with authorities. The Japanese American Citizens League (JACL) affirmed the national security "necessity" of the measures taken against
them, denouncing any attempt to represent detention as injustice. "We
are going into exile as our duty to our country because the President and
military commander of the area have deemed it a necessity. We are gladly
cooperating because this is one way of showing our loyalty."[42] They op-
posed resistance and issued warnings and threats againt Japanese who
were uncooperative. Some Japanese Americans organized an intelligence
service of their own. "We intend to protect the country and ourselves by
reporting any un-American activity to the proper authorities." On the
basis of informants' reports men were sent to segregated detention centers from which they could be deported. For Japanese who willingly reported others, informing was a calculated, unforced choice.[43] Assessing
this network of informers, one historian characterized what passed for
information as "rumor, innuendo, hearsay, or information leaked in
spite."[44] This is a history of authorities inviting betrayal and making it
simple to do. The fact of the matter is also simple: "Not one case of sabotage or espionage among the Japanese immigrants and Japanese Americans has ever been proved."[45]

## White Neighbors: Betrayals at Home

Alongside the story of official betrayal is the quiet face of personal betrayal by neighbors who watched the frightened family next door packing up what they could carry and being bused away. Neighbors who turned away. Who did not offer a word of sympathy or support. These neighbors were not informers, but they were not passive either. Effective withdrawal of recognition as "decent folk" is deliberate and communicative. It amounts to an active alteration in status. It is the mundane counterpart of public repudiation of Japanese Americans as citizens, and in its way, as painful.

There had been forewarnings: posted curfews for Japanese insured that neighbors saw them hurrying home in the evening. The evacuation itself was a public spectacle. "The sign had appeared overnight. On billboards and trees and bushes and the backs of bus-stop benches. It hung in the window of Woolworth's. It hung by the entrance to the YMCA. It was stapled to the door of the municipal court and nailed, at eye level, to every telephone pole along University Avenue."[46] Neighbors were witnesses to the public injustice and contributors to the personal devastation.

Some neighbors took the evacuation order as license for destruction and violence. "The night before we left we got vile phone calls all through the night. Dirty Japs, get out of town."[47] Japanese were assaulted in drive-by attacks by people known to them. Neighbors vandalized and set fire to property: "As soon as we were taken away, our family nursery was pillaged." Neighbors profited from the forced sale or abandonment of shops, small businesses, farms, machinery, personal property, homes. "Neighbors swooped down like scavengers."[48] "People, *neighbors*, came and stole pipes, hoses, windows, light fixtures, floorboards — everything."[49] Japanese suffered catastrophic losses,[50] giving the government's bad-faith claim that "relocation" was "for your own protection" a veneer of credibility.

Apart from predation and arrant destruction, and as cruel in some respects, is turning away. Neighbor relations may have been rudimentary, even uneasy, but Japanese were settled at home, an achievement that only became clear when it was undone in what amounted to personal abandonment. Julie Otsuka's novel *When the Emperor Was Divine* is based on the experience of her grandparents and American-born mother, then age eleven. At the time of evacuation the family had been living a middle-class life in Berkeley, California. Neighbors saw the father of the family arrested and led across the lawn in his bathrobe and slippers by three men in suits with FBI badges. Readying the family for removal, the mother packed up the house, aware that her neighbors were watching, and aware of their silence. Neighbors see them go to the Civil Control Station at the First Congregational Church, see the identification numbers pinned to their collars, see the buses:

> They had all seen us leave, at the beginning of the war, had peered out through their curtains as we walked down the street with our enormous overstuffed suitcases. But none of them came out, that morning, to wish us goodbye, or good luck, or ask us where it was we were going (we didn't know). None of them waved.[51]

Many Japanese may have had only bare-bone relations with white neighbors before the war, and turning away from them is not turning on them. Still, encounters marked by the democracy of everyday life were abruptly cut off—direct personal confirmation that they were mistrusted, viewed as enemy aliens. Betrayal by government—denial of rights and civic standing—can be protested, resisted, or faced with resignation. Neighbors turning away is personal betrayal.

The poet Maya Angelou was thirteen years old and living in San Francisco's Fillmore District: "The Asian population dwindled before my eyes," she wrote, "As the Japanese disappeared, soundlessly and without protest, the Negroes entered with their loud jukeboxes and just-released animosities, and the relief of escape from Southern bonds." Her family evinced neither sympathy nor interest: "No member of my family or one of the family friends ever mentioned the absent Japanese. It is as if they never owned or lived in the houses we inhabited." Angelou reflects on this patent indifference: "The Japanese were not whitefolks. Their eyes, language, and customs belied the white skin and proved to their dark successors that since they didn't have to be feared, neither did they have to be considered. All this was decided unconsciously."[52]

Even so, good neighbor remained as ideal and practice. Memoirs describe a surprise party with gifts of heavy pants and nightgowns to wear in the camps, a dinner on the evening before removal with neighbors who laid out their best china and linens, offers to care for possessions, people down the block simply letting them know that "they felt sorry for us." [53] Neighbors who did no more than interact in ordinary ways for as long as possible did not see themselves as dissenters in political opposition to national security policy. If they refused to join in the general enthusiasm for evacuation, if they expressed confidence in the family nearby as "decent folk" and were appalled that they should be presumed to be "enemy aliens" and interred, their supportive behavior was private, unobserved. They saw themselves doing what they could to relieve stress, minimize material loss, blunt degradation. It is impossible to overstate the significance of good neighbors carrying on as normal—or the "as if" of normal.

In the eclipse of the democracy of everyday life we see clearly—perhaps more clearly than by assessing public policy directly—the damage of this political state. Recall that as ideal and often enough in practice recognition as "decent folk" entails disregard for our neighbor's status in other social spheres and disregard for ascriptive characteristics—national origin, family history, religion, race. The criterion for good neighbor is modest: trustworthy engagement in mundane give and take. The politicization of daily life deranged all this. It erased the boundaries loosely defining this separate sphere so that everything suppressed for the sake of the quality of life at home could flood in, and did: family history, citizen status, race, and political loyalty. The family next door was seen through the lens of racial and political categories, and through the miasma of mistrust thrown up by war. The public political sphere and the informal sphere of good neighbor nation were conflated. Pluralism gave way to totalism.

"*They're afraid*, our mother had said" of neighbors who turned their backs, affecting to see nothing. They may have been warned that anyone who offered support or wrote letters to people in the camps was guilty of helping the enemy, she conjectured.[54] Or perhaps the mother was trying to soften the experience of betrayal for her children. Perhaps the neighbors never expected them to return.

## Camp Neighbors

The eclipse of the democracy of everyday life marked interactions in the camps as well, where Japanese families were neighbors by force. The camps were small towns of 8,000 to 18,000 organized into blocks. There was no privacy: small spaces, cramped quarters, flimsy construction with partitions that did not extend to the ceiling, sheets hung on wires across the room, open latrines and communal showers, and mess halls. A world without walls. A world enclosed by a wall: barbed wire and guard towers. Armed guards searched for contraband (flashlights, radios, hot plates, alcohol, knives, scissors). Whites who ran the camps were characterized as "operators," "racists," and "damned sociologists."[55] Some administered physical abuse and flung racist epithets.[56] We get the sense of disorientation, uncertainty, and ennui—internees accused of nothing, time weighing on them, rattled by rumors that circulated incessantly:

> The men and women would be put into separate camps. They would be sterilized. They would be stripped of their citizenship . . . They would be sent to a desert island and left there to die. They would all be deported to Japan . . . They would be held hostage until every last American POW got home safely. They would be turned over to the Chinese for safekeeping right after the war.[57]

Detainees were thrust into a total environment of mistrust. Uncertain of "what anyone would do, here," ordinary vices had free reign and normal offenses were amplified in this habitat of unwanted, unrelieved intimacy. Internees stole, harassed, acted out grievances. There were opportunities for offensiveness and for taking offense: the lack of privacy for physical ministrations, for example, and the impunity with which detainees could violate the rudiments of domestic order. ("One morning I saw some women emptying bed pans into the troughs where we washed our faces.") Nerves frayed. "I felt stifled and suffocated" by neighbors inches away. "Internal squabbling spread like a disease." "Family life began to show signs of strain almost immediately."[58] The mental and emotional deterioration of people living close by was frightening—the suicide rate was high. The material and emotional resources for ordinary reciprocity dissipated.

Beyond amplifying ordinary offenses, the structure of camp life created its own frictions. Internees were viewed as collaborators for accepting jobs in camp operations. Neighbors divided over whether to speak out about conditions in the camps, and conflict simmered or erupted into violence between cautious internees ("She did not want to cause any trouble . . . The nail that sticks up gets hammered down"[59]) and those who made demands, challenged camp officials' decisions, or engaged in minor acts of resistance.[60] "All you have to do is behave" evokes Vaclav Havel's grocer putting the "Workers of the World Unite!" sign in his window to signal "I know what I must do. I behave in the manner expected of me. I can be depended upon and am beyond reproach . . . and therefore I have the right to be left in peace."[61]

The spark that erupted into severe infighting among internees—quarrels, accusations, informing, and episodes of violence—was the government's "loyalty review program" initiated in 1943. The Army decided to recruit Japanese Americans for military service, and the questionnaire asked men of military age whether they would pledge loyalty and volun-

teer for combat duty. To some detainees agreeing to serve signified acquiescence in the injustice done them and "no" was a protest, or "no" was
motivated by not wanting to serve in a segregated unit. Detainees fearful
of being released craved the safety of the camps; they said "no" in order
to remain wards of the state. And militants in the camps threatened revenge against men who answered "yes" and registered for the army.[62]

These sources of enmity energized informing. Neighbors informed on
one another to authorities out of malice, resentment at an insult or humiliation, or to obtain some personal advantage; opportunistic incentives
were at work. Crippling relations more than anything else, then, was betrayal by camp neighbors. It was a constant fear. The belief that neighbors
had informed had its own logic: it could explain otherwise inexplicable
searches of possessions to which a detainee was summarily exposed, or a
work assignment, or a move. What seemed like arbitrary arrest (for going
to the latrine during curfew; agitating for better medical care and up-
graded food) was exacerbated by whispers that a barracks neighbor had
reported these actual or invented violations. "I still don't know why my
name was on that list of agitators put into the stockade," but this detainee
had suspicions.[63] Informing was a real danger. Informants assisted the
FBI in removing "troublemakers."[64] Men were betrayed by camp neighbors who saw anything but compliance as a betrayal of internees who
kept their heads down. "Stool pigeons" identified "known agitators" who
could be separated from the rest.[65] On the other side, gangs formed in
some camps, "outing" suspected informers. "If I or anyone was friendly
with the authorities, we were suspected of being an *inu*" (a "dog" or
informant).[66]

"Camp analysts"—social scientists assigned to the camps, many of
them anthropologists—had a hand in betrayal. Tasked with studying
"how the social and cultural reactions of the Japanese Americans to the
imprisonment and relocation varied," their reports describe fear of force,
fear of forced relocation, and a litany of other unsurprising responses.
This much is unexceptionable, except insofar as it provided "a scientific
patina" to the image of "a thoughtful and caring administration."[67] The
moral debasement of professional work is striking; it emerges clearly in
analyses of "Japanese character," which contributed to the young field of
national character studies and became part of the arsenal of psychological warfare employed against the enemy (and later applied more
broadly).[68] More immediately, the social scientists screened those who
had answered "no" to the loyalty questionnaire for removal to the segregation center. Some compromised themselves further, providing names

of dissidents and other information "useful in maintaining authoritarian control."

All this underscores the absurdity and insult of efforts to represent internment as benign and for internees' own good. Volunteers, mostly members of the peace churches and conscientious objectors, "dreamed of helping create 'peaceful and harmonious' communities."[69] Instructions handed out to detainees read: "Here we say Dining Hall and not Mess Hall; Safety Council, not Internal Police; Residents not Evacuees."[70] The delusion represented by these assurances could not be sustained. "I was brainwashed," one detainee reflected, "But when I hear about people who were in prison, I think, 'Hey, wait a minute, so was I.' It's take a long time to realize that."[71] The sculptor Isamu Noguchi gives a cold-eyed account of this charade. Noguchi lived on the East Coast not in an evacuation zone, but at the invitation of the head of camp he voluntarily entered Poston in 1942 with a plan to design parks and recreation areas. Though the WRA eventually failed to support the project, Noguchi had months to observe and remarked acidly on the camp head's ludicrous fantasy: "Though democracy perish outside, here would be kept its seeds,' cried Mr. Collier through clouds of dust."[72] The program of civic education imposed in camp schools was another insult. "Every school activity was to be evaluated for its social worth ... Does it promote better assimilation into our American society?," Erica Harth recalls.[73] Her account, "Democracy for Beginners," expresses the double affront of assuming that Japanese Americans were democratic beginners and that their improvement could be effected in detention. The educational goal of "better assimilation" anticipated the poisonous aim of the government relocation policy after the war and the trauma of resettlement.

Perhaps astonishingly, many Japanese regarded internment as an aberration.[74] A university student wrote to the *Daily Californian*: "Our wish to those who remain is that they maintain here the democratic ideals that have operated in the past. We hope to come back and find them here."[75] Hope attached to restored civic status and enforceable rights, of course. "We hope to come back and find them here" also applied to the democracy of everyday life at home among neighbors.

## Resettlement: Recovering the Democracy of Everyday Life

The meaning of internment (meanings in the plural, really) was affected by the experience of return. American democracy had betrayed them and its counterpart was betrayal by neighbors and the abrupt eclipse of the democracy of everyday life. Resettlement was a moment of "no more" and "not yet." Whatever prewar encounters with neighbors had done to encourage expectations of reciprocity was in the past. Superceded. "No more." Over time (and generations) Japanese Americans would became the "model minority" and desirable neighbors; the democracy of every-day life came out of eclipse. But "not yet."

Management of relocation was in the hands of government officials, and we can understand internees' mix of wishfulness and fear. Despite "lack of favorable community acceptance" and public protests in "receiv-ing areas," the WRA determined to resettle internees outside the West Coast exclusion zone in cities and towns in the Rocky Mountains and Midwest. The rationale for resettlement was a transparent combination of hostility and sentimentality about neighbors. The thought was that by transplanting Japanese among American good neighbors, they would be rehabilitated. Internees were advised not to congregate with other Japa-nese, to assume a "low profile."[76] "Obey all rules, regulations, and laws . . . Be quiet and well behaved. . . . you must be inconspicuous."[77] Adapt to "what anyone would do, here." The WRA slowed the flow of return to the West Coast,[78] and only about a quarter of internees returned to the city where they had lived before the war. Many faced homelessness; hence this poignant reaction:

> I'm not leaving! They forced us in here and now they're forcing us out. Where are we supposed to go? I don't have any place to go. They made me lose my grocery store, my home—everything. I don't have money— no job—nothing. What am I supposed to do? I'm seventy-two years old . . . What am I supposed to do? Goddamn those bastards. They'll have to kick me out! I'm not leaving!.[79]

The experience of remaking a home was variable and in no small part dependent on the response of neighbors. When circumstances were rela-tively comfortable and neighbor relations hospitable, return to quotidian life was a balm. Internment, the injustice and betrayal, was seen as some-thing they had gotten through. For others, though, internment was just the beginning of ongoing stigmatization and mistrust, and resettlement has been described as "the most traumatic experience of all for the evacu-ees."[80] Otsuka recreates one family's disturbing return. In the camps, the young boy had played war games: "Kill the Nazis! Kill the Japs!" and nursed a rosey vision in which nothing had changed: "the tree-lined streets at sundown, the dark green lawns, the sidewalks, boys throwing balls in backyards." "When the war is over," the boy's mother told him, "we can pack up our things and go home." After almost three-and-a-half years, with the allotted twenty-five dollars (the same amount given to criminals released from prison), they returned. She had left their home in the care of an unscrupulous lawyer, who leased the house to people who vandalized it and pocketed the rent money. The children would occasionally catch sight of their former possessions around the neighborhood: "Wasn't that our mother's Electrolux Mrs. Leahy was pushing back and forth across her living room floor? Didn't the Gilroy's mohair sofa look awfully familiar?" Now, when the family ran into these neighbors on the street, "they turned away and pretended not to see us."[81]

For some, openness to reciprocity among neighbors as "decent folk" was psychologically impossible. The father in Otsuka's novel had spent the war in a detention camp separated from the family, writing letters that arrived blacked out and marked "Detained Alien Enemy Mail." We can try to conjure his state of mind. To the best of his ability, and like so many immigrant men, he had conducted his life according to the rules: the working and saving, dedication and patience, "no drifting, no laxity, no laziness, faithfully meeting every obligation."[82] He came to see these expectations as delusions. The father rarely spoke to anyone after his release. He did not like to use the telephone. He would not eat out in public. The advice he gave his children was the advice of someone ashamed, perhaps, for not protecting his family, certainly irreparably mistrustful: "You never know who might be listening . . . Why go looking for trouble?" "And don't think for a minute that they're your friend."[83]

For those who returned to their former homes, the experience of neighbors' gestures of acceptance as "decent folk" was profound. Some did more. Neighbors who cared for the family's musical instruments, and returned them after the war, for example. Or Bob Fletcher who worked three fruit farms for families in the camps. He paid the bills, keeping only half the profits for himself, and lived in a bunkhouse out of respect for the privacy of the owner's home—all the while "ignoring the resentment of neighbors" and enduring harassment himself. This is kindness amounting to rescue. It is also, more specifically, a declaration that the Japanese families he knew were "decent folk." "I did know a few of them pretty well," he explained, "They were the same as anybody else. It was obvious they had nothing to do with Pearl Harbor."[84] Patrick Hayashi tells of a neighbor who had a nursery like his grandfather's. "The day my family was taken away, he came to our nursery and took some cuttings from some of our azaleas . . . And the day my family returned, he brought them over and said to my grandfather, "Here are your flowers. I've kept them for you so you can start your life again."[85] This too is kindness, and more; its import goes beyond sympathy and assistance. For the Hayashi family it revived the expectation of neighbors as "decent folk" and confidence that they would be regarded that way. America may exhibit its character as good neighbor nation when it fails as a democracy to protect even basic rights.

Yet return to quotidian life at home did not encourage breaking the silence. "Let it go" was the common aftermath. "I have come to understand why it was necessary for me to forget those years, that it is a natural human reaction to disaster and trauma."[86] Detainees joined in the general national muteness. Silence came in several emotional hues. Better not to speak out about the mohair sofa in the neighbor's living room; the predictable result would be bitterness, accusation and denial. For some, humiliation colored silence. Takemoto's mother explained much later: "Well, when you have something bad done to you, you get to thinking you were bad. That it was your fault. That's the psychology."[87] Repressed bitterness played a part: "For fifty years I never allowed myself to think it was immoral. Unjust. I never allowed myself to think that. I kept it out of my mind.... Otherwise it would have crushed me."[88]

Silence was also seen as the price of restoring neighbor relations.

> No one outside the camps could quite grasp what we had gone through, and it was a subject that made everybody uncomfortable. Moreover, most did not want to know. We hardly had the language to describe these places and experiences, so most of us maintained a distance, a silence.[89]

Returning to the three-stool soda fountain where he had been a regular, Sato Hashizum reflected:

> Doc Watson, always a gentleman, probably didn't want to broach the prickly subject of our forced removal into concentration camps and I, an awkward teenager, wouldn't be sure how to respond if he did ask.... I was largely glad he hadn't asked, but a small part of me wished he had.[90]

When a neighborhood librarian inquired about his time in the camps, a young detainee recalled his response: "'It was fine, ma'am.' I was supposed to put the best foot forward. When she turned around and told her assistant, 'You see, some people in camp enjoyed it,' I felt betrayed. That was not the response she was supposed to give her assistant."[91]

It took forty years for a Congressional Commission, formed reluc-
tantly under pressure, to investigate federal internment policies. The report published in 1983 as *Personal Justice Denied* attributed internment
to "racism, wartime hysteria, and the failure of political leadership."[92] It
took still longer before a redress and reparations movement agitated for
compensation and an official apology. There was no great rush to "face
history and ourselves," it seems. Political time and personal time were
separated by decades. There was no widely publicized occasion for witnessing—for victims to be heard and to confront those who wronged
them. There was no holding to account the perpetrators of large-scale
deprivation of rights. A record of who turned individuals in to the FBI as
"enemy aliens," who informed on them to camp authorities, who vandalized or seized their homes and businesses was not a post-war goal.

Even after resettlement, when reciprocity among "decent folk" was
tentatively reasserted, careless accusations would arise out of the blue,
stunning their targets. The son of an internee describes his father's experience: "His neighbors at Ahwautukee Retirement Village—playing poker
at the rec center, putting over the golf course, or leaning over backyard
fences" were a picture of the mundane. But after the 1988 Civil Liberties
Act authorized a $20,000 token restitution, one neighbor told him: "It's
not right," "Why should you get *all that dough*?"[93] This is moral obtuseness. It is the echo of that earlier denial: "You see, some people in camp
enjoyed it."

Perhaps it is "incontestable that nothing is more uplifting in all of life
than righteous anger,"[94] but not every one feels it or expresses it if they
do. Like the father in Otsuka's novel, some turned anger against themselves. Interviews with former detainees many years later reveal bitterness, but not such that there was need for a national commission to temper it and hold vengeance in check. Instead, the struggle for self-respect
and normalcy after the war typically translated into "just leave it behind
you."[95] "We didn't talk about it." "Just put it behind you." "Let it go,"[96]
and people did. Karen Karematsu tells the story of her high school reading assignment about a man who had challenged his evacuation order in
court. The man was her father, but she had never heard about his imprisonment during the war or about that Supreme Court case from him.[97]

We might hope that beneath silence and "just put it behind you" lay a
stoic assertion of independence rather than passive resignation to bearing the indignity of internment and uncompensated losses. We might
hope that "let it go" signaled refusal to be damaged by events—a way of
freeing themselves from the effects of betrayals. But it is hard to believe

that many men and women were unscarred, and little is achieved by ascribing heroic recovery to them. "You really don't know so you kind of let it go" is an admission of unresolved conflict.

Still, "just put it behind you" looks determinedly ahead. Returning home or making a new one, a focus on settling and being a good neighbor expressed the desire for of quotidian life and an iota of hope for its possibility. Neighbor was foregrounded. Minimal reciprocity, the disposition to regard the people next door and to be regarded as "decent folk," signaling the intent to live and let live, speaking out in ordinary ways against ordinary offenses—the elements of the democracy of everyday life do specific and important work. Insofar as it was revived, the recovery had both personal and collective significance. The democracy of everyday life is no substitute for rights and political activity, for nondiscrimination, or for justice, of course. And "just put it behind you" was not politically constructive; it pushed the question of public betrayal into the background and put off national reckoning. It may have kept internees from finding meaning in expressing grievances and agitating for apology or reparation. But Havel's words are apt: "The most important thing is always the quality of that life,"[98] defined here by the democratic ethos of give and take among neighbors. It is a democratic bulwark rooted deeper than a public culture of rights and available when institutional and principled resources are overwhelmed, weakened, narrowed, or eliminated. That is why the derangement of life at home is its own incomparable moral and social disaster, why the appearance of hardy shoots of good neighbor is always noted and expressly valued, and why recovery of the democracy of everyday life from eclipse through the actions of neighbors aware of what they do is life-altering.

In the next chapter, "Killing," I probe the darkness that descends when democratic officials encourage or condone murderous violence. Histories and memoirs show African Americans vulnerable to lynching by people they know, hoods or no. Neighbors killed and mutilated them; other neighbors signaled recognition of mutual vulnerability, shared their misery, provided comfort, sometimes offered safe haven. They provided what is always possible and meaningful: gestures of recognition as neighbors and "decent folk."

# 8

# Killing

"We all carry within us our places of exile, our crimes and our ravages, but our task is not to unleash them on the world."[1] When we fail at Camus's task, men and women set their demons on neighbors, often with impunity. Murderous neighbors—the thing is hard to grasp, no matter how many firsthand accounts by survivors and witnesses we study. We may be able to put ourselves in the shoes of those who inform on neighbors in a political atmosphere suffused with mistrust, under pressure from authorities, and where an institutional apparatus makes betrayal easy to do. But murder at close hand, savage and intimate, is outside our ken. Unintelligibility is at a pitch when it is not mechanized, bureaucratic mass killing but brutal and personal, the work of people we recognize and thought we knew, and who knew us. Survivors express incredulity; they say that the violence was unpredicted, that we neighbors had gotten on together. James Cameron, survivor of a lynching in 1930, declared emphatically: "There was not a race problem in our town."[2] His fall from what he thought was the secure status of neighbor as "decent folk" seems to him precipitous and total. He finds himself viewed by these hateful neighbors through their warped mirror of "decent folk," which functions in cases of racism and exclusion to remove whole categories of men and women from the compass of the democracy of everyday life. Indeed, the cruelty of intimate violence impels us to say that the perpetrators do not see their victims, at that moment, as human. The reality is that in repudiating the inclusive democratic ideal of "decent folk," they have cast themselves out.

Civil wars, in particular "irregular wars," produce betrayal and murder among neighbors on a large scale. There, violence is a technique in the competition for local control. These two-sided political conflicts are different from unilateral cases of genocide or from lynching where defense-less men and women are terrorized, mutilated, and killed by neighbors who call up from the depths "cowardice, treachery, murderousness, and violence against the weak."[3]

The circumstances and reasons for organized killing of vulnerable neighbors vary, but some things are constant. For killers to do their ghastly work police, sheriffs, mayors, judges, governors, and civil servants must remove legal and political obstacles to torture, mutilation, and mur-der. Political as well as moral restraints on abject cruelty must be lifted. Killing is a public spectacle, and in any case a matter of local knowledge, but perpetrators are not charged, witnesses are intimidated from appear-ing in court or perjure themselves, and juries exonerate the accused. Of-ficial complicity is expected and condoned. The whole affair is a public secret. Men who lynched two boys drove by the victims' homes, repeat-edly shouting, "Yes, we hung your son-of-a-bitch son! You can't do any-thing about it, either."[4]

Another constant is that in the constellation of explanations proposing to make sense of neighbors killing neighbors, scholars point to some deep subterranean cleavage that subsists beneath quotidian encounters long before it erupts in murderousness.[5] The long list includes racism, tribal-ism, ideological polarization, sectarianism, and "post-colonial identities" where a majority casts a minority as an alien presence ("for the Hutu who killed, the Tutsi was a settler, not a neighbor").[6] The question raised in these accounts is what set of combustible conditions unleashes vicious derangement of ordinary give and take?[7] What "evil spirit had to come along in order to wake the sleeping monster inside the people and move it to action"?[8]

Moral psychology is interwoven with political factors—this too is a constant. "Our moral resources either turn out not to work in a particular context, or else they are deliberately neutralized or overridden."[9] It takes socialization into killing to overcome normal inhibitions on violent ag-gression, and this process is distinctive among neighbors because of the absence of institutional frameworks. Unlike military combatants, the kill-ers are not specially trained or stripped of their civilian identity; they are not distanced from their victims or remote from the "moral landmarks" of everyday life. Also, and importantly for my theme, individual psychol-ogy and political factors are interwoven at the level of personal history. Violence that appears to simply mirror deep social cleavages on the one hand or to be random and indiscriminate on the other is, on closer inspec-tion, often linked to the history of individual encounters, which plays a part in the selection of victims. We know, after all, that neighbor relations are not all benign. Individual acts of aggression short of violence are commonplace. Neighbors, like the noise bully, may be cruel, arbitrarily deranging life at home. Animosities, grudges, feuds, rivalry, and envy get acted out all the time. They are the cause and sometimes just the occasion for offenses and conflicts. It's been said that "the original target of our hatred was probably always our neighbor,"[10] and that hostility between neighbors "is so common that it can seem to be the human condition."[11] That said, violence against neighbors is normally held in check, which is what gives Berger's Earl Keese's demonic wrangle with his neighbors its element of absurdity and vicarious release. Under atrocity-producing conditions, however, the personal history of encounters enters malignantly and with force. Grievance meets opportunity.

There is a distinct quality, call it a moral temper, when it is neighbors who murder. The difference lies in part in proximity to home and the opportunities neighbors have to murder or to protect. It has to do, too, with the fact that killing neighbors occurs in full view of family and others living nearby; it is not sequestered in camps or on battlefields. So killing neighbors represents a total breakdown. We have reason to think that the "moral resources" of sympathy and moral imagination by which we see others as "human" or as "decent folk" are taxed least where we live. If "the ethics of preventing atrocities are an extension of the ethics of everyday life,"[12] the domain of life around home is the final bulwark against atrocities, and when it is overwhelmed and violence is unleashed, the rupture is critical. Of course, the language of decency and humanity rightly applies; all such atrocities are morally abominable. But universalistic terms are imperfect substitutes for invocations of neighbor, which has specific resonance. When neighbors participate in atrocities, or applaud the violence, or turn silently away, the transgression has specific added meaning. The terror at destruction of the known world around home is incomparable, a kind of extreme, outer limit. "Was it inevitable that the Jews, looking their last on this world as they rode in the death trains speeding from different parts of the country to Treblinka or other places of slaughter, should have had to witness the indifference or even joy on the faces of their neighbors?"[13] Killing neighbors is the outer tail, the far reach of the eclipse of the sentiment of common humanity. It is also the ultimate violation of the domain around home and suppression of the disposition to view neighbors as "decent folk." The convergence is a unique horror.

In a related way, rescue by neighbors has a distinct moral temper. Acts of rescue often make explicit reference to neighborliness, as I will show.

The radical rupture that is neighbors killing makes us deeply, achingly aware of the inestimable, now-not-to-be-taken-for-granted value of everyday life. When rescuers describe what they did as "what anyone would do," as they do, they affirm and reassert the quotidian. In insisting that they did nothing special, they invoke, preserve, and remind themselves of their (and the victims') identity as neighbor. Moreover, even modest neighborly gestures quite apart from rescue have extraordinary impact. "Every human gesture or act of generosity across the tribal barriers may lodge in someone's memory."[14] The dynamic interaction between aid and protection on the one side and everyday life at home on the other works in two directions, then, mutually reinforcing. Rescue is cast as a reclamation of the ordinary, and mundane exhibition of the ordinary has heightened meaning and effect.

I'm not saying that murder or rescue by neighbors has greater moral or political significance than killing and saving as soldiers in war, or combatants in civil war, or brutality and protection in other settings. It does have a distinct moral temper, though. Intimate violence is its own identifiable experience, as reports by survivors and perpetrators make plain. And it illuminates a surprisingly common association made by rescuers themselves to ordinary neighborliness. A close look at our touchstone case of neighbors killing and rescuing supports these claims.

## Lynching

America's homegrown version of murderous neighbors is lynching of African Americans by whites. After slavery itself, lynching was "America's national crime." It was a peculiarly American crime.[15] Lynching often went beyond killing and was accompanied by torture, cutting, disemboweling, dismemberment, castration, butchering, and roasting the dead body. Lynchings were "feasts of blood."[16] This was intimate violence at the hands of people known. Lynching was never an extermination campaign and southern whites did not aim at eliminating or "cleansing" African Americans (labor lost as a result of black migration north was an unintended and costly consequence of terror). Lynching was not massacre, either. It was local, intimate violence on a small scale. Nonetheless, the newly coined term "genocide" would capture the cruel deliberateness and potential inclusiveness of the atrocity. In 1951 Paul Robeson presented *We Charge Genocide: The Historic Petition to the United Nations for Relief from a Crime of the United States Government against the Negro People* to the recently established United Nations. In a "crystallization of my destiny" lynching survivor James Cameron founded what he called America's Black Holocaust Museum. [17]

Lynching has a prehistory before Reconstruction and white-on-black violence in the South. It was a form of vigilante justice on the frontier. Lynching of African Americans by other African Americans occurred too, in part because whites did not accord black victims legal justice. [18] Lynching extended outside the South to the Midwest and West—one of the most studied murders took place in Marion, Indiana.[19] That said, the "vast wave of homicidal violence"[20] that resulted in thousands of murders of African Americans (women as well as men) began with the end of slavery, ran from its peak in the 1890s to just a few killings in the 1930s, and was mainly a southern phenomenon.[21] General terror surrounded the 1930 Marion lynching: "Most of the black people in town had stayed awake the whole night . . . They all thought they were going to die. Sadie had seen the bodies hanging." [22] The infamous lynching of Emmett Till occurred in the 1950s, and James Byrd was lynched in Jasper, Texas in 1998.

Among rival explanations for lynching in the years after Reconstruction are Democratic efforts to rout the Republican Party (in the 1860s and '70s targets were politically active black men, blacks who held office, and black Republican voters);[23] as a way of resolving "the crisis of communal solidarity" caused by Populists forging coalitions of class across racial lines; labor discipline; frustration with legal due process;[24] southern disconnection from modern civilization.[25] Underlying all of these was the determination to make subjugation of free blacks permanent through terror. Put simply, masterless blacks threatened the economic, political, and cultural status of whites.[26] The apt descriptive phrase is Eric Foner's: "counterrevolutionary terror."[27]

So lynching should be seen as one element in a broader pattern of intimidation and humiliation, insult and injury, meant to keep African Americans subordinate: burning churches and schoolhouses, killing livestock, victimizing white educators, and much more. Ida Wells-Barnett's lifework was to show that lynching was no aberration.[28]

[The New South's] white citizens are wedded to any method however revolting, any measure however extreme, for the subjugation of the young manhood of the race. They have cheated him out of the ballot, deprived him of civil rights or redress therefore in the civil courts, robbed him of the fruits of his labor, and are still murdering, burning and lynching him.[29]

In this repertoire of viciousness, lynching was a powerful demonstration of African Americans' defenselessness.[30] "Hopelessly outnumbered, outgunned, and out-fanaticized," rebellion (or just invoking civil rights) was "suicidal." It is also true that neighbors were the "terrain of struggle"[31] — African Americans absconded, destroyed property, and committed arson, murder, and sometimes armed resistance to lynching.[32] The Rosewood Massacre of 1923 was spurred by black Masons who fought back against a mob bent on lynching a black man accused of raping a white woman. Exceptions aside, lynching was an exhibition of black vulnerability. For any insult or offense — real or imagined or deliberately trumped up — was cause, and the arbitrariness and disproportion between offense (even supposing it was real) and response (since "punishment" is an inaccurate term) is precisely the point. It served the purpose of control through terror. Again, lynching is criminal violence but it is not ordinary homicide. It is not assassination. It is not a crime of passion. It is political violence, though its larger purpose was not always announced. Control through terror was the "surplus" meaning on top of the specific rationalization for each act.

Brundage's taxonomy is useful: "private lynching" in backwoods, off a road, or hung from railroad trestles; "terrorist mobs" ("moral regulators"); and lynching as a public spectacle, described as "the measure of legitimacy of lynching in the South."[33] Mutilation as well as killing, killing by a group not by an individual alone, the murderers' purported anonymity, and the presence of spectators define the classic lynching. "Scourged from his home, hunted through swamps, hung by midnight raiders, and openly murdered in the light of day," Ida Wells surveyed it all.[34] "I could not suppress the thought," James Baldwin wrote on seeing the red clay hills of Georgia from an airplane, "that this earth had acquired its color from the blood that had dripped down from these trees."[35]

## Intimate Violence

Lynching was intimate violence, and the contours of neighbors killing neighbors are set by the several senses of intimacy. First and literally, it was close-up and hands-on. Lynching was not mechanized mass killing but physically immediate. The settings — often village greens outside jails — were small scale and familiar.

It was intimate because it penetrated the psyche of blacks (and doubtless whites as well). "The threat of lynching is likely to be in the mind of a Negro child from the earliest days."[36] For Richard Wright, "the things that influenced my conduct as a Negro did not happen to me directly; I needed but to hear of them to feel their full effects in the deepest layers of my consciousness."[37] In a 1934 poem he imagines the scene of a lynching. Notice the domesticity of his description: the "design of white bones slumbering forgottenly upon a cushion of ashes . . . And upon the trampled grass were buttons, dead matches / butt-ends of cigars and cigarettes, peanut shells, a drained gin-flask . . . and the lingering smell of gasoline." From these homely material remnants Wright evokes the disorienting force of even an imagined lynching: "The dry bones stirred, rattled, lifted, melting themselves / into my bones." "And the sooty details of the scene rose, thrusting / themselves between the world and me."[38] No single phrase is more telling of lynching's effect on those who had no direct encounter with it: the sooty details of the scene "thrusting themselves between the world and me."

Finally, lynching was intimate because often enough victims and murderers knew one another and the reasons for targeting *this* black man or woman were personal. The core of intimate violence lies here, then, lynching by neighbors, people known to one another and living in close proximity, with a history of encounters, their connection a matter of local knowledge. Not always, of course; outsiders, strangers, were murdered too. But underscore neighbors. In lynching as in betrayal, political violence is privatized, personalized. "Rather than just signaling the politicization of private life . . . intimate violence also reflects exactly the opposite process: the privatization of politics."[39]

The specifics of choosing victims is understudied, and the personal face of lynching can be lost sight of in a literature focused on broad social and political themes. It makes no appearance, or only indirectly, in the Tuskegee Institute's classification of the causes of lynching. [40] The microhistory of personal encounters that targeted victims is necessarily one of inference. We have no exhaustive examination comparable to Jan Gross's of Jedwabne, which I discuss below. But memoirs and firsthand accounts make this aspect of intimate violence plain. Lynchers chose their targets. The violence was discretionary. Public lynching may have been ritualized, but there was no standard of selection. Murderous rage (or calculated cruelty) was directed at individuals who were rude, or threatening, or against whom the killers had a grievance. The immediate rationales were as varied as everyday encounters gone awry. Ida Wells-Barnett, the one-woman crusader, attempts a list: "hanged for stealing hogs," "lynched because they were saucy," "lynched for a quarrel." The title of one chapter of her tract *On Lynching* is "Lynched for Anything or Nothing."[41]

Insolence and disobedience as provocations are personal by definition (insolence as a legal offence has a long history in the South[42]). It was arbitrary whether any particular act or gesture, word or demeanor was accepted, ignored, or dealt with by some lesser violence. Murderers assumed the authority to define the offense—to read the mind of the offender and judge his attitude. There were a host of personal reasons for lynching neighbors besides insolence, of course. Black neighbors knew whites' secrets, and fear of revelation set a white neighbor against them.[43] They were scapegoats caught in the middle of violence surrounding a white neighbor's adultery, for example.[44] Add sharecropping to the catalogue: a system of close relations that provided a whole set of motives for murder[45] including conflict over wages, credit, and debt.[46] Landowners hustled and cheated tenants whose only recourse was to slip away at night, and when they tried, whites retaliated. (Black "snitches" who tipped off whites about a neighbor's intention to flee were also motivated by private grievances.)[47]

The official rationale for lynching, of course, was purported crime, above all rape or attempted rape of white women "The anxiety over interracial sex was so great it fostered the related notion that sex with white women was the real objective behind all black aspiration"[48] such that any form of challenge to caste was liable to be interpreted as "the opportunity to enjoy, equally with white men, the privilege of cohabiting with white women."[49] The participation of white women in lynching has been interpreted as an expression of "their desire to move freely without the threat of sexual violence." It was "a perverse demonstration of . . . [women's] desire for authority and autonomy" and an occasion for white women's solidarity across social class.[50] Through it all the concern with racial purity was in one writer's words, a "sincere self-delusion."[51]

Correspondent Martha Gelhorn found herself present at a lynching in 1936. She was driven there by one of the organizers who knew both the victim and the woman who'd been "screaming off her head bout it [rape] since this afternoon." Hyacinth was a nineteen-year-old black teenager; the accuser a middle-age woman: "Jees, you ought to see her. They could stick her out in a field and she'd scare the crows to death." A horrified Gelhorn realized that the woman was lying about being raped and that the killers knew it. In response to Gelhorn's outcry, her driver put it plainly: "She says he did it that's enough for us. You gotta take a white woman's word any time before you take a nigger's. Helluva place it'd be if you said white folks lied and niggers told the truth."[52] "Lies and lynching," as one scholar put it. [53]

Lynching was arbitrary but not random violence, in short. Random violence and terrorization of a population occurs during war with wholesale bombing or shootings in which killing is general and unpredictable.[54] Stilll, its unpredictability was psychologically similar to indiscriminate murder. Victims were chosen, often by those who knew them, for no other reason than that they lived nearby. Relatives and neighbors of the target were lynched as proxies if the "offender" was hidden or out of reach. We could call it guilt by association on the basis of proximity and race. That the standard rationales were smokescreens emerges in accounts of stories invented precisely because they would spark a lynching. There was no safe way for African Americans to avoid becoming a victim. Sheer arbitrariness makes innocence irrelevant and compliance impossible as a course of safety. Blacks were reduced to trying to read whites' minds. "Is he irritated?" "Is he looking for action?" "Is he in the mood for a friendly conversation?"[55] Blacks could develop a false sense of security until they were targeted: "But you know me!" After the fact, the sober recognition: "This was Marion, Indiana, where there was little room for foolish Black boys."[56]

Victims knew the people who mutilated and killed them. Murderers knew their victims. Locals knew who the killers were. James Cameron's survivor memoir begins this way: "It is impossible to explain the impending crisis of sudden and terrifying death at the hands of people I had grown to love and respect as friends and neighbors." Of the crowd at the lynching:

> I recognized a few faces from homes near my own neighborhood. I saw customers whose shoes I had shined many times. Boys and girls I had gone to school with were among the mob . . . neighbors whose lawns I had mowed and whose cars I had washed and polished.

He describes the mayor of Marion taking part. "Surely Edwards must have realized that I recognized him . . . Why didn't the mayor mask his face?"[57] "Dick Hinds had on a disguise," remarked an Alabama freedman who saw his son cut to pieces with a knife. "I knew him. Me and him was raised together."[58]

We can say as Kalyvas did of civil war that violence is "a reflection rather than a transgression of neighborliness—though a perverse one."[59] What is the significance of victim and murderer living in proximity as neighbors? It is the most flagrant denial of something everyone recognized even under this system of racist segregation: black and white neighbors were mostly "decent folk." Cameron's family lived in a shotgun house; the people who lived in front of their three little rooms were white: "wonderful landlords, neighbors, and friends."[60] Lynching effects the transformation of neighbors into "white savages" and black bodies barely recognizable as human.

### "Feast of Blood"[61]

Written descriptions and a library of photographs attest that lynching almost never ended with murder. W.E.B. Du Bois studied the lynching of Sam Hose and learned that "Hose had been 'barbecued' and his knuckles were for sale in a grocer's window."[62] Murder—brutal and face-to-face is one thing. Torture, mutilation, physical devastation is another. Here is an account of Mary Turner's lynching in the eighth month of pregnancy. "Her ankles were tied together and she was hung to the tree head down. Gasoline was taken from the cars and poured on her clothing which was then fired . . . a sharp instrument was taken and she was cut open in the middle, her stomach being entirely opened. Her unborn child fell from her womb, gave two cries, and was then crushed by the heel of a member of the mob. Her body was then riddled with bullets from high-powered rifles until it was no longer possible to recognize it as the body of a human being."[63]

That is crucial: "*It was no longer possible to recognize it as the body of a human being.*" Descriptions fasten on this point: "Tommy was a bloody mass and bore no resemblance to a human being."[64] Everywhere dehumanization is a concomitant of atrocity. It is a condition of atrocity. Dehumanization explains killing the same person repeatedly in what amounted to the mock hanging of dead bodies. "Shipp was dead long before the hysterical mob ever got him to the tree. Smith fared no better. Both were killed several times over."[65] An old man in the crowd at the Carunna lynching said, "You have done your duty now gentlemen. For God's sake let well enough alone. Go to your homes and leave the body where it is. There is nothing more for you to do here."[66] In fact, every excess and punishing mutilation of the dead in this "feast of blood" *was* necessary. This was well understood. "Local authorities routinely allowed bodies to remain on display . . . sometimes for days."[67] ("Here is a strange and bitter crop."[68]) Dismemberment, burning, reducing the body to a pulp was necessary because killers "need to escape the restraints of moral identity: of their sense of not being a person who would wound or kill"[69] and spectators need to escape the restraints of not being the sort of person who would acquiesce in the killing. Deformation made the person who murderers and spectators may have known unrecognizable.[70] It eradicated the physical traces of the individual and made connection with the victim, this victim, unthinkable. It obliterated the possibility of recognizing him as neighbor and "decent folk." He had to be beyond recognition and therefore beyond connection—not just in universal terms as human but also as "Cameron" who mowed their lawns. Mutilation had to be extreme because neighbor was a strong identity in its own way, and familiarity and proximity required erasure. There was more to do here. There was a lot to obliterate. Achieving unrecognizability was necessary before killers could "let well enough alone" and "go on home."

## What Anyone Would Do, Here?

"Death at the hands of persons unknown," the legal phrase had a particular meaning in the context of lynching. It was a lie, cover for authorities' refusal to prosecute. There was often no question of who the perpetrators were; they seized victims in full public view.

> We do it in midday; we do it after full, not to say formal, notice, and so thoroughly and generally is it acquiesced in that the murderers have discarded the formula of masks. They go into the town where everybody knows them, sometimes under the gaze of the governor, in the presence of the courts, in the presence of the sheriff and his deputies ... take the prisoner, take his life, often with fiendish glee and often with acts of cruelty and barbarism.[71]

A memo to the Governor after the Mary Tate lynching names the murderers: "It is my information that S. E. McGowan has publicly boasted of his part in the lynching."[72] *Detroit Free Press* reported on a lynching at Corunna in 1898: they "did not conceal the fact that they had helped Sullivan to his death, but on the other hand they declared themselves at every opportunity." (The Sheriff is reported to have said, "We tore the masks from many but would not remember their faces.")[73] Locals knew the "respectable citizens"—attorneys, planters, ministers, editors, town officials—who participated in the brutality, put up bail for arrested Klansmen, propagandized in support of lynching. If they did not take part themselves they "could not stop their sons from murdering their inoffensive neighbors in broad daylight."[74]

The 1897 lynching of Frazier Baker, appointed postmaster of Lake City, South Carolina, spurred the first federal intervention since Reconstruction. "Prosecutors faced a wall of silence and non-cooperation." As a result several of the accused were acquitted for lack of evidence, and a hung jury set the rest free.[75] Historians report case after case of survivors and witnesses being threatened if they revealed what they knew.[76] Ralph Ellison's "The Birthmark" tells the story of a brother and sister identifying the body of their brother who has been hideously deformed by lynching. The coroner insists that he was hit by a car. Clara objects: "They asked us last month to sign a piece of paper saying we wanted things like this to stop . . . Now look at my brother, he's laying there looking like something ain't even human. And these white folks talking 'bout a car hit him. He was lynched . . . I'm gonna tell everybody, HE WAS LYNCHED!" The patrolman: "Nigger, we tole you that boy was hit by a car, understand?" "He's telling you right, boy," the coroner adds, "He was hit by a car . . . And you better remember that, nigger. And your sister better remember that, too. 'Cause a car might hit you. Understand what I mean?"[77]

"At the hands of persons unknown" is a public secret, and the scale of the lie is significant. "Every word, if it does not have to be a direct lie, is nonetheless obliged not to contradict the general, common lie."[78] The public secret distorts neighbor relations beyond even the deeper distortion of intimate violence itself. It represses not just reporting but communication more generally. Among African American neighbors, sharing information is dangerous, and private conversation about this dominating fact of local life is inhibited. So besides being obstacles to justice, public secrets inflict specific injury on everyday life. By their nature public secrets "torque them with psychological conflict."[79] For both blacks and whites, silence is "what anyone would do, here," and anger is directed at anyone who speaks out about what is generally known but not acknowledged—who the murderers are, the complicity of officials, and the killers' connection to the victim. The public secret is, then, a form of intimidation that infects private as well as public encounters.

The public secret has political meaning too, of course. It creates the impression that lynching is "what anyone would do, here." It underscores the didactic message that everyone condoned the killing. From this standpoint, Klu Klux Klan hoods were less about masking identity than indicating the collective nature of the act. This show of anonymity, like the public secret, communicates solidarity. The extended meaning of "death at the hands of persons unknown," in short, was that "no persons had committed a crime because the lynching had been an expression of the community's will."[80] After one 1916 lynching in Abbeville, South Carolina, the killers published a letter in the *Scimitar*:

We are ALL responsible for the conditions that caused Crawford's death ... There were several hundred who participated in this lynching, and nearly ALL the others were well-wishers, therefore to pick out a few to satisfy a newly imported mawkish sentiment is pitiful and cowardly.... so let's not ask only eight to shoulder the whole burden ... Answer a mawkish sentiment generated by hypocrisy and craven fear with the ringing verdict, Not guilty.[81]

By the 1930s lynching was in "irreversible decline." Local activists and national organizations—the NAACP, the Association of Southern Women for the Prevention of Lynching, and the Commission on Interracial Cooperation—publicized lynching nationally, circulated photographs in the media, prodded officials to uphold the law, and spurred investigations.[82] The images of lynched bodies were imbued with a narrative focused "not on black victimhood but on the savagery of white mobs, mobs that stood as abominations to American democratic ideals."[83] And ongoing support for lynching focused on this growing national attention; the frame of discussion switched from race to local pride and state sovereignty. Resentment at northern intrusion was fierce enough to be called "oppression psychosis."[84] Isolated lynching continued, notably murders of strangers, "outside agitators." Emmett Till, the fourteen-year-old visitor from Chicago, was lynched in 1954. By then, the public secret was not kept. Killers were not immune to prosecution. They were acquitted, but the town did not rally around Bryant and Milam. The two became outcasts, ostracized by the white community. As one interviewee explained, "Men who are capable of murder do not make very lovely neighbors. Even contributors to the ... defense fund wanted those killers to get out of the county."[85] In making this half-turn, people cast them out, invoking the modest measure of neighbors as "decent folk."

Before this turn, after which lynching was no longer presented as "what anyone would do, here," it could seem as if everyone did. How might we think about the men and women who participated in the "feast of blood," and the fact that victim and killers were often neighbors?

## "A Crowd of Decent Folk"

In Alan Tate's 1911 poem "The Swimmers," we hear the voice of a boy watching the corpse of a lynched man drift down the river:

My breath crackled the dead air like a shotgun
As, sheriff and the stranger disappearing,

The faceless head lay still. I could not run
Or walk, but stood. Alone in the public clearing
This private thing was owned by all the town,
Though never claimed by us within my hearing.[86]

"*This private thing was owned by all the town*" ... it could seem so. [87] Not all townspeople attended lynchings; some evaded, avoided, shirked, refused to participate.[88] But we know little about whites who shunned them yet kept the public secret: "never claimed by us within my hearing."

It is useful to try to differentiate the experience and state of mind of neighbors who kill from those who attend the lynching. The term "mob" is applied as a matter of course, but evoking hysteria and spontaneous unorganized violence is misleading insofar as the classic public lynching required planning, staging, and rallying spectators. In any case, "mob" makes sense applied to the group who kidnapped, mutilated, hung, and burned,[89] and to those on the periphery who took a turn kicking the body ("the weaker ones had to be content with spitting and throwing things at me."[90]) Distributing pieces of noose, clothing, and body parts among spectators was common,[91] and collectors might be included in the "mob."

Spectators who did not take an active part are participants of a sort as well. They were not murderers, and we can suppose that many considered their role benign.[92] Should we take attendance as condoning the violence; were they all "well-wishers"? This view is encouraged by descriptions of lynching as unexceptional popular entertainment.[93] "Lynching was an undeniable part of daily life, as distinctly American as baseball games and church suppers. Men brought their wives and children along to the events, posed for commemorative photographs, and purchased souvenirs of the occasion as if they had been at a company picnic."[94] Killers were intent on making this point: lynching was "what anyone would do, here," and what everyone did.

Lynching was not so common that it can be characterized as unexceptional entertainment, however, and other reports paint a quite different tonal picture in which spectators are struck silent. As Gelhorn describes the scene: "The crowd stood still; you could hear the mosquitos whining." Hyacinth begged for mercy and "the crowd had trembled now, stirred by his voice." After the hanging, "there had been a noise a sudden guttural sound as of people breathing a deep breath."[95] Silence is the center of Auden's poem, *The Shield of Achilles*:

A crowd of ordinary decent folk
Watched from without and neither moved nor spoke

As three pale figures were led forth and bound
to three posts driven upright in the ground.[96]

"A crowd of decent folk." The assumption that people attending lynchings were "witnesses" in the strong sense of conferring spiritual or social
significance on the event, testifying by their presence[97] is a standard inference. But attributing the intention to support lynching from attendance
and attributing unconflicted attitudes to spectators almost certainly
claims too much. Some people were accidental bystanders. Some were
frightened by the lawlessness and repulsed by the sight and sound. One
white man confessed to being afraid and "desperate to get out of town
before it started . . . he went fishing with a friend at Deer Creek, just south
of town." But the friend eventually persuaded Blaine to go back to have
a look.[98] Spectators were seen by all the town too, recognized by one another. Gelhorn reports the men calling to each other after Hyacinth's
murder: "So long, Jake," "See you t'morrow Sam," "Just saying goodnight
to each other and going home."[99] Moral restraints can be weakened by
neighbors aggressively enforcing their view of "what anyone would do,,
here." Lynching was not just an individual moral process; it was a social
and political project.[100]

In his 1901 essay, "The United States of Lyncherdom," Mark Twain attributed the acquiescence of a "crowd of decent folk" to "man's common-
est weakness, his aversion to being unpleasantly conspicuous, pointed at,
shunned." Its other name is "Moral Cowardice." "They come only because they are afraid to stay at home, lest it be noticed and offensively
commented upon." He is emphatic about the dynamic: "Each man is
afraid of his neighbor's disapproval." People at lynchings do not enjoy the
spectacle:

> It cannot be true: all experience is against it. The people in the South
> are made like the people in the North—the vast majority of whom are
> right-hearted and compassionate, and would be cruelly pained by such
> a spectacle—and would attend it and let on to be pleased with it, if the
> public approval seemed to require it. We are made like that, and we
> cannot help it.

Twain underscored his point by refusing to publish the essay: "I shouldn't
have even half a friend left down there, after it issued from the press."[101]

Spectatorship without more doesn't mean the "crowd of decent folk"
applauded or condoned the killing, but it is acquiescence. That said, failure to act or to speak out or to turn away where atrocity is happening

before one's eyes by and to people known is a particular state that the term "passivity" does not capture. Passivity refers to external inaction and doesn't illuminate state of mind. Acquiescence requires a great deal of internal activity. It takes emotional and psychic energy to repress the ethics of everyday life. Twain's insistence—"It is thought, as I have said, that a lynching crowd enjoys a lynching. It certainly is not true; it is impossible of belief"—points to what must be a painful, agitated inner state. People in attendance at a lynching, or who pass by the fresh site marked by rope and blood, must overcome resistance from the bit of their identity that is, apart from this moment, a regular neighbor. It requires what one psychiatrist has called "doubling," to proceed from witnessing or perpetrating atrocity to carrying on in mundane fashion the rest of the day—where "carrying on" includes harboring the public secret and at the same time continuing ordinary give and take with neighbors.[102] Witnessing atrocity is compatible with returning home to mundane back and forth with both black and white neighbors. Even killing is. We are fully capable of compartmentalizing the brutality. Lynching did not eradicate quotidian encounters at home; neighbors could revert to reciprocity among "decent folk," white and black.

White / black relations during (and long after) the period of lynching were not guided by the regulative ideal of the democracy of everyday life. It would claim too much to say the democratic ethos was in any way reliable. White supremacy, black codes, pervasive segregation in public places were its civic and legal antithesis. Still, the notion of good neighbor was not absent, including recognition of "decent folk" and day-to-day reciprocity. It was present within racial communities. And it made appearances across racial lines. Even racism and a caste system are compatible with particular neighbors regarding one another as "decent folk" for the purposes of daily give and take. This feature of the phenomenology of neighbors emerges strikingly when spectators turn protectors.

## Rescuers

Invoking the abolitionists, Mark Twain spoke of the efficacy of "a brave man in each affected community to encourage, support, and bring to light the deep disapproval of lynching hidden in the secret places of its heart—for it is there, beyond question." But he admits that there are not enough morally brave men in stock, and he proposes recalling Christian missionaries from China to cow and scatter southern lynch mobs; they have the necessary martyr personality.[103]

In fact, some neighbors were protectors and rescuers. Here too we have memoirs and historical accounts, but no comprehensive record of whites and blacks who hid the hunted, tended injuries, helped men and women escape. James Cameron's survivor narrative is a rare source. He attributed the interruption of his lynching, which came after he was already strung up in a tree, to a "miraculous intervention," the voice of the Virgin Mary, saying, "Take this boy back. He had nothing to do with raping or killing . . . No mortal could have commanded such obedience and submission from the angry ten to fifteen thousand white supremacists."[104] Witnesses offered alternative accounts. Some attributed it to the uncle of the alleged rape victim declaring himself "satisfied" with the two lynchings of Shipp and Smith earlier in the day; others recall several of Cameron's white schoolmates persuading the crowd to stop; still others pointed to a police captain's intervention.

As always there were exceptions, then, people who did not permit themselves a failure of nerve and risked speaking out, or refused to keep the public secret and testified in court.[105] Local sheriffs sometimes faced down mobs storming the jail and protected prisoners. In the lynching of Claude Neal in 1934, the sheriff had moved Neal from jail to jail to try to save him from gathering crowds. Proof of innocence did not matter though: after acquittal his "freedom lasted only a few minutes. A gang of white boys waylaid the black boy as he was walking home from the courthouse, tied his feet to the back of a car, and drove all the way from Clarksdale to Marks with the black boy's crushed, bloody head bouncing along the road bed."[106]

Even in a caste system, some neighbors signaled "I know you" and "I will do no harm." This signal is not a perfect equivalent of live and let live, which entails recognition of mutual vulnerability. There was no symmetry here. But acknowledging neighbor relations may be the prelude to rescue. During the Florida massacre in 1923 that killed six blacks, burned the entire black section of Rosewood to the ground, and sent people running for refuge into the swamps, white neighbors took in women and children to protect them from the gunfire, hid them, and got them onto trains to safety. Moving firsthand accounts describe the interruption of viciousness as men and women recover their own identity as a neighbor and recognize black neighbors as "decent folk." A memory, a familiar gesture in the present, the appearance of a person they know from home—something mundane returns me to the person I am there where I live. A Klansman at the Marion lynching approached a thirteen-year-old black girl walking toward the jail, put her in his car, and removed her from the scene:

He told me they were bringing people out of the jail and was going to lynch them. And he says, you got no business down here. Now you get over here out of the street lights, out of the car lights, and when I hit my headlights that third time, you'll know it's me, and you run and get in the car, and I'm gonna take your butt home. Now that was his exact words.[107]

Harper Lee's *To Kill a Mockingbird* dramatizes intimate violence interrupted by the moral force of reclaiming identity as a neighbor, and I return to this scene. Atticus Finch sits outside the jail guarding the prisoner Tom Robinson who is falsely accused of raping a white woman. Jem and Scout, the Finch children, recognize the neighbors who drive up and threaten to storm the Maycomb jail. The crowd disperses when Scout—whom I cast as the model of the emergence of the democracy of everyday life in the segregated south—engages the armed men in conversation. "I go to school with Walter . . . We brought him home for dinner one time. . . . Tell him hi for me."[108] The dynamic of disarming is clear: bringing men with a grievance and opportunity for atrocity back to their everyday selves.

Mutual aid among black neighbors is particularly hard to document or quantify. We have one account of a family saved from a mob by Lewis Barns who hid them under a wagonload of hay and corn.[109] Neighbors hid fugitives, covered their tracks, and provided information about who was hunting them. We know that neighbors were crucial to any rescue.[110] Indeed, for blacks, neighbors predominated in every type of social relation,[111] for social connection and geographic proximity were bound together. From slave times through emancipation and the era of lynching, African Americans constructed neighborhoods, mapping their own lay of the land on and between the plantations where they lived and worked. Their bonds were not some general racial or communal solidarity but rather connections among neighbors. The domain open to African Americans was severely restricted, of course, and mobility was limited: Black Codes, laws against vagrancy, chains of debt, landlords' patrols. The decisive response by African Americans, the physical reaction, was exodus to the North, whose scale "made race a national issue."[112] For those who did not leave, neighbors were their support and protection in struggles with debt and labor disputes, capricious and vicious treatment.

Rescue aside, recognition as "decent folk" was sustaining. Under extreme conditions, the appearance of the ordinary is significant—testimonies to this fact are legion. Cameron's memoir makes much of the white neighbors who assisted his mother during his time in jail and near-lynching. "Had it not been for their loving goodness and concern, no one knows what would have happened to us. Their sympathy and words of encouragement gave my mother strength to carry on."[113]

Official apologies for lynching came, as they had in the case of Japanese internment, much later.[114] A 2005 Congressional resolution "expresses the deepest sympathies and most solemn regrets of the Senate to the descendants of victims of lynching, the ancestors of whom were deprived of life, human dignity, and the constitutional protection accorded all citizens of the United States."[115] The national apology for the Senate's failure to heed Ida Wells-Barnett's plea to pass federal antilynching legislation was warranted. But in official apology the specific horror of intimate violence and neighbors killing neighbors is lost to view. Lost, too, is the specific self-understanding and moral temper of neighbors who rescue, and I reflect on this shortly.

## Jan Gross's *Neighbors*

Perhaps the most analyzed instance of murderous neighbors is the massacre of an entire Jewish population of the Polish town Jedwabne. The study confirms the common outlines of atrocity among neighbors. Occurring in the context of war, occupation, and Nazi control, the scene of slaughter is different from continuous, small-scale lynchings throughout the American South. The "bloodlands" of Eastern Europe before and during World War II has no counterpart in the United States,[116] though lynching was a "feast of blood." These atrocities share defining features, nonetheless. Victims and killers are locals and civilians, not armed combatants. The perpetrators are numerous enough and ordinary enough that murder appears to be "what anyone would do, here." And officials condoned the horror. The killing was done close up, by primitive means, by neighbors with their own hands. Gross's study underscores core themes of lynching as intimate violence, including the appearance of neighbors who rescue.

*Neighbors* documents the day in July 1941 when half of the population of a small Polish town murdered the other half—1,600 Jewish men, women, and children. Gross reports the names of the dead and details the massacre: stoning to death with bricks, knifing, plucking out eyes and cutting tongues, drowning, burying alive. Finally, in order to make sure they had murdered everyone in the time frame permitted by recently arrived German authorities ("Was eight hours not enough for you to do with the

Jews as you please?") neighbors rounded up those remaining, gathered them in a barn, doused them with kerosene, and burned them alive. As others have observes, "Killing turned out to be supremely easy, it does not entail any uncommon expenditure."[117]

Only a handful of Jews survived. They affirmed in interviews the same belief in the dependability of neighborliness often expressed by victims of lynching: the sheer surprise of it. Jedwabne Jews had believed the Poles to be good neighbors: "Here there were no such big differences in opinion or whatever, because they were in this little town, on good terms with the Poles. Depending on each other. Everybody was on a first-name basis, Janek, Icek . . ."[118] Survivors tell a story of cooperation between a Catholic butcher and his Jewish neighbor to share a freezer; a woman who grew up playing and attending school with the seven children of her Jewish neighbor in the old market square.[119] Anti-Semitism was hardly absent, but was attributed to "local hooligans," not neighbors.[120] Yet, as soon as the first Germans arrived in Jedwabne, the local authorities asked, "Is it permitted to kill the Jews?" The unexpectedness of violence at the hands of neighbors, the terrible puzzle of it, is a *cri de coeur* repeated in other situations—the Rosewood massacre of African Americans in Florida elicited this from a survivor: "We ain't had no problems back there, not with the white folks, not with no one. Ain't had a bit of problems. I don't understand why them peoples did us like that."[121]

This was not the organized Nazi killing machine, but it was the way a large percentage of Jews in the region were eliminated. "Not anonymous men in uniform, cogs in a war machine, agents carrying out orders, but their own neighbors, who chose to kill."[122] The atrocities in Jedwabne were the result of decisions made by the Polish residents, organized by the town mayor, Marian Karolak, and with the participation of the entire town council. Gross's purpose in *Neighbors* is to show that histories of the period are mistaken in attributing the Jedwabne murders and many others to the German occupiers alone with only logistical help from local townspeople.[123] His "microhistorical perspective" "restores agency to individuals who are usually portrayed just as cogs of bureaucratic machinery or inert particles of the human mass."[124] No one was forced to participate, yet participation was high. "The few Jews who survived the burning or who heard about it from eyewitnesses accuse their neighbors and fellow townspeople from Jedwabne and from other nearby villages, of the crime."[125] Several days after the massacre Leon Dziedzic was ordered by the Germans to gather up the remains: "We used rakes to push the piles of corpses into a great ditch dug along the north wall of the barn. I recognized people I knew."[126] "There were things people could have done at the time and refrained from doing; and there were things they did not have to do but nevertheless did."[127] "Mass murder" denotes the number of dead but also the number of perpetrators; it is similar to lynching in creating the impression—here the documented reality—that killing was what "anyone would do, here."

There were here, as there are in hellish situations, brave exceptions. The massacre was planned, and some Jews were warned in advance by Polish neighbors. The shtetlach was surrounded by farms and despite risk to their families and property, some peasants hid Jews in heaps of manure, haystacks, swamps, forests, in the mortuary of a cemetery. Some Jews bought help with possessions or money. Sometimes rescuers asked for nothing. No one could have survived without assistance. In testimonials of rescue and escape (including the famous story of the Bielski brothers), relations forged with neighbors were key:

> A comparison between what happened in the Polish kresy and what happened in other European countries under German control makes it very clear that the attitude of the host populations to the Jews was one of the main determinants of the Jews' fate. This is true of most genocidal events.[128]

This "infinitely small minority" of rescuers had to oppose both the Germans and their Polish neighbors, and Poles who helped save the pitifully few who escaped were reluctant to testify later under their own names.[129] Still today, they remain hesitant to reveal what they had done.[130] This was self-protection, not modesty. Stigma continues to attach to protectors, who were ostracized and despised. Their lifesaving acts appear not to be viewed by their Christian neighbors as righteous but rather as betrayal. So this similarity to lynching as well: rescuers did not announce themselves; they did not act overtly; they did not give away the public secret of who murdered; they knew that their acts of protection and rescue would be seen by white neighbors as betrayal.

There were rescuers even in Jedwabne, then, recognized by the Yad Vashem authority as the "Righteous Among Nations." "Righteous" does not suffice to capture the particulars of rescue. By itself it does not single out rescuing neighbors from strangers, though that is a mark of Jedwabne and of lynching in America. Indeed, acts of protection and rescue, I argue, invoke neighborliness so often and explicitly that it needs explaining. It is as if neighbor is a stand-in for decency and humanity. In America, where good neighbor is shaped by the democracy of everyday life, both falling off from it and enacting it has a specific, added resonance.

## Rescue

Rescue, like atrocities themselves, seems to elude understanding: why do some people overcome intimidation and elementary self-protective impulses to save others? Here I move tentatively and speculatively beyond lynching to consider rescue broadly. I keep the focus on aid and protection in the context of extreme political violence, not the rescue of a skater falling through thin ice or lifesaving assistance during disasters (my subject in the next chapter), and I keep the focus on protection afforded by men and women individually, not organized collective action. Rescuers insist that they are doing "what anyone would do, here." Historical accounts, interviews, and memoirs converge on this point: they represent their extraordinary actions as ordinary. It is a refrain in Miep Gies's autobiography, *Anne Frank Remembered: The Story of the Woman Who Helped to Hide the Frank Family*. In what would become the best-known case of rescue, Otto Frank had asked, "Miep, are you willing to take on the responsibility of taking care of us while we are in hiding?" "Of course," she answered.[131] Representation of rescue as "what anyone would do, here," resonates with being a good neighbor.[132] In fact, whether they offer protection to neighbors or to perfect strangers, rescuers' often invoke neighborliness in recounting their experience. How does the resonance of ordinary neighborliness contribute to understanding altruistic acts that from outside seem extraordinary?

A standard starting place in thinking about rescuers is to identify the moral principles that guide their action. Philosophical discussions set out the normative grounds, the "ought," of why we should save. Philosophers or not, we typically follow this line of thought and explain a rescuer's action in terms of her commitment to human rights or human dignity, the sanctity of each life or the abomination of deliberate cruelty. Even if they are articulated and consciously adhered to, however, general moral principles by themselves are only one facet in making sense of rescue. Principles are not self-enforcing, after all. And often enough, general principles are neither present in the moment nor figure centrally in rescuers' reflections after the fact.[133]

Kristen Monroe's study provides another window onto people who aid, protect, harbor, and save. The heart of their altruism, she finds, is not principle but a certain "perspective" on the world: rescuers describe feeling connected to all men and women. The scope is universal. Grounded in religion or (somewhat surprisingly) more often absent appeal to religious belief at all, rescuers experience "love your neighbor as yourself" as imperative, where neighbor is everyone.[134] Closely related is Jonathan Glover's argument in *Humanity* that men and women who resist atrocity are able to call up the basic "human responses" of sympathy and respect.[135] They say of the people they saved, simply: "they were human beings" who needed my help.

The intensity with which people experience the moral "ought" is variable, and a necessary complement to principle, perspective, and sympathy is the internal dynamic that gives the imperative force and compels action. It consists, we know, of the felt necessity of acting in a way that corresponds to one's values. Better put, the felt imperative to act in a way that is consistent with one's sense of self,[136] with who we are, in our own minds. Rescuers would not be at peace with themselves, they would be wracked by inner conflict, if they did not try to save. Integrity is a name for this. It points to the energy, the internal force or spur that brings moral principle or the perspective of common humanity or sympathy to active life in the world.[137] "Only certain options are available to us because of who we are, or more precisely, who we perceive ourselves to be."[138] "Well, I never thought about it."[139] "I had no choice." Inaction was morally and psychologically unavailable.

Moreover, to rescuers' minds, what they did was not special. Moral philosophers, and the rest of us too, draw a line between ordinary and supererogatory obligations but in the moral psychology of rescuers the line between ordinary action and extraordinary altruism appears to be erased. More than that, *ordinary* is underscored. "I don't think that I did anything that special. I think what I did is what everybody normally should be doing."[140] Here is where good neighbor enters. Invoking neighborliness, as rescuers do often and spontaneously, is a way of emphasizing that to their minds what they did was "what anyone would do, here." "The idea of helping neighbors" was very much a part of his outlook, Monroe reports of one of her subjects.[141] We should take this recurrent claim seriously.[142] Rescuers know, of course, that most neighbors did not save Polish Jews and that neighbors, black and white, rescued targets of lynching only rarely. But good neighbors would, and that is part of the rescue narrative. The self-understanding of people who save under conditions of political violence may not refer to good neighbor explicitly in every instance, that would claim too much, but often enough that we discern an integral connection.

From our standpoint outside, rescuing is not neighborly reciprocity, not at all. It appears instead as one-sided, the unconditional height of good works, and plainly not what "anyone would do, here." We might even think that associating rescue with neighborliness diminishes the act by failing to appreciate the rare virtue of those few who save. But phenomenologically, from inside, the continuum with ordinary neighborly reciprocity seems obvious. It is a common element of rescuers' self-representation and self-understanding. What is this impulse to invoke neighborliness?

In ways I have demonstrated, neighbors "holding our lives in their hands" in the context of intimate violence is distinct from situations in which strangers or officials are positioned to make life and death decisions. Neighbors killing neighbors represents a total breakdown of life as normal, in that most important and vulnerable place, home. The radical rupture in everyday life where we live has specific meaning and impact. It is the ultimate transgression. In the American shame of lynching by neighbors, rescue by neighbors is its direct negation. True, from the perspective of moral philosophy and of many rescuers, every effort to save is absolute and universally required—neighbor or stranger. And general moral terms like decency and humanity do describe rescue. But universal terms do not do the same work as "neighbor." Good neighbor is more than a homely synonym for moral decency. Neighbor is another layer of moral identity and has specific resonance activated in atrocity-producing situations. Something of the moral temper of direct, immediate resistance to the radical rupture of life at home seems to play a part in these situations. So much so that it transfers from rescuing actual neighbors to saving per se.

"Neighbor" entails "canonical expectations about what constitutes normal behavior,"[143] and casting rescue in these terms evokes and reasserts the normal. Rescuers will the restoration of the inestimably valuable everyday. Declaring saving as "what anyone would do, here" is a way of reclaiming the ordinary. It does this very concretely. "Neighbor" allies rescue with the safety of home, the horror of being pursued and stripped of home, where getting people to a safe place is the whole objective. It recalls the everyday setting, the face-to-face character of encounters, the nod of recognition, the disposition to view neighbors as "decent folk" and to live and let live. Again, "the ethics of preventing atrocities are an extension of the ethics of everyday life,"[144] and in America that ethic takes the form of the democracy of everyday life. We can infer from rescuers' own language that the threatening environment did not erase identification as a good neighbor; their moral responses were not weakened or overwhelmed. And it must be solace for rescuers themselves to see their own acts in terms of neighborly reciprocity, and to imagine that their neighbors would do the same. "Of course" Otto Frank would care for Miep Gies in hiding.

The valence of good neighbor works in two directions. It translates extraordinary rescue into what anyone would do, evoking quotidian life at home. It also makes ordinary encounters among neighbors extraordinary, its own vital form of assistance. I've made this point before: the affective power of ordinary give and take under extraordinary conditions. Neighborliness as we experience it day to day can't protect or save in times of atrocity and mistrust. Yet gestures of recognition and solicitude, however modest, become precious. They are noticed, keenly. Their impact is indelible. Never more so than in circumstances where every other vestige of ordinary relations is erased, as in this fictional recreation of an encounter between a Jewish *Sonderkommando* and the wife of the death camp commandant:

> One morning I am in the lane passing the Kommandant's garden, and I see Frau Doll setting off for school with her daughters. She looks in my direction and she says something quite extraordinary to me. And I recoil from it as if I have smoke in my eyes. Five minutes later, standing bent behind the main guardroom, I am able to shed tears for the first time since Chelmno. "Guten Tag," she says.[145]

The moral tenor of the neighborly gesture is captured perfectly in Vasily Grossman's "The Old Teacher," quoted earlier:

> Standing by windows, gates and doors, the doctor's former patients watched his last journey. No-one, of course, wept, took their hat off or came out to say farewell. No-one during this terrible time was moved by blood, suffering and death; what surprised and shook people was kindness and love.[146]

The narrator in Camus' *The Plague* made the point: we neighbors are "just the same as ever": this is our strength and innocence.[147] Or neighbors act *as if* they were "just the same as ever." The homeliness of encounters resonant of neighbors around home can "act as a catalyst for the wild, vagrant hope—especially vulnerable in mean-spirited times—that things need not be as they are."[148]

"That things need not be as they are"—precisely. Lynching declined by the 1930s. The emergence of the democracy of everyday life as a regular characterization of encounters between blacks and whites would come, where it did come, much later. We see the comparative solidity of this democratic ethos in examples like Crown Heights where under mistrust-creating conditions neighbors are disposed to see one another as "decent folk," engage in reciprocity, speak out, and live and let live. The American ideal of good neighbor is coherent and reliably widespread in practice. It does not take root everywhere. It can go into eclipse. But it is not entirely absent from neighbor relations and is a resource during the worst moral calamities. It is at work during natural disasters as well. Neighbors are "first responders" in the aftermath of floods and earthquakes. What neighbors do—and what *only* they can do—is the final chapter of "Holding Our Lives in Their Hands."

# 9

# Disasters

This ghastly examination of personal and political betrayal and killing reminds us of the comparatively benign parameters of neighbors good and bad in America today. Absent mistrust-creating, atrocity-producing conditions, we are not tempted to murderousness or betrayal. We are not pressed to "forge [our] fate daily at the price of [our] lives."[1] Nor are we ordinarily tasked with rescue, or with offering protection. Settler and immigrant odysseys evoke historical moments when neighbors were all the resources we had for assistance, and reciprocity was necessary for getting by. We are no longer dependent on an "economy of mutual favors." Government programs and voluntary associations provide necessary services and social safety nets, or should, and the good turns neighbors perform for one another do not amount to permanent welfare. There are exceptions, too many of them, when poverty gives rise to an ongoing state of mutual dependency, as I showed in Chapter 3, "Reciprocity among 'Decent Folk.'" But for the most part neighborly assistance is not a necessity of life, and our expectations of "what anyone would do, here" are geared to the quotidian. We don't hold one another's lives in our hands.

In emergency situations and in natural disasters, we do. In cases of accident, injury, illness, and fire only family or neighbors can render effective help on the spot and possibly avert the worst. Neighbors are a lifeline in the event of a heart attack, burglary, or domestic violence, which we may be able to interrupt by a knock on the door or call to the police. Availability is what matters in the moment: proximity, presence, and speed in applying CPR or dialing 911.

Disasters are a different matter. They are large-scale catastrophic events, sudden and sometimes unexpected, unstopped if not unstoppable, in which the nature and scope of danger and destruction are unpredictable and, for the victims at least, unimaginable.[2] Availability and speed are key to survival as they are with accidents and fires. Similar, too, is the fact that our personal responses are largely untutored and unplanned. In institutional contexts, drills and protocols come into play, but once again we neighbors are on our own. "How you act results in life or death, for yourself or others, as in everyday life only more so."[3] In disasters, however, calling for help or intervening on our own—critical as it may be—is not the whole story. In addition, our response is a matter of improvised cooperation. Floods, earthquakes, major storms, heat waves, and unnatural catastrophes (nuclear accidents, chemical contamination that pollutes and befouls, electrical outages, explosions) propel neighbors out of their homes, into one another's company, and into action. There are innumerable examples of neighbors taking matters into their own hands to protect, rescue, sustain, salvage—often in advance of local officials and always as a necessary supplement to both government efforts and organized volunteers. Neither officials nor voluntary associations can be on the scene fast enough or know the terrain well enough to save someone elderly trapped in a back room by high water or to rescue a family's dog. Neighbors have local knowledge. They come up with responses that are imaginative in their practicality—using whatever is at hand and digging into their emotional resources. Thousands survived Hurricane Katrina and its aftermath because of the conduct of neighbors. "First responders" are not the first.

Exhibitions of altruism on the part of ordinary people—strangers as well as neighbors—are the positive face of every disaster. The field of "disaster studies" examines this phenomenon. Solicitude and care in emergencies, like rescue in the face of political atrocity, are liable to be reduced (or elevated) to universal human decency or altruistic good works, and this is not wrong. Strangers rescue too, of course. Immediately after the thirty minutes or so it took for the twin towers of the World Trade Center to collapse on September 11, a reversal occurred and "people began moving toward the disaster rather than away from it."[4] By afternoon, thousands of volunteers, along with firefighters and police, were "attacking the debris by hand, forming bucket brigades, and climbing over the smoking pile that in some places rose fifty feet above the street."[5] During Hurricane Sandy in New York City, where I lived at the time and was part of the exodus from lower Manhattan, encounters with strangers were transformed. People on the street and in the subway showed interest in one another and a compulsion to talk about what was happening. For those few days, detachment was rare and ordinary anxieties and preoccupations dissipated in the atmosphere of shared disaster.

Something is lost, however, if assistance by neighbors in the domain of home is assimilated to the acts of strangers, and if the democracy of everyday life operating in emergency situations is lost to view. Here too, the experience of good neighbors is its own story, a complement to the larger picture. And once again, a touchstone case gives us a necessary angle on the picture. From accounts of Hurricane Katrina I draw a chronology of what neighbors do and by detailing these steps provide an understanding of their special importance. The significance of neighbors' presence is practical, of course, but also moral. Their actions are made possible in part by good neighbor as a facet of moral identity and by past experience with encounters shaped by the democracy of everyday life. Disasters bring to bear neighbors' local knowledge, their experience of reciprocity among "decent folk," of spontaneous rallying and improvised collective action. Disasters call on the sort of self-governing that is an element of neighbors' interactions under ordinary circumstances. We are eager to hear these stories about neighbors rescuing and aiding in emergencies because they confirm our sense of good neighbor as an element of personal identity and conception of America as "good neighbor nation."

## Katrina

The flooding of New Orleans after the breach of the levees and of other cities and towns of the Gulf Coast in August 2005 was a large-scale disaster, not a small, local emergency. Katrina "had an impact zone of approximately 90,000 square miles across Louisiana, Mississippi, and other states, more than a million displaced victims, over 1,300 deaths, and gave rise to economic costs exceeding $80 billion."[6] Mandatory evacuation of New Orleans came too late and without adequate planning.[7] Eighty percent of the city was under water. Vital services were down. People were drowning or perilously stranded, without power, food, water, phones, medication, physical security. Before the influx of organized volunteers, and before city hall and state and federal agencies acted, neighbors did. They rescued people who lived nearby from rooftops, saved pets, took in the homeless. They attempted to get medical care and provided what care they could themselves. Katrina "put tremendous pressure on improvisation."[8]

Spontaneous aid and rescue stand out here just because government agencies failed, and prevention, planning, evacuation, and relief went so wrong. Social scientists have analyzed this secondary, political catastrophe. When survivors and onlookers speak of "Katrina" they are referring to the storm as a personified agent, of course, but not just that. Too much hubris, error, indifference, political infighting, and malfeasance were apparent to attribute the disaster to the hurricane alone. Victims, certainly, do not forget officials who disavow responsibility, transfer blame, offer no apology, shield themselves with lawyers—political decisions before and responses afterwards are made by men and women, not brute nature.[9]

In fact, during Katrina authorities were often seen as an obstruction; they abandoned, criminalized, and effectively imprisoned residents of New Orleans. Police and military "dumped us in the middle of nowhere. It was never about evacuation. It was about putting everybody in one spot so they can keep an eye on him or her."[10] They turned "this massive encampment of suffering people at the intersection of Causeway and Interstate 10 . . . almost all people of color, except for the National Guard and police . . . [with] people sitting outside without food and water in near 100-degree heat just waiting for buses" into hell.[11] As one survivor put it:

> Never in my life had it been clearer to me that the people in charge didn't have a clue what they were doing. And that realization gave me and my fellow citizens freedom. Once we got over the horror of watching President Bush ignore us while our Governor and Mayor locked themselves in a power struggle at our expense, we began to take care of business in the most efficient and cooperative way.[12]

Disasters are said to be the great equalizer, but demographics are part of the autopsy of disaster. Politics and social environment are risk factors in every catastrophe, and the victims "are primarily social outcasts—the elderly, the poor, and the isolated . . . invisible people."[13] Where "equality of survival" *is* an actual democratic commitment, government agencies prepare well, and they prepare all of us: inscribing procedures and assigned roles, specific obligations, and recurrent practice in the most self-conscious way so that the "force" of habit is activated in emergency. Elaine Scarry's model of this "special repertoire" is the Swiss Shelter System designed to save the population in the event of nuclear war.[14] During and after Katrina nothing like the principle of "equality of survival" prevailed—the best evidence being lack of evacuation planning.[15] ("The city wasn't offering no free way out. I mean you had to pay for a bus ride, a plane ride, a train.")[16] The equalizer in the disaster was the behavior of neighbors alert to their mutual vulnerability.[17] Assistance by neighbors stands out against the patent unfairness not of the natural event per se, which is always arbitrary, but authorities' effective abandonment of the worst off.

Neighbors' actions during and after Katrina stand out too against the "elite panic" that predicted widespread hysteria and violent "herd reactions." Authorities and the press anticipated and in some cases conjured up savagery, looting, rape, and murderous gangs. The New Orleans Police Department "adopted a defensive posture more appropriate for a 'war zone' than the site of a natural disaster,"[18] and the ugly memory of armed soldiers and national guardsmen and police is a standard feature of survivors' reports. "Humvees . . . driving up the street, all filled with soldiers. They all jumped out and positioned themselves all over the block . . . they all pointed guns at me."[19] Another resident recalled: "A woman from St. Bernard Parish fainted next to Lora. When she approached a state trooper to ask for help, he informed her that he wasn't there to help, he was there for security."[20] Governor Blanco proclaimed: "These are some of the forty thousand extra troops that I have demanded. They have M16s, and they are locked and loaded"—with the result that New Orleans became a prison from which desperate people who could have walked away were prevented from escaping.[21]

In this fury and chaos neighbors are the first human presence and the first to take action. What did neighbors do? And what meaning did they give their actions?

## Witnessing, Saving, Improvising Order

There is a pattern and chronology to neighbors' response to disasters, which I have synthesized from survivor reports and social science accounts. Response proceeds in three steps: witnessing, immediate aid, and improvised collective action. Taking these in turn provides a vivid picture of "neighbors rising" and of the resilience of the democracy of everyday life in a disaster.

Before neighbors take any action they are witnesses. They take in, if that is not too strong a formulation, the physical derangement of the lay of the land, the devastation. "It was like an atomic bomb had gone off"—only that image suffices.[22] They often see grotesque death around them. Survivor memories from Katrina are explicit: "She stayed on that torn-up attic a while longer and saw coffins and bodies, livestock and wildlife, alive and dead, go floating by."[23] Interestingly, many initial observations are of animals: the fate of pets, of course, but animal life generally. [24] "The ants were training up by the thousands up higher and higher. You could see them on the glass. Those little reptiles . . . were suctioned up to the top of the glass and freaked out like everything else."[25] "There's the carcass of a horse 25 feet in a tree."[26] Immediate awareness too of the absence of life: "Everything was gray. Everything was dead, There were no bugs, birds; nothing was alive." This witness continues, "And it was just me; there wasn't anybody else around."[27] Until there was.

In "On Some Mental Effects of the Earthquake," his essay about the California earthquake of 1906, William James described "the awful discontinuity of past and future, with every familiar association with material things dissevered." [28] A Katrina survivor put it simply, "Everyone woke up the next morning and everything was different."[29] At almost the same moment, neighbors' presence provides grounding and orientation. Where physical destruction obliterates known landmarks, these faces are recognizable. They are the terrain on which we reemerge. People move onto the street as they can and regard one another, their emotions mirrored in one another's faces. The woman from down the block is a touchstone for what has happened to me. The uplift that comes from the sight of people living nearby does not depend on having a close history of give and take; recognition suffices—a familiar figure in this disorienting present. Disasters throw us full force into the totally absorbing "right now," and old grievances and settled patterns of interaction are erased.

Neighbors' presence on the deranged terrain around home where "every familiar association with material things [is] dissevered" provides more than physical orientation. Congregation on the street stimulates an awakening. "'Man, its gonna be okay,' said his neighbor, wrapping his arm around Monte's shoulders. 'Danielle and the kids are alive. You're alive.'"[30] Neighbors' presence is immediate proof that they are not the sole breathing speck in this universe, desolately alone. "We sort of checked out how many people were still on our block and the next block. . . . it was very dark."[31] Later, witnessing will lead to shaping stories and drawing meaning from them, but first there is just the mutual recognition that we are here. James's theme is "the subjective phenomena" of the disaster, and he observes that people "sought the greater safety of the street and yielded to the passionate desire for sympathetic communication." He concludes that this is a universal psychological tendency. Misfortune almost always comes with loneliness, but the earthquake spared victims that particular pain:

We lose our health, our wife or children die, our house burns down, or our money is made way with, and the world goes on rejoicing, leaving us on one side. . . . In California every one, to some degree, was suffering, and one's private miseries were merged in the vast general sum of privation.[32]

Neighbors in New Orleans report feeling: "Everybody is present to everybody." [33] In the initial phase of the Buffalo Creek disaster victims exhibited a similar response:

For one dread moment they thought that the world had come to an end, that they had been "left naked and alone in a terrifying wilderness of ruins," as Anthony F. C. Wallace put it. But "a stage of euphoria" quickly follows . . . as people come to realize that the general community is not dead at all.[34]

Only then, after presence stimulates orientation and awakening, come purposive responses. That is the second step in my chronology of neighbors in disaster: aid and rescue. Tommy "didn't see the elderly couple from the room next door. They were in their eighties . . . the woman standing helplessly with her husband almost neck-deep in brown water as their dog floated on a mattress nearby." With a two-by-four Tommy shattered the glass, and they swam through.[35] People with boats rescued neighbors from roofs and trees, scared off alligators, siphoned gasoline and drove neighbors out of immediate danger. William James again: "Everyone seemed doggedly bent on achieving the job which he had set himself to perform."[36] This is crucial: resistance to immobilization. "Setting myself a job" is a vital compensatory impulse, a drive to agency.

Then the third step: initial individual efforts turn quickly into enlarged cooperation. Neighbors compare and confer. They improvise. William James's account, said to be "in many ways the first good empirical investigation of human nature in the crucible of disaster,"[37] emphasizes "the rapidity of the improvisation of order out of chaos."[38] As Katrina shows, some people on the block emerge to take the lead. They are fixers, "making things happen." They are "natural order-makers."[39] "Prosocial behavior" in disasters is not always lawful: "requisitioning" or "commandeer[ing] which is now a common word in the New Orleans parlance"[40] diapers, medicine, water, food, pet food, and distributing supplies in the neighborhood "without riots or fights." Prudently gathering mops, hoses, bleach, disinfectants to deal with the scourge of waste, the swamp of sewage, mud, infection. Also liquor and cigarettes. One group called itself the

"Robin Hood Looters."[41] People "who shared their food and water, who genuinely cared for another in need . . . and comforted those in moments of despair."[42] Reciprocity in short, under extreme conditions.

No logic requires that suffering would translate into spontaneous collective rescue and aid among neighbors, as it did. That owes to the democracy of everyday life. Neighbors' responses are unplanned but not entirely unprecedented. Cooperation among neighbors in response to disturbing situations is after all a sequence familiar from mundane encounters. Resources for improvised action already exist. Under ordinary circumstances, faced with an intransigent offender like the noise bully in my building, we want the matter to be "collectively dealt with." We neighbors define the offense, identify and assess the delinquent, rally one another, and settle on a course of action. We act without rehearsal. Absent rules, authoritative interpreters, and designated enforcers, we neighbors legislate the bounds of "what anyone would do, here," and take the decision to act and to enforce "local knowledge." Neighbors rally without the organization, authority structure, and decision-making procedures of formal or informal democratic practices. This dynamic is recognizable in disasters: neighbors call on one another to act—rapidly, without preparation or structures, rules or routine. Elaine Scarry challenges the assumption that quick action is inconsistent with thought or that ordinary people are immobilized cognitively, overcome by an attitude of hopelessness. These erroneous assumptions are themselves immobilizing, she argues; they create the expectation that during disasters ordinary people surrender elementary forms of responsibility and self-governance.[43] Studies of disaster show that familiar practices of speaking out and taking action prevail. The democracy of everyday life is resilient. I don't mean to say that neighbors' collective action is shaped by conventions or scripts or assigned roles. But the hard-won habit and *disposition* to speak out, rally people nearby, recognize mutually vulnerability, and take action is at work.

The point about improvised cooperation among neighbors deserves repeating. As we know from everyday experience, we seldom anticipate the difficulties and offenses neighbors throw at us, or how we will finally navigate the treacherous terrain. Often enough we are taken by surprise. We make judgments and decide on steps. Uncertainty is compounded in disasters, of course, and so are the requirements of improvisation. What defied imagination must now be confronted. Neighbors during Katrina did not have to deal with the gargantuan ruins of the Twin Towers where the scale and weight (more than 1.5 million tons) of "heavy steel and debris lay densely compacted there, tied together like steel wool and complicated by the existence of human remains." Even there, Langewiesche writes, for whatever reason, "probably cultural, probably profound . . . the learned committees were excluded and the soldiers were relegated to the unhappy role of guarding the perimeter and civilians in heavy machines simply rolled in and took on the unknown."[44] None of this, he notes, "reflected the normal operation of the U.S. emergency-response system."[45] Something analogous describes neighbors in Katrina, venturing out into a chaos that was unimagined, with no instructions or protocols, judging immediate necessity and taking action. Neighbors "simply rolled in and took on the unknown."

One thing more: in disasters neighbors rally and improvise in defense of their lives and homes. Mutually vulnerable, they are aware of the depth and intensity of their interests in home and the material elements of personal life. A home is, often enough, a part of oneself and the pain of damage and loss is commensurate with that. Derangement is experienced as something close to a total devastation, which it may be. ("This is everything I have.") So neighbors figure uniquely in disasters like Katrina as grounding, witnessing, awakening, rescuing, salvaging, and later reconstructing. Neighbors often figure in the longer-term trauma suffered by people permanently evicted from their homes as well. These "refugees" mourn for lost houses, possessions, and familiar good and bad turns with the people who lived nearby. And as residents trickled back to New Orleans in the months following the disaster, neighbors provide orientation in the altered lay of the land. Where "the daily tasks of receiving mail, purchasing groceries, and navigating from place to place became foreign . . . Much like immigrants, New Orleanians turned to their neighbors for aid in negotiating the new landscape."[46]

## "Decivilization"

Not everyone moves from awakening to devastation into action. Some people are in shock, paralyzed, affectively overwhelmed, their senses muted and dulled. The word trauma applies. People "wandered emotionless through the wreckage . . . not reacting to the destruction, just moving. They had a blankness in their eyes I'd never seen before."[47] There is inevitably lawlessness and opportunism ("food, jewelry, clothes, every tennis shoe in the city was stolen"). But to draw the conclusion Timothy Garten Ash did of Katrina, that "the crust of civilization on which we tread is a thin wafer," is exactly wrong. Wrong because he is referring not to the

vulnerability of electrical grids or clean water or the virtual disappearance of effective government; these breakdowns of civilization were true
enough. Instead, Garten Ash uses "wafer thin" to refer to personal encounters: "One tremor and you've fallen through to scratching and gouging for your life like a wild dog." In characterizing the response to Katrina
as a violent, nasty, brutish Hobbesian state of nature, he is repeating
claims made so incessantly at the time by officials and the press that they
were assumed to capture the reality. In retrospect many of these reports
turned out to be urban legend, fantastical allegations.[48] The mayor and
police chief reported "that snipers were shooting at helicopters, tourists
and the police."[49] A guest on Oprah Winfrey's television show reported:
"We had little babies in there . . . Some of the little babies were getting
raped." Mayor Nagin reported "hundreds of gang members in the Super-
dome, raping and murdering."[50] *New York Times* columnist Maureen
Dowd described New Orleans as "a snakepit of anarchy, death, looting,
raping, marauding thugs, suffering innocents . . ."[51]

Garten Ash misreports; he sees bedlam. He also echoes the ancient
(and recurrent) thought that "human beings [do not] lose their social and
political structures in an emergency simply because they have suddenly
been subjected to an asocial and anarchic framework but because they
are, in their own deepest impulses, asocial and anarchic."[52] "Most people,"
he writes, "most of the time, engage in a ruthless fight for individual and
genetic survival. A few become temporary angels, most revert to being
apes." [53] The eternal question of human nature aside, empirically his proportions are all wrong. Most people did not revert to being apes. And
"temporary angels," is dramatic, sentimental. Rescuers attest that they
did "what anyone would do, here." As important, they see their neighbors
reciprocating: "He would do the same for me."

So pause to consider this moment of presumptive "decivilization." Survivor narratives give meaning to the disastrous events. Everyone has a
story, and "the anguish of formulation" is part of the reparative process.[54]
The stories collected after Katrina are just a sample, and not a random
one since they feature survivors who have done well in the sense that they
have integrated the disaster into their understanding of their lives and
selves. They want to tell their stories. Still, notably, we read repetitive narratives of good neighbors "rising." "Everyone shared. It was what kept us
from losing out minds. It was what reassured us that, contrary to what
CNN was suggesting to the world, we had not devolved into animals."[55]

The positive counterpart of "decivilization" as an account of disaster—
the exact inversion of "scratching and gouging for your life like a wild

dog"—has it that ordinary people's response to disaster provides "an extraordinary window onto social desire and possibility."[56] In one description: "Citizens themselves in these moments constitute the government," and disasters produce the outlines of "beloved community." [57] A radical social critic, Rebecca Solnit represents mundane life in the United States as a social disaster of disconnection that is disrupted with positive consequences by actual physical disasters; she compares the experience of 9/11 to the uplifting experience of the Civil Rights Movement: "The affinities with disaster communities are obvious: activist communities come into being in response to . . . discrimination, destruction, deprivation—and sometimes generate a moment or a fragment of a better world."[58] Disasters show that "the citizens any paradise would need— the people who are brave enough, resourceful enough, and generous enough—already exist."[59]

This counterpart to "decivilization" is unembarrassedly utopian. It draws attention to the euphoria some neighbors do feel doing together what they must do in the moment: rescue and aid are adrenalin-producing acts, achievements of stamina and practical and moral imagination. A Katrina survivor puts it this way: "I didn't know what anarchy would be like, but for us, in this little corner of the world, our anarchy was people banding together and hanging out together for safety and just for community—sharing food, sharing information. Because all we had was each other, and that was the really beautiful thing of it."[60] "Beloved community" is an overstatement, though: the wish to see disaster as transformational opportunity is belied by actual experience. For one thing, neighbors' actions are direct and personal—neither part of a social movement nor anticipating one. They are not prefiguring a better world. Nothing is further from their minds. They do what they must do under dire circumstances. The spirit of rescue and aid is not a peculiarly "civic temper" either, and there is little evidence that disaster generates an appetite for permanent, energetic civic engagement.

"Beloved community" is an overstatement, too, because the community—no matter what definition we apply to that protean term—is damaged. Its workings are broken and its residents are dispersed. Overall social bonds are rarely strengthened by disaster, on the contrary.[61] After initial survival and improvisation comes the dreadful business of physical recovery, salvaging the remains of home, battling insurance companies and government programs, coming to terms with our neighbors' comparative good fortune. Disaster brings fresh opportunities for conflict. A heightened form of the democracy of everyday life comes into its own at the moment of adversity and soon after the disaster but it is overtaken by the entry of large-scale, organized efforts at rescue and restoration. My point is that there is no obvious moral or psychological step up from witnessing, awakening, rescue, and improvised cooperation to participatory democracy. Neighbors—even neighbors taking collective action in emergencies—are neither anticipation nor model of citizenship. For victims of disaster, the appetite—indeed the craving—is to return from urgency and fierce cooperation to reabsorption in mundane affairs. Neighbors in disaster do not foreshadow "citizens of paradise." But they do exhibit and foreshadow the modest but essential practices of the democracy of everyday life.

Afterwards, after witnessing, saving, and improvised cooperation, and after time for resettlement and adjustment, many people do attest to undergoing personal change. Some remain overwhelmed by their losses but others report new "balance and ability within themselves."[62] "I have learned something about my own ability to persevere. It has helped me to appreciate the small everyday things."[63] On this point the contrast between Katrina narratives and the stories told by Japanese Americans after internment is striking. Things were done *to* Japanese internees. They were of necessity mostly passive; the democracy of everyday life was effectively untapped. They went on with their lives after resettlement at the end of the war, but the principal narrative of that time is of lost time, the dominant temper is resignation, and the lesson drawn is "Just put it behind you ... Let it go ... All you have to do is behave." [64]

## Neighbors Superseded: Civic Voluntarism

Heightened energy and activity among neighbors in disasters like Katrina is short-lived. After all, "Can the methods of a nineteenth-century barn raising drag a twenty-first century disaster area from the mud and muck?"[65] Disasters require assistance on a large scale, in accord with established procedures, and with resources that do not depend on mutual aid. "Disaster administrators" take over, and in the process officials quickly cabin, supplant, disrupt, and even squelch neighbors' efforts. The surge of cooperation and improvisation is displaced. Survivors become beneficiaries, recipients of public and private assistance. "We're totally dependent on the federal government now for assistance ... It's just ... It's an everyday battle."[66]

So, along with government agents, into the disaster arena come organized groups of volunteers. The process is called "convergence."[67] Neighbors' spontaneous cooperation is supplanted by the activity of church groups and volunteer fire fighters, small aid groups and large profession-ally led relief organizations. Their work is not improvised; efforts are planned and rehearsed. Routines and systems of "best practices" are ap-plied, as they should be. The democracy of everyday life evident during disasters is carried on by neighbors at a level "below" organized groups, on an intimate scale, in a spirit distinct from civic voluntarism, and with-out material resources except for what is felicitously at hand.

Separation of spheres—here I'm referring to the separation of life at home among neighbors from organized civil society—is a defining char-acteristic of pluralism in America. I want to set off the terrain around home from the terrain of civic voluntarism, and insist that locating rough boundaries between these spheres as I do is not an arid analytic exercise. The moral uses of pluralism are meaningful for us personally, and moral identity as neighbor is its own identity, which cannot be assimilated to doer of good works or good citizen.

## Good Neighbors / Good Works

It is easy enough to blur them; we do it all the time. We borrow the luster of the proverbial good neighbor to describe good works that have noth-ing to do with proximity, regular encounters, and reciprocity among "decent folk" in the context of life at home. We characterize one-way provision of assistance by members of a voluntary association as "neigh-borliness." This conflation is long-standing and apparently irresistible. In 1868 Charles Bosanquet advised that because "philanthropic endeavours that resembled 'the original neighbourliness' were most successful ... those offering assistance should describe themselves as neighbours, high-lighting their differences from district visitors."[68]

What separates good neighbors from doers of good works, and why is the distinction worth attention? Under ordinary conditions the domain of neighbor is marked by reciprocity among "decent folk"—that is the defining difference. Reciprocity is endemically difficult, as we know; we neighbors "wear our fingers rough" trying to balance loaves and balls. Moreover, the content, extent, and proportionality of giving are con-strained by these relationships.[69] We likely experience too much solici-tousness as disturbing and unwelcome. For relations around home are skewed by any hint of charity or suggestions for improvement, whether they are performed in a spirit of beneficence or a spirit of reproach. Both subvert the democratic ethos of neighbors. Excessive favors and incessant advice fail the test of rough equivalence. In plain contrast to neighborliness, unbridled generosity may have a place in families and between friends, and it is admirable when applied to organized good works. Good works performed individually or through voluntary associations are unburdened by considerations of reciprocity. As volunteers or donors our purpose is typically to benefit strangers, sometimes anonymously, and without any expectation of return. The shift of phrase is telling. "Good turns" says that neighbors' interactions are personal and reciprocal; almost by definition "good works" are one-way, captured in the standard insistence that it is better to give than to receive.

In an attempt to salvage the assimilation of good works to good neighbor and to interpret doing good as reciprocity, we can frame activity (as philanthropists especially do) as "giving back" and speak of reciprocating a benefit received: this school or religious fellowship "made me who I am." What is served by casting good works as reciprocity, "giving back"? It draws attention to life history and emphasizes personal commitment— her school was literally her alma mater. The giver also modestly wards off the label altruist. Philanthropy is not reciprocity, however; it has nothing of neighbors' rough equality of concrete give and take. So moral and phenomenological differences exist between neighbors' beneficial give and take and good works performed by and on behalf of strangers. Obviously, this is not to deny that neighbors too perform charitable acts. The elderly woman next door may require assistance, especially if she is impoverished or isolated, and our solicitude counts as a good deed, a "mitzvah." As Proverbs 27:10 has it, "A close neighbor is better than a distant brother."

## Good Neighbor / Good Citizen

I continue down the path of contrast, pressing the distinction between neighbors' good turns on the one hand and good works carried on through voluntary associations on the other. Collectively, voluntary associations comprise a large sector of civil society. ("The most conservative national estimates (from the Census Bureau) suggest that more than one quarter of all Americans volunteer every year, contributing on average roughly 2.5 hours per week.")[70] Americans work through organizations local and parochial, national and international, and their good works are not restricted to (indeed they are comparatively rarely directed to) aiding the worst off.[71] For most goods provided by voluntary associations, including churches, are "club goods" not public goods. This suggests that the "association" part of "voluntary association" is crucial. Unlike neighbors, whose good turns are personal and individual and arise from the accident of proximity, membership joins like-minded people with shared interests and purposes.

To push the distinction between the domain of neighbor and civil society further, the business of voluntary associations is linked to politics in a way that neighbors' good turns are not. Americans invent worthy causes (and not-so-worthy ones), identifying a problem that government addresses inadequately, and this volunteerism takes on the color of civic activism and advocacy.[72] Voluntary associations also press the public worth of what they do because their funding comes from government grants, contracts, and public-private partnerships. The growth of voluntary associations and the growth of government activity have gone hand in hand, and civil society is mislabeled the "independent sector." [73]

So it's not surprising that civic voluntarism and "good citizen" are often fused, and that the notion of "participation" has migrated away from formal political activity like voting toward "efforts to start a hospital or help the homeless."[74] In this spirit, democratic theorists assign membership in civil society groups a democratic role. They define civil society as a realm of "concrete and authentic solidarities"[75] and as a principal source of "social capital," which presumably spills over from religious groups, athletic teams, etc., into public, political life. Going further, democratic theorists cast membership groups as direct preparation for citizenship: "It is only through group organization that the individual learns . . . to be an effective political member."[76] Requisite civic skills and dispositions are developed in voluntary associations cast as schools of due processes, fairness, a sense of political efficacy, and more. From Tocqueville to Progressives at the turn of the twentieth century to participatory democrats and not a few conservative thinkers today, democracy is said to depend on the "art and science of association."

My insistence on separate spheres is not meant to suggest that they are walled off from one another. Voluntary associations recruit members, and members sometimes recruit their neighbors. Katrina's aftermath spotlights this feature of democratic life in America: after the improvised cooperation of rescue was past, some residents organized neighborhood and ward planning groups in an attempt to have a voice in reshaping a city that required massive reorganization and rebuilding.[77] That said, the channel that leads from neighbor to civic activist should not obscure the independence and distinct value of the sphere of neighbors' good turns. It should be clear that neighbor relations shaped by the democracy of everyday life are misunderstood if they are seen solely or principally as preparation for civic activism. There is no necessary continuity at work, no dynamic imperative moving from our good turns as neighbors to collective civic action—not empirically and not morally. Continuity with citizenship is not the chief value good neighbor has for us individually and it is not its chief value to democracy. To anticipate the thrust of my final chapter, "Thoreau's Neighbors," and the theme of my conclusion, the democracy of everyday life is the remainder when government and political institutions and the organized associations of civil society seem distant or corrupt or failed. Disasters tell us that. When "decivilization" threatens, the democracy of everyday life is a "saving remnant."

**PART IV**

Minding Our Own Business

# 10

# Thoreau's Neighbors

The phrases "minding our neighbors' business" and "minding our own business" serve as shorthand for engagement and disengagement with people living nearby. Minding our neighbors' business is a state of attention we bring to reciprocity, to taking offense and speaking out, and to enforcing "what anyone would do, here." We are alert and minding our neighbors business when we live and let live, and never more so than when we hold our neighbors' lives in our hands. What about minding our own business, though?

Minding our own business is no simple proposition. The phrase is commonly taken as a rebuke when we trespass, snoop, interfere, admonish, advise, correct, and enforce. It is a demand to back off. Among neighbors, minding our own business is often strictly impossible, for wanted or not we have opportunities to learn things about the people nearby. Then, minding our own business is mainly a matter of what we do with what we know: keeping what we know to ourselves. It commends reticence. Sometimes minding our own business entails self-protective retreat from a wearisome excess of give and take, or withdrawal from demanding neighbors who want to engage us in some affair of correction or improvement or reproach.

In more general terms, minding our own business owes to our separateness and our need for privacy and control over our lives at home. The poet Auden writes:

> a toft-and-croft
> where I needn't ever, be at home *to*
> those I am not at home *with* . . . .
> Nor a windowless grave, but a place
> I may go both in and out of.[1]

In Frost's words, again, "We're too unseparate. And going home / From company means coming to our senses."[2] "Coming to our senses" — the phrase suggests that detachment is not all negative or reactive. It denotes a restorative return. It invites us to spend time in our own company, to be a neighbor to ourselves.

If we take the phrase literally, minding our own business is not only about discrete distance or detachment but also about attending to ourselves. What relation does minding our own business bear to our neighbors? It may involve them profoundly if our observations and encounters spur self-awareness. "These neighbors have brought out certain traits I didn't know I had," Berger's Earl Keese observes, "That may be all to the good, mind you."[3] Neighbors provoke self-questioning and even self-transformation. This may seem surprising, since we normally locate the source of personal insight and change in the drama of the family romance. We attribute turning points and self-knowledge to critical developmental stages in the life cycle, or to traumas, including political violence and disasters. But mundane encounters around home are provocations to self-awareness too. Observation and the compulsion to compare can stimulate resolution and correction — we're not condemned to fruitless repetition. From our vantage point as spectators to our neighbors' lives we gain insight into our own vulnerabilities, moral resources, and the terms of our happiness.

## Our Neighbors, Ourselves: Two Stories

Two beautiful, poignant narratives turn on the dynamic of learning about ourselves from minding our neighbors' business. Something happens that startles us into thought. We are inadvertently exposed to dramas taking place in houses and apartments around us. We hear obscenities, screams, thuds. Or we hear music and gaiety. We find that we can't turn away from the sights or tune out the sounds. We eavesdrop. We learn more than we thought we wanted to know. Listening in, we find ourselves confronted with something these neighbors reveal about our own lives.

This is the conceit of John Cheever's story, "The Enormous Radio." Jim Westcott's gift to his wife is a radio that mysteriously broadcasts the goings-on in neighboring apartments. At first it channels operational noises: the rattling of elevator cables, the ringing of phones, the "lamentation of a vacuum cleaner." Then the radio transmits voices: "a monologue on salmon fishing in Canada, a bridge game ... a bitter family quarrel about an overdraft at the bank." Then more: carnal love, vanity, faith, despair. Irene Westcott listens, rapt and appalled. What she hears is news to her. The radio transmits intimate human disasters she somehow neglected to know existed, certainly not in her neighborhood. We can call this innocence or complacency. She is also startled to discover her appetite for raw emotion.

Irene begins to draw comparisons to her own life. She is helpless to stop the thoughts from coming. In her household no one screams or flings obscenities; if the radio were to broadcast her family's domestic sounds, the neighbors would hear nothing startling, nothing intimate or personally revealing. But denial is not functioning well. She becomes anxious that discord may lie beneath the polite surface of her life. She seeks reassurance from her husband:

> Life is too terrible, too sordid and awful. But we've never been like that, have we, darling? Have we? I mean, we've always been good and decent and loving to one another, haven't we? And we have two children, two beautiful children. Our lives aren't sordid, are they, darling? Are they . . . We're happy, aren't we, darling? We are happy, aren't we?

Jim replies, tiredly, "Of course we're happy."

Then, seizing the moment, he "surrenders to his resentment": "What's turned you overnight into a convent girl?" He challenges his willfully naïve wife with the fact of their own money problems, exacerbated by her profligacy. He ticks off a list of vile actions: stealing her mother's jewelry before the will was probated and not sharing the inheritance with her needy sister; making a friend's life miserable; and in a final terrible cut, her abortion: "You packed your bag and went off to have that child murdered as if you were going to Nassau." Irene feels "disgraced and sickened."[4]

We don't always have the wherewithal—the imaginative probing, patience, or common sense—for self-reflection. We don't attend to ourselves. Neighbors may draw back that curtain of inattention and prod us into minding our own business.

"Eli the Fanatic" is a tender, mournful account of radical self-transformation through the path of neighbors. Philip Roth's story figured earlier in my discussion of neighbors as enforcers in Chapter 5, "What Anyone Would Do, Here." Recall: a small group of orthodox Jewish immigrants including a Hasidic survivor of a death camp have bought a house in suburban Woodenton, New York. Neighbors commission Eli

Peck to warn the new arrivals that they are unwelcome unless they conform to local etiquette. Either the Hasid sheds his black hat and gets a new suit and appears as a modern American or they will enforce the zoning ordinance the newcomers have violated and have them evicted. They state their motive for their aggressive intervention plainly: these secular Jews fear that their standing in this progressive Protestant suburb is provisional on fitting in.[5]

Eli takes on the assignment, but after several visits, the residents of the dark house on the hill seem to cast a "spell" on him. He absorbs the fact that the black-suited survivor has lost everything. "A mother and a father? . . . No. A wife? No . . . A little ten-month-old baby? No! A village full of friends? . . . That leaves nothing, Mr. Peck. Absolutely nothing!" Eli is stunned to come face-to-face with his inattention to this catastrophe. "Normal" life in progressive Woodenton permits obliviousness, as if the Holocaust had not happened. And he is stunned into further self-awareness. The Hasid is Eli's age; nameless and faceless in the dark shadows of the house, he is Eli's double, and their encounter awakens him to his own deviation from "what anyone would do, here" and to yearnings he had not admitted having.

From the first, Roth tells us, Eli has been an object of concern in the neighborhood. He doesn't fit in. He is too nervous, too sensitive. He drifts away. His neighbors preach "common sense" as "the ruling thing," and Eli is unaccountably resistant. At every exhibition of their adamant "normal," he feels empty. Now, confronted with this survivor who has nothing, Eli realizes that for everything he has (a wife, a baby on the way, a suburban home, friends and neighbors), he knows something of nothingness. He has been diverting himself from his unlived life. He has been underliving. So when the weary death camp survivor agrees to compromise and to wear Eli's appropriate suit for running errands in town, the progressive neighbors are gratified and remark that in his green suit, he seems to belong! But to Eli he seems to be saying, "Here, I give up." Eli discovers his own need to reject the terms on offer and to live as who he is "down to his marrow." His "Judgment Day" arrived, he puts on the Hasid's black suit and walks Woodenton's main street as if it were a desert wilderness. His neighbor, the survivor, reveals him to himself; his neighbors, the assimilated suburban Jews, provoke him to live as himself, to "come out."

"The Enormous Radio" and "Eli the Fanatic" present neighbors as unwitting spurs to self-knowledge. Minding their business well can be a provocation to minding our own. But once again, what is our business? We have a guide.

## Walden

John Winthrop's "Model of Christian Charity" is the American taproot of "minding our neighbors' business." The taproot of "minding our own business" is another "American scripture,"[6] Thoreau's *Walden.* Thoreau projects his own "city on a hill": "I please myself imagining a State at last which can afford to be just to all men, and to treat the individual with respect as a neighbor."[7] Neighbors are part of Thoreau's exacting account of "how I lived and what I lived for." His experiment in solitude at Walden Pond and his return to Concord from the woods assign central place to shifting turns of attention outward to his neighbors' business and inward to his own. Thoreau explores the terms of engagement and detachment. He reports on the worth and the limits of ordinary reciprocity, and the possibility of giving and getting greater favors. He assigns moral gravity to minding our neighbors' business and minding our own. The path to care of the self runs through them. So does the democracy of everyday life. With the right state of attention, the right degree of distance, and the right give and take, Thoreau imagined, good neighbor is the solid substrate of democracy in America.

## "That Old Musty Cheese That We Are"

Life in the woods, which as Thoreau reminds us more than once began on Independence Day, 1845, is an experiment in the art of living. "I lived alone, in the woods, a mile from any neighbor, in a house which I had built myself, on the shore of Walden Pond, in Concord, Massachusetts, and earned my living by the labor of my hands only." Thoreau's withdrawal from town began with the question whether "the near neighborhood of man was not essential to a serene and healthy life"[8] and "made the fancied advantages of human neighborhood insignificant?" Thoreau poses this as a question, not an assertion. He requires solitude, it turns out, but cannot be solitary. "Virtue does not remain as an abandoned orphan, Thoreau cites Confucius, "it must of necessity have neighbors."[9] Neighbors are everywhere in *Walden,* a recurrent theme.

The first pose Thoreau assumes toward neighbors is aversive: he calls his cabin in the woods his "withdrawing room." There is the oppressive press of proximity, the surfeit of distracting news and gossip. "To be in company, even with the best, is soon wearisome and dissipating."[10] With neighbors we are mostly killing time. "We meet at very short intervals, not having had time to acquire any new value for each other . . . and give each other a new taste of that old musty cheese that we are."[11] Thoreau prescribes a certain distance, then: "Individuals, like nations, must have suitable broad and natural boundaries, even a considerable neutral ground, between them."[12] The problem is not antagonism, which can be bracing, but banal encounters. "Why go to his house ... Why be visited by him at your own? ... Leave this touching and clawing."[13] Minding our own business demands inattention to the "confused *tintinnabulum* from without."[14]

Purposeful innerness to what end? To entertain the questions how to live and what to live for? This philosophical definition accurately describes his enterprise:

> Morality is not exhausted by our relations to others, by codes of moral behavior ... It also concerns the ways in which individuals relate to and regulate themselves—the ways in which we practice self-government ... Ethics is the care of the self.[15]

"Do what nobody else can do for you," Thoreau urges, "Omit to do anything else."[16]

## Care of the Self

"Let every one mind his own business, and endeavor to be what he was made."[17] What is the meaning of this obscure imperative? Some fortunate natures do not need self-examination. The woodchopper who visited him at his hut and other "strong and valiant natures" "mind their own affairs ... not knowing how they live." [18] That is, these unreflective natures have a mysterious, engrained clarity and certain purpose. Call it integrity. For the rest of us whose internal compasses do not work spontaneously and inerrantly, care of the self requires minding our own business. It must be a deliberate endeavor. Thoreau's discipline, detailed in *Walden,* shares characteristics with nearly every philosophy of care of the self: preparation, exercises in concentration, asceticism, proportionality between capacities and desires, rituals of awareness, daily writing and recording.[19]

As a start to minding our own business, then, we must give ourselves permission to disinvest from the costly ways in which we let ourselves be diverted by minding our neighbors' business. There is nothing easy about distancing: "Wherever a man goes, men will pursue and paw him,"[20] and physical withdrawal by itself does not insure attention to our own business. But separation is a start. "My purpose in going to Walden Pond was not to live cheaply or to live dearly there but to transact some private business with the fewest obstacles."[21] First, then, is detachment and the "deficiency of domestic sounds."[22] "No cockerels to crow or hens to cackle in the yard. No yard! But unfenced Nature reaching up to your very sills . . . Instead of no path to the frontyard gate in the Great Snow,—no gate—no frontyard,—and no path to the civilized world."[23]

Thoreau does have company in the woods, first of all his own. Doubling is a hallmark of his thought.[24] "With thinking we may be beside ourselves in a sane sense . . . and I am sensible of a certain doubleness," he wrote.[25] Thoreau conceives of his relation to himself as interpersonal. Inner dialogue is a common concept in philosophy, beginning with Plato's parts of soul ("The good life belongs to him who . . . becomes his own friend and harmonizes the three parts" of his soul[26]). Doubling is often characterized this way in terms of friendship: we are friends to ourselves. Strikingly, Thoreau employs the different vocabulary of "neighbor" to himself. It is the American signature. As a neighbor, he has an eye on himself. He is proximate. He lives beside himself companionably. Thoreau "treats himself with respect, as a neighbor," the phrase he will use to define American democracy.

## Neighbors Doing Good / Being Good

In the opening paragraphs of *Walden* Thoreau lists questions people put to him about his life in the woods: "what I got to eat; if I did not feel lonesome," and "what portion of my income I devoted to charitable purposes." No surprise that Thoreau's neighbors accused him of self-absorption: "But all this is very selfish, I have heard some of my townsmen say. I confess that I have hereto indulged very little in philanthropic enterprises."[27] As we know, Thoreau discredited great swaths of contemporary society: all that "getting and spending," the "lying, flattering, voting, contracting yourselves into a nutshell of civility or dilating into an atmosphere of thin and vaporous generosity." Nothing he wrote undermines conventional morality more thoroughly, however, than his subversion of neighbors "devoted in so many ways to the good of their fellows." Thoreau explodes this ideal and substitutes for good works his own notion of reciprocity.

His deflation of good works begins this way: "You must have a genius for charity as well as for anything else. As for Doing-good, that is one of the professions which are full."[28] With "profession" he charges hypocrisy; good works are a bid for social status.[29] And "there is no odor so bad as that which arises from goodness tainted. It is human, it is divine, carrion."[30] With this Thoreau foreshadows Nietzsche unveiling the perverse moral psychology of "humanitarianism" (and perhaps the radical pose of Foucault in detecting in humanitarian reform a fresh form of cruelty.)

Thoreau goes on to unravel the familiar fabric of doing good completely. "The greater part of what my neighbors call good I believe in my soul to be bad"[31] was written at the time of the fugitive slave law and his neighbors' acquiescence in the foundational American evil. There could be no clearer evidence of cant and sheer incomprehension of good and evil. Professing charity, his neighbors are complicit in the greatest injury.

With this, Thoreau brings us back to minding our own business—in place of doing good he substitutes the prescription: set about *being* good.[32] Instead of "thin and vaporous generosity" we should give the poor, or anyone, the aid they most need:[33] a strong dose of ourselves.

> I want the flower and fruit of a man; that some fragrance be wafted over from him to me, and some ripeness flavor our intercourse. His goodness must not be a partial and transitory act, but a constant superfluity, which costs him nothing and of which he is unconscious.[34]

This way of thinking may "easily make us poor neighbors and friends sometimes," Thoreau concedes.[35] That is, he discards for now "what anyone would do, here," including good works. It does, however, make him a good neighbor on his terms, and if we accept these terms we can make sense of his histrionic claim: "Probably I should not consciously and deliberately forsake my particular calling to do the good which society demands of me, to save the universe from annihilation."[36] His particular calling is care of the self, and who I am is the valuable good I bring to others. Thoreau turns the phrase round and round: "going about the world in his own orbit, doing it good" or rather, as a truer philosophy has it, "the world going about him getting good."[37]

## "They Are Our Austrias and Chinas, and South Sea Islands"[38]

We know what comes from Thoreau's undisturbed attentiveness to care of the self and the natural world of Walden Pond. He explores the "true necessaries" of life and in the course of this critical activity everything ordinary, including neighbors, is transfigured. This is a feature of every transcendental experience, of course. For Thoreau it meant finding "amid the pine boughs ... a delicate sense of their neighborhood."[39] In the woods he was introduced to "brute neighbors."[40] He was "neighbor to the

birds." He became sensible of "such sweet and beneficent society in Nature . . . an infinite and unaccountable friendliness." [41] The startling illumi-
nation of the quotidian—the beneficent society of pine boughs—extends
to his Concord neighbors. We rarely see our neighbors for who they are,
Thoreau cautions. Terribly, we depreciate them. "We live thick and are in
each other's way, and stumble over one another, and I think that we thus
lose some respect for one another."[42] Thoreau reports that he can "know
neighbors," see them with fresh eyes, so that they appear unfamiliar. He
can perceive their essential foreignness:

> We dream of foreign countries, of other times and races of men placing
> them at a distance in history or space [but] we discover often, this dis-
> tance and strangeness in our midst, between us and our nearest neigh-
> bors. *They* are our Austrias and Chinas, and South Sea Islands.[43]

With this we get an advance glimpse of Whitman's radical, infinite individuality: if we recognized our neighbors' foreignness, "we should live in
all the ages of the world in an hour."[44]

Thoreau did not expect his neighbors (or his readers) to imitate his life
in the woods. But anyone can experience attentiveness as he has set it out
for us, he believes, and readers of *Walden* know this is true. Thoreau does
not tell us anything beyond our own actual, dimmer experience. It is not
impossible "sometimes" to alter the face of everyday objects and events,
and to make each moment worthy of reporting. There is our imagined
geography around home: the "lay of the land" we create for ourselves on
our walks can carry us far away. We defamiliarize our beaten track. Imagined geography transports us. Here, for a moment, are our South Sea
Islands.

Neighbors' society is "cheap," then, only if we fail to see their proximity as fortuitous and fail at least sometimes to orient ourselves to their
foreignness. If we are open and attentive, we may receive what Thoreau
and Emerson both called the "flower and fruit" of a man.[45] If "the fancied
advantages of human neighborhood [are] insignificant," or deleterious,
the real advantages are luminous enough. Neighbors expand our world:
"Nature and human life are as various as our several constitutions."[46] Appreciation of one another's foreignness and separateness is a way of taking neighbors as they take themselves, as we all take ourselves—as absolutely distinct and individual, in all our particularities and eccentricities.

Heroics are endemic to transcendentalism, and Thoreau was prone to
the epic: "Men come tamely home at night only from the next field or
street . . . We should come home from far, from adventures, and perils, and

discoveries every day, with new experience and character."[47] We encountered just this magnification of neighbors in Augie March's characterization of people in his Chicago tenement: "The resonance of great principle filled the whole kitchen." The elevation of neighbors in this way is distinctively democratic, as Augie observes when looking back he continues to see nobility in them, "our teeming democrats": "Without a special gift of vision, maybe you wouldn't have seen it in most of us." Thoreau is not alone in this confident possibility of encountering strangeness and greatness in neighbors, and through them "living in all the ages of the world in an hour." This chord is played over and over in American writing, not only in the best of times but also in times of loss and despair, coming from the hearts of "poor misanthropes" as well as insouciant Augie Marches. Ralph Ellison in *Invisible Man* captured this capacity for openness, for seeing the extraordinary in the ordinary: "What about those three boys coming now along the platform, tall and slender, walking stiffly with swinging shoulders ... It was as though I'd never seen their like before ... who knew but that they were the saviors, the true leaders, the bearers of something precious?"[48]

## Visiting

Thoreau never let up blasting superficial give and take, missed opportunities "to affect the quality of the day, that is the highest of arts."[49] In "Visitors" he introduces other positive aspects of reciprocity available to neighbors. During his time in the woods, he tells us, he was a visitor at the poorest, grossest shanty and "drank to genuine hospitality the heartiest draught I could."[50] He recounts what he got and gave: water, conversation, the gift of "inaudible harmony."[51] We get and give company for our thoughts. We mind one another's business without disturbing it. He records, that is, the grace and reticence of live and let live.

> Having each some shingles of thought well dried, we sat and whittled them, trying our knives, and admiring the clear yellowish grain of the pumpkin pine. We waded so gently and reverently, or we pulled together so smoothly, that the fishes of thought were not scared from the stream.[52]

"Visiting" is time in one another's presence at home, with no instrumental purpose. It is the moment of "how are you feeling today?" prolonged — that moment of affecting the quality of the day. "Visiting" sets limits: not too close or long, preserving the separation and neutral ground Thoreau sees as the art of neighborliness.[53]

Notice one more thing about neighbors' beneficial presence. One of his visitors, the Irishman Seeley, Thoreau tells us, "was there to represent spectatordom, and help make this seemingly insignificant event one with the removal of the gods of Troy."[54] Which is to say, when they are not intrusive or out for gossip or trying to reproach and improve us, the audience neighbors provide is a "true necessary." We need spectators to our lives. Interiority and doubling are not enough. Neighbors can provide assurance that our business is worthy, that it holds interest. "Perhaps it is the most generous course to permit your fellow-men to have an interest in your enterprise," and reciprocity moves us to perform the good turn of taking an interest in theirs.

## Leaving Walden

Thoreau made a great romance of withdrawal to nature but we know that his cabin was visible from the road, neighbors from town stopped by, and he returned to Concord regularly during the two years he spent in the woods. His life and writing were exhibitionistic and confrontational. He is chanticleer, waking his neighbors up to the state of American society and government and to their own part in America's national crime, slavery. Also to true philanthropy, and to care of the self. Thoreau did not remain in the woods, or ever intend to: "Can we not do without the society of our gossips *a little while* under these circumstances?"[55] Even his experiment in independence produced old musty cheese over time.

> I left the woods for as good a reason as I went there . . . It is remarkable how easily and insensibly we fall into a particular route, and make a beaten track for ourselves.[56]

So Thoreau returned, "a sojourner in civilized life again."[57] He observed local etiquette and did not begrudge most of doing "what anyone would do, here." Not every moment is transfigured, and the stuff of ordinary reciprocity among neighbors could be "comparatively good." He said of the woods and pond as he had said before of life among his Concord neighbors, "Thank heaven, here is not all the world."[58] "Perhaps it seemed to me," he wrote, "that I had several more lives to live." Thoreau, and we, move back and forth among different spheres over the course of our lives, and over the course of the day. We are at home with and flourish from the moral uses of pluralism. As condition for the endeavor of care of the self and as practical necessity, we require these several worlds. We have several lives to live. One is the democracy of everyday life among neighbors; another is the public life of democratic citizens. Thoreau brings them together.

### "Treating the Individual with Respect as a Neighbor"

Thoreau is living out, extravagantly in his fashion, the defining elements of the democracy of everyday life: reciprocity, speaking out, and live and let live. Here it all is, amplified by his profound self-reflection and gorgeous language. Thoreau is also advancing my argument by working out the indissoluble, morally significant relation between good neighbor and democracy proper.

One way to see this connection is, perhaps surprisingly, by considering the starting point: Thoreau's mode of detachment. Retreat from society is a common theme in literature and philosophy. The artist's loathing of philistine society and rage at unrecognized genius drives the romantic soul to retire to the garret. There is aristocratic disdain for bourgeois society, and there is the quest for spiritual purity. All commend detachment and all seek out only the rarest company.[59] Thoreau had a problem justifying withdrawal that the romantic artist, aristocrat, and saint did not have. The problem was democracy.[60] Critical as he was, he did not set himself above others nor, finally, apart from everyday society. His way of representing a certain distance without disparagement was to cast American democracy in terms of neighbors. Thoreau speaks of being a good neighbor to himself; he pronounces neighbor the singular relation in which we demonstrate respect for one another; and he casts good neighbor as the democratic recourse we have when the Constitution and government fail.

> I please myself imagining a State at last which can afford to be just to all men, and to treat the individual with respect as a neighbor; which even would not think it inconsistent with its own repose, if a few were to live aloof from it, not meddling with it, nor embraced by it, who fulfilled all the duties of neighbors and fellow-men.[61]

Coming at the end of *Civil Disobedience*, this passage ("not meddling with it, nor embraced by it") can be read as special pleading, as if Thoreau claims an exceptional status for himself. Because he is self-sufficient and property-less, on this reasoning, he declines the protection of government and incurs no obligations as a citizen. He can live aloof. But the passage is not about his own standing only; it reads generally. "All the duties of neighbor," as he has explored them, constitute moral education for American democracy. He challenges authorities to treat us as the status of neighbor demands: "How shall he ever know well what he is and does as an officer of the government, or as a man, until he is obliged to consider whether he shall treat me, his neighbor, for whom he has respect, as a neighbor and well-disposed man."[62]

The importance of Thoreau's "respect, as a neighbor" cannot be overstated.[63] He elaborates its meaning in *Walden*: distance, strangeness, giving and getting strong doses of one another as true philanthropy. In *Civil Disobedience* the meaning of "respect as a neighbor" lies in contrast to what he saw as the relation between citizens and government in a slaveholding, war-mongering democracy. Government turns citizens into cogs, machines, dependent impersonal parts. It is "a wooden gun to the people themselves."[64] At worst (that is now, or when Thoreau wrote), "government is a demonical force ... a monster ... a semi-human tiger or ox, stalking over the earth with its heart taken out and the top of its brain shot away." It makes citizens, terribly, agents of injustice. That is the most profound disrespect.

Acts of civil disobedience announce the intention to make our obligations as citizens conditional. But Thoreau does not actually "dissolve the union" between himself and the state. It is one thing to reject as he did membership in voluntary associations like Brook Farm or the Congregational church or any antislavery society ("I did not wish to be regarded as member of any incorporated society which I have not joined"[65]). It is another to disassociate from democracy. And Thoreau does not want complete separation. "Neighbor" is the right name for the status of ongoing connection when in desperate times "to speak practically and as a citizen" is not an acceptable moral standpoint. When identity as a citizen or "officer of the government" is not something we can accept for ourselves, then Thoreau speaks as a "well-disposed man" and a neighbor. He retains association, common ground, reciprocity. He acknowledges all the "duties" of neighbors. Neighbor is for him the foundational, residual democratic status.

We've seen what treating neighbors with respect entails. If only we pay attention, we see our neighbors in the round as absolutely unique individuals, we receive their "flower and fruit." We create some distance and space for care of the self, neither meddling nor embracing. We know this much from *Walden,* respect for neighbors requires a vantage point from which we see not the "old musty cheese that we are" but rather the accident of proximity, separateness, and foreignness. The final respect we pay is minding our neighbors' business as a spur to and ingredient of minding our own. Care of the self runs through them. The actual practices of citizenship, on Thoreau's severe view of democracy in America as he knew it, contribute nothing to this. "All the duties of neighbors" can't be itemized, but as neighbors, in contrast to citizens, we can take the measure of the commitments we consent to (the terms of reciprocity, speaking out, the critical moments of live and let live) and we can elect detachment.

Thoreau lays out several perspectives on democratic government — all of which are available to us:

> Seen from a lower point of view, the Constitution, with all its faults, is very good; the law and the courts are very respectable; even this State and this American government are in many respects, very admirable and rare things, to be thankful for, such as a great many have described them; but seen from a point of view a little higher, they are what I have described them; and seen from a higher still, and the highest, who shall say what they are, or that they are worth looking at or thinking of at all?[66]

Each of these standpoints provides understanding, and each is necessary to democracy in America. The highest standpoint from which we may question whether "this American government" is worth looking at or thinking of at all, has made its way troublingly into American thought. Thoreau was writing at a moment of crisis, anticipating the coming moral and political catastrophe. But this rejectionist stance has fueled a strain of profound antipathy toward government even if it is not unjust. Shorn of Thoreau's severe ethical strictures and blind to his several concurrent perspectives on the state, it spurns the (also true) standpoint from which our political institutions are in many respects "very admirable and rare things to be thankful for." It invites contemptuous disregard for the shaping, protective force of government when it operates fairly in society and in the background of life at home. Thoreau's deprecation of coercive political authority that turns citizens into agents of injustice is contorted in the strain of unrelieved anti-governmentalism that taints American political thought.

"Respect, as a neighbor and well-disposed man" need not take on an antipolitical life of its own, though. In fact, it is essential to democracy in America, Thoreau knew, especially when democratic government and fellow citizens make us instruments of terrible injustice, and instigate betrayal and violence. The meaning and value of the democracy of everyday life among neighbors is evident when democracy proper is disfigured. When democratic politics leaves us at the end of our tether, Thoreau's demand to treat one another with respect as a neighbor emerges as democracy's "saving remnant."

It is not hard to recognize in Thoreau's reflections on neighborliness the democracy of everyday life as I have set it out. All the elements are there, transposed by his gorgeous, "extra-vagrant" terms. What are his incessant warnings against the petty private despotisms that produce lives of "quiet desperation" but reasons for speaking out? "Giving a dose of ourselves" is reciprocity—though neighbors' status as rough equals and "decent folk" is aestheticized. And what is Thoreau's distance and neutral ground, his "let every one mind his own business, and endeavor to be what he was made"[67] but a rich form of live and let live? The democracy of everyday life is transfigured by Thoreau, of course; that too is his business—making ordinary "decent folk" strange, foreign. But we see these alterations for what they are: neighbors refracted through a great intelligence and with perfect confidence in the possibility of self- and mutual transformation. Throughout, there is the moral significance of the quotidian: the art of affecting the quality of the day. *Walden* and Thoreau's great political essay are enduring because they are at once a script for "how I live" and a scripture for "good neighbor nation."

# CONCLUSION

# Political Theory and the Democracy of Everyday Life in America

At the end of *Politics as a Vocation* Max Weber advises: "Those not up to the task of politics would have done better to cultivate neighborly contacts with other people, individually, in a simple and straightforward way, and . . . to go about their daily work without any fuss."[1] There is nothing solely individual, simple, straightforward, or without fuss about neighborliness. Good neighbor does not ask less of us than citizenship, and it is no easier. This much is certain: Citizenship is well theorized but not very well practiced. Neighborliness is well practiced but not very well theorized. My aim is to construct a moral and political theory of good neighbor.

Robert Ellickson has it that "the overarching substantive norm of the rural residents of Shasta County is that one should be a 'good neighbor,'"[2] and so it is with most of us, most of the time. In America, good neighbor is shaped by the democracy of everyday life as a regulative ideal. Its elements—reciprocity, speaking out, and live and let live—apply to weighty, often fraught relations in that vital, sensitive place, home. It demands judgment day after day, and a fair amount of self-discipline. Proving ourselves trustworthy can be difficult, and assessing others is often difficult too. The internal tension between minding our own business and minding our neighbors' is taxing. Where the democracy of everyday life fails to shape our encounters, we recognize plainly and painfully that the quality of life is deranged.

The democracy of everyday life has a place of its own, then, around home. That is its domain. After we take account of organized political life, work, membership groups, social circles, friends, and family, there is this "remainder." Its importance owes to the depth and intensity of interests and values attendant to life at home, in proximity to neighbors. There, daily trespasses and kindnesses are inescapable. There, neighbors' encounters and claims are concrete and immediate, not at all distant or abstract as our rights and obligations as citizens often are. We shouldn't underestimate the significance of neighbor relations, just because and not despite the fact that they are mundane. Again, "To affect the quality of the day, that is the highest of arts," and encounters with neighbors brighten or degrade the day, every day.

Psychological and empirical accuracy requires taking the democracy of everyday life into account; at stake is a fuller picture, I won't claim a complete picture, of the democratic ethos in the United States. And political theory requires taking into account its relation to democracy proper. In this Conclusion I hone in on the value of the democracy of everyday life for democracy in America.

## Neighbors and the Moral Uses of Pluralism[3]

In the Introduction I wrote about the intimate biography of a political theory. Personal experience with a neighbor, the noise bully down the hall, motivated this project, I said, and that is true. Working out the elements of the democracy of everyday life had an additional powerful impetus for me as a political theorist—to affirm the moral uses of pluralism. Appreciation for the *experience* of pluralism drove me to attend to life at home, among neighbors. It underlies my insistence on the moral distinctiveness of day-to-day encounters there. For the democracy of everyday life is one piece of the structure and experience of pluralism in America. Modern society as a whole—certainly contemporary democracies with flourishing civil societies—is marked by differentiated spheres with their own identifiable norms and institutions. Various domains of social and political life are parceled out among, indeed they are constituted by, differentiated systems of law, modes of authority, and internal organization. Less often studied than this fact of plural spheres is the personal experience of pluralism.

Here is what I mean. We work with others. We belong to voluntary associations. We are nested in circles of friends and family and informal social groups. We are quite aware that we fall within the jurisdiction of several layers of government: official providers of public goods and services and enforcers of rights and obligations. We move back and forth among these spheres, and with this comes what I call the personal, moral uses of pluralism.[4] We are many-sided, if not protean, personalities for whom shifting involvements among spheres is not only unavoidable, a fact of life in society, but also a condition for moral development and change. For self-understanding and self-esteem. For compensation in one domain for deficits and deprivations suffered in others. For cultivating vital aspects of character that have little to do with specifically democratic traits and dispositions. For providing a safety valve for unconventional relations and behavior. For recuperation. For experimentation. For individuality. Our identity as good neighbor is not coincident with our self in other settings. We are not of a piece. Shifting involvements among separate spheres is required by pluralism as we know it; more, it is an exhibition of human capacity. It draws on and fuels our complex, resilient moral psychology. "I left the woods for as good a reason as I went there. Perhaps it seemed to me that I had several more lives to live, and could not spare any more time for that one," Thoreau wrote.[5] We can say, with him, of every domain including home: "Thank heaven here is not all the world."

Preservation of multiple spheres is the great promise and charge of liberal democracy distinguished by personal freedom, made meaningful by the possibility of shifting involvements. In contrast, a social structure — even if it is pluralist and complex, but made rigid by caste and class and other entrenched walls and divisions — inhibits shifting involvements. Segmented pluralism shares something of the dangers of holism. In short, the fact of differentiated spheres is insufficient; what matters is the moral uses of pluralism.

I affirm all this because underlying my attention to the distinctiveness of the democracy of everyday life is aversion to social and political holism as an error of simplification and more importantly as a threat to moral personality and liberty. A great deal is at stake.[6] Something is lost if the democracy of everyday life is overlooked, or flattened out, or seen as valuable only insofar as it instantiates public democratic principles and practices. Something is lost by assimilating neighbor relations to civic ones. That is why I "think against" tendencies to flatten out our social and moral world. It is why I have attended especially to discontinuities between the democracy of everyday life and the public realm of democratic institutions and practices. Navigating relations with neighbors as I theorize them—the specific way we move out of ourselves there—should be understood as an integral aspect of the moral uses of pluralism.

Within the wide compass of plural spheres, the domain of life around home has another distinction. It is one we all occupy. Even those of us without employment or workplace, who are not members of any organization or association, who are detached from civic life—even the most isolated among us. With tragic exceptions, we all have a home (not excepting a makeshift camp under a highway overpass) and with it neighbors, a mental map of this terrain, and the task of navigating encounters there. The domain of life around home in proximity to neighbors is the one sphere in our various, variegated life worlds that affords a common experience—not in terms of particular encounters, of course, but in terms of identity as a neighbor. Minding our own business and minding our neighbors' is a challenge we all know. The democracy of everyday life is a source of commonality in a way that work, or membership, or political participation is not. Reciprocity among "decent folk," speaking out, and live and let live, shape our experiences of home and their meaning. They affect us too, it is abundantly clear, by their absence or eclipse.

## Isn't Unadorned Neighborliness Enough?

Of course, not every aspect of neighbor relations must be understood in terms of the democracy of everyday life. Some conduct is adequately characterized in general moral terms that apply regardless of relation or proximity. The obligations neighbors have to warn of danger and to avoid acts of arrant cruelty, for example, are obligations in every setting; neighbors just have more occasion than others to look out for trouble and more occasion to make people nearby miserable. The same is true of the imperative to assist in critical situations: neighbors or not, we are enjoined to offer help in emergencies or special situations of need. Even so I've argued that rescuing, warning, saving, and consoling have specific meaning beyond their practical consequences when performed by neighbors; they are profoundly affecting evidence of normalcy. So even here the democracy of everyday life adds something to the obligations to warn, and do no harm, and provide rudimentary assistance that hold for us all, everywhere.

My account also challenges the notion of an ethic of neighborliness that goes a step beyond general moral decency in its demands but fails to entail the democracy of everyday life as I've laid it out. We can sketch a general ethic of friendliness, helpfulness, and the requirement to take one another's basic interests into account that applies widely if not universally.[7] I have no quarrel with this (though except for "love they neighbor" I have not found any such ethic articulated in moral philosophy). I have not made a comparative study of neighbor relations, but I can say with confidence that nothing in a general norm of neighborliness as we might propose it promises a democratic ethos. Reciprocity posed in terms of rough equality among "decent folk" is a characteristic of good neighbor here, where in other places give and take is not characterized by (and does not aim at) disregard for, class, status, ethnicity, and so on. In many places the matter and manner of friendliness, helpfulness, and reciprocity are regulated by social rank or hierarchy or tribe or tradition or clientelism. Similarly, neighbors in many places may speak out to enforce "what anyone would do, here," but the delineation of offense and procedures for responding are set by authority, or appeal to the wisdom of a local elder, or by strict adherence to tradition rather than neighbors' self-governing enforcement. Or, to take one more example: minding our own business, and live and let live, have little meaning in settings where neighbors are kin or bonded by ethnic or religious solidarity, their lives tightly intertwined, or where constant interactions are a matter of sheer economic or political necessity. In all these circumstances, neighbors expect to know and communicate the details of one another's lives, and absence of privacy and personal control is an unexceptional state of affairs.

The democracy of everyday life shapes experience and our identity as a good neighbor in the domain of home, then. Good neighbor is a true democratic ideal here, but a false model for democratic citizenship. I have stressed this point because conflations of neighbor and citizen make regular appearances in democratic theory. Inattentive to the separate and distinct sphere of life around home and to the moral uses of pluralism (or not inattentive but intent on diminishing its significance in favor of some greater democratic holism), political theorists are prone to collapse the distinction between the democracy of everyday life among neighbors on the one hand and citizens exercising rights and duties and participating in civic life on the other. They look for and prescribe consistency and do not attend to the valuable differences and discontinuities I have brought to the foreground.

Continuity between the democracy of everyday life and formal democracy might be stated in abstract terms like these: "efforts to relate individual well-being with collective well-being," for example, or "figuring out how to live in relations of equality with others whom we did not choose." These formulations are correct but not clarifying, and they are far from capturing the experience of either neighbor or citizen. But two versions of the democratic wish conflate neighbor and citizen in a more specific way. One version depoliticizes democracy; the other politicizes neighbors. The domain of neighbors outside of and beyond politics either swallows up democratic government and citizenship or neighborly private life and sociability is swallowed up by public principles and practices. Visualize the first as bottom-up: neighbor is cast as model or metaphor of good citizen. Visualize the second as top-down: pubic principles and practices dictate neighbor relations, or should. Both are totalizing—insufficiently appreciative of the moral uses of pluralism.

## The Democratic Wish #1:
## Good Citizen = Good Neighbor

Main currents of American political thought cast neighborhoods as the premier site of political participation.[8] A persistent political romance sees neighbors as the best hope for democracy. The term "citizen," evoking as it does *civis* and the ancient city, encourages images of democratic politics as face-to-face and (adjusted for historical changes in social standing and racial and gender norms) inclusive. Small size, accessible arenas, fewer cognitive demands, and the presumed responsiveness of local officials combine to make neighborhoods appear to be the ideal site of active citizenship. And, the argument continues, national democracy is built up from the structures of localism.[9] This recurrent democratic wish, Jeffersonian in origin, tied to Progressivism by John Dewey, and echoed repeatedly since, represents the neighborhood as democracy's "regenerative kernel."[10]

Nowhere is the determination to regard neighbors as building blocks of democratic participation more insistent than in Mary Parker Follett's Progressive faith in "the homely realities of the neighborhood meeting."[11] "People should organize themselves into neighborhood groups to express their daily life, to bring to the surface the needs, desires and aspirations of that life, that these needs should become the substance of politics, and that these neighborhood groups should become the recognized political unit."[12]

Follett's charge to neighbors went well beyond occasional cooperation in building a playground. "The right method of attacking all our problems" is at stake: regular meetings, group discussion, neighbors' initiatives.[13] What could be more romantic—by which I don't mean utopian but rather bound up with a wish for harmonious holism—than Follett imagining that neighborhood organization "gives us the best opportunity we have yet discovered of finding the unity underneath all our differences ... of living the consciously creative life"?[14]

Follett knew what she was up against:

> Whenever I speak of neighborhood organization to my friends, those who disagree with me at once become violent on the subject. I have never understood why it inflames them more easily than other topics. ... They tell me of the pettiness of neighborhood life, and I have to listen to the stories of neighborhood iniquities ranging from small gossip to determined boycotting.[15]

She cautions that by itself being a good neighbor is no preparation for civic engagement. Neighbors' value to democracy depends on forming and joining associations and on the transformative effect of participatory membership. Put contentiously, neighborhood groups are "boot camps of citizenship" that convert neighbors into self-governing citizens. When social scientists today refer to civic activists as "good neighbors" we hear an echo of Follett's Progressive imagination.

Of course, neighbors do enter the civic sphere. Case studies track the steps from informal complaining and rallying in the hallway to collective problem-solving and advocacy in civic groups. Of course, the "needs, desires, and aspirations" of daily life can (Follett writes "should") provide substance for politics. The course from speaking out against an offensive neighbor to local activism has been travelled often enough. As one classic study argues, a key to any sort of political involvement is being asked, and activists may recruit the people next door.[16] I have no wish to diminish the fact that neighbors sometimes enter political life on the basis of domestic concerns and at the urging of people living nearby. But there is no necessary or automatic inclination or impetus leading from the democracy of everyday life to civic activism. Part of my effort has been to give neighbor relations their full due by recognizing that the day-to-day business of reciprocity and speaking out does not normally spring from or generate political concerns. Nor does their chief meaning and value—not even their value for democratic public life—lie as a stimulus to political participation. When our encounters revolve around sewers and schools, when neighbors move from confronting the bully down the hall to organized associations seeking improvement by political means, we no longer view one another in the simple guise of neighbors and "decent folk." We make claims on one another that go beyond mundane reciprocity, speaking out, and live and let live. Of course, when we act in public life on matters that touch on the environment around home we don't cease to be neighbors. But in organized political activity we may very well cease to identify ourselves principally as neighbors and we may cease to be seen as acting qua neighbor by the people next door. We are advocates and partisans. We are not attending, now, to the business of neighbors—to whether the character of our everyday encounters ensures or degrades the quality of the day.

There is this empirical fact to contend with, too: whether the measure is voting, attending meetings, contacting officials, or something else, local participation falls short of the democratic wish that sees neighbors as democracy's "regenerative kernel." We might expect the limitations of actual practice to discourage equating good citizen with good neighbor, but over and over in democratic theory neighbors figure as model. The ideal sometimes takes this form: citizens should relate to one another *as if* they were neighbors, extending habits of reciprocity to the nation as a whole. The thought is that citizenship on the model of neighbor would illuminate our connections to one another and undergird more robust social justice. But neighbors' commitments are voluntary and limited; our encounters do not aim at the provision of public goods; rough equality of reciprocity is not a homely application of justice. Neighborly give and take is a poor touchstone for shared sacrifice and solidarity. Neighbor relations, personal and individual as they are, do little to clarify and a lot to obscure the motives, interests, justifications, and decisions entailed by justice among strangers, which citizens are.

The problem with political theory that sees neighbors as democracy's "regenerative kernel" is methodological, too. If theorists would straightforwardly pursue the analogy between citizens and neighbors, they would do what I have done throughout: examine the conditions and limits of claimed similarities and differences. The importance of juxtaposition and analogical reasoning for political theory is precisely that it requires us to spell out distinctions and differences: friend/neighbor, neighbor/citizen.[17] Without it, we do not see what is inappropriate or mistaken or illusory in the connections and continuities we assert.

The identification of citizen with neighbor seems to be indestructible, however, a perennial aspiration. The impulse to borrow the luster of good neighbor for citizenship approaches sentimentalism. It adds an accessible, homely tenor to democracy. It personalizes and miniaturizes political life. It softens the severity of demanding contributions to national security and distributive justice. It rejects at a stroke the characterization of political participation as partisan or ideological

Worse than sentimental, citizen as neighbor is unsober, and in its way dogmatic. For reciprocity among neighbors as "decent folk" turns on the real possibility of disregarding precisely the social inequalities, racial and sectarian differences, and conflicting ideological commitments that citizens bring to public life. The good neighbor ideal, practiced often enough, disregards these differences, which cannot and should not be disregarded in public affairs. They just are the circumstances of politics. They provide the perspectives and the substance of political decision-making, which is always partial and partisan. In short, the collapse of citizen into neighbor obscures the purposes, motives, interests, and justifications that shape democratic politics and government.

There is one more, intractable problem with taking neighbors as model citizens and democracy's "regenerative kernel." As neighbors we can effectively initiate and respond to give and take, speak out against offenses, offer warnings, award people living nearby the assurances of live and let live, and more. Being a good neighbor is open to everyone; it is not constrained by status or resources. This experience of rough equality and sense of personal efficacy—the democratic ethos of good neighbor—are rare in political life. Appeal to neighbors as model or metaphor obscures citizens' usual remove from sites of decision, inequality of assets and political opportunity, the power of elites. Put strongly, neighbor as model diverts attention from the absence in our lives as citizens of anything like an experience of self-governing. Setting formal juridical equality aside, citizenship is deeply, irremediably differentiated. These critical facts should be inescapable—but the equation good citizen = good neighbor permits escape. The dogmatism in taking as a model neighbors for whom rough equality of reciprocity among "decent folk" is realizable is that it can perpetuate as if it were actual the unrealized notion of equal citizenship. Neighbor functions as an easy gloss.

## The Democratic Wish #2: The Logic of Congruence

"Thinking against"—my persistently contrastive treatment of the democracy of everyday life—is trained at a second version of the democratic wish. Here, the conflation of neighbor and citizen is reversed, and good neighbors are seen as artifacts of the penetration of public democratic principles and practices into the domain of life around home. This follows, indeed enshrines, a familiar tenet of social science and democratic theory: "the logic of congruence."[18]

The orthodoxy has it that political stability, good government, and the reproduction of democratic citizens depend on the infusion of public principles, institutions, and processes "all the way down" into civil society and private life. Democracy is weakened if citizens suffer cognitive or moral dissonance, the argument goes, and only legal saturation and insistent civic education can generate civic virtues and capacities and commitment to democratic values. Political equality, for example, demands habits and sentiments that cannot be realized without public democratic culture pervading the voluntary associations of civil society.[19] Today, the standard imagery is vertical, the prescribed direction top-down. In short, the logic of congruence poses democratic institutions and practices as primary and assigns other domains value as necessary supports.

Democratic theory offers up something approaching a holistic vision, one too inattentive to the multiple facets of moral personality. One that undervalues the moral uses of pluralism—including our capacity as neighbors to make a collective effort to lead a private life. In the "logic of congruence," pluralism gives way to totalism. The democratic logic of congruence is not totalitarian, of course; it aims at inclusive and egalitarian civic identity. But it reflects holistic impulses, and from that perspective, my account of the democracy of everyday life is incompletely saturated by public principles.

I don't mean to say that the democracy of everyday life is *incongruent* with public democratic principles and practices, or only "softly" so and only episodically. The democracy of everyday life does not pose a direct challenge by proposing an alternative civic ideal for public life; its strictures apply in the domain of neighbors. And the claims it makes on us are normally complementary with political obligations. But because of the weightiness and intensity of the specific interests and values we ascribe to private life around home, there are tensions. The democracy of everyday life and demands of citizenship sometimes pull apart and bring conflicts of value to the surface. Live and let live prescribes hesitance to report the undocumented immigrants next door, for example. Or, the claims of privacy among neighbors go well beyond those recognized by law; our rooms with a view produce their own demanding ethic of reticence. My point is simply that political democracy and the democracy of everyday life are bound up with one another in ways more nuanced than congruence theory and a single causal direction of influence—top-down—suggests.

If I have attended more to discontinuities than to continuities between democracy and the democracy of everyday life, it is out of faithfulness to reliable though not invariable felt experience and as a corrective to the imperial impulses of the "logic of congruence." But I don't want to over-correct. Most of the time, in most encounters among neighbors, the public political dimension is out of mind. Not always, however. In the past when neighbors used racial covenants to exclude blacks, they applied public principles of segregation to the private sphere. People exposed to preju-dice today may be hard put to distinguish a neighbors' detachment and her claim to be minding her own business from discrimination. For so-cially vulnerable minorities, the zone of politics and the zone of neighbors may not seem discontinuous, and the question of public principles of jus-tice is not out of mind in encounters with neighbors. Inviting vulnerable neighbors to let down that guard, signaling that we recognize them as "decent folk," is part of the immensely important work of live and let live.

My point is that there is little danger of democratic theorists overlook-ing the fact that legal intervention in the personal and private may be required; applications of "the logic of congruence" are their focus. But there is a danger that the meaning and value of the domain of everyday life disappears in any but the political sense. In focusing on the democracy of everyday life and practices of reciprocity, speaking out, and live and let live, I bring that world of experience beyond politics back into focus.

Today, "adaptive change" advances in the direction of the top-down "logic of congruence." The incursion is evident in the spread of legally binding arrangements governing neighbor interactions. Homeowner as-sociations, co-ops, and condominium covenants submit residents to for-mal rules, elected authorities, quasi-majoritarian governance structures, itemized rights and duties, and mechanisms for legal appeal. Do these mandated practices crowd out the democracy of everyday life? They af-ford it less scope. Is this a loss? From the moment the first Puritans landed in Massachusetts Bay, "before the soil of Old England was off their boots, they were extolling 'the cheapnesse . . . great hospitality . . . kind neigh-borhood . . . and valiant acts of *former* times,' fretting that there were 'no such now a dayes.' "[20] Melancholy and nostalgia are constants. But no-where is truncation of informal relations total. The "logic of congruence" is always, necessarily incomplete. There is always a remainder of encoun-ters shaped by the democracy of everyday life, and, of course, occasions for miserably falling off from it. Experience tells us there is always a large and morally significant remainder.

I have focused just there, on aspects of neighbor relations outside of institutions and formal rules, where appeal to authorities is unavailable; where even exhaustive homeowner covenants do not tell us what to do about the noise bully, or whether and in what "temper of reproach" to enforce "what anyone would do, here." The moral identity of good neighbor and the ideals of the democracy of everyday life have their own history and present power. We know this, finally, from the intensity of our personal experiences with neighbors, and from the agitated stories we tell about life in proximity to others around home.

## The Phenomenology of the Democracy of Everyday Life

Analytically, then, I've differentiated good neighbor from good citizen. The distinctiveness of the democracy of everyday life as we conceive it and experience it for ourselves is as important, and I have taken my bearings from "inside." My description of the moral psychology of neighbors is neither random nor exhaustive; I've simply taken experience and made it less fragmentary and confused, and a little more complete. Every move from internal experience to narration involves interpretation.[21] The democracy of everyday life, I argue, captures experiential meaning and contributes to this meaning.

From this standpoint, the temptation to represent relations at home in terms of formal democratic principles is at odds with the internal meaning of what we do. With exceptions I have noted, we just don't think in these terms.[22] We do not invoke civic rights or obligations or democratic processes of decision-making in our encounters with neighbors day to day. We don't use these concepts to narrate our interactions or to explain or justify our conduct, not to ourselves and not to others. When we acknowledge through acts of reciprocity the rough equality of neighbors as "decent folk," we are not expressing commitment to political equality or social equality either; rather, we are disregarding these categories. We don't understand speaking out against the bully down the hall as a shadow or anticipation of organized political participation, and in responding we don't think to replicate processes of democratic decision-making that are required in other settings. Rather, we take it as spontaneous protection against a neighbor who degrades life at home. We conform to the regulative ideal live and let live without invoking the principle of toleration or necessarily valuing a generally open and tolerant disposition. Rather, we are responding to these particular neighbors in this situation, recognizing our mutual vulnerability, offering the assurance of quotidian encounters without fear.

Good neighbor is remote from the sense citizens correctly have that public democratic principles and practices of fairness or due process are impersonal and apply generally, without exception, and with little discretion. Reciprocity, speaking out, live and let live come into play in the course of a history of encounters with particular individuals, and qua neighbors we do not feel obliged to be inclusive. We can detach, withdraw. Elective affinity is consistent with the democracy of everyday life so long as leaving this neighbor out is not stigmatizing. Put simply, we are fully aware that in encounters with neighbors we can modulate demands and try to grasp and control the full measure of our commitments that as citizens we cannot.

## Democracy's Saving Remnant

In mapping the terrain, I've argued against, pressed the negative: what the democracy of everyday life is *not*—*not* reducible to simple decency or some general ethic of neighborliness. And, once its democratic ethos is affirmed, *not* reducible to a pale, incomplete version of civic relations. Conflating public principles and practices and the democracy of everyday life is an error. More than an error, it is a counterfeit account of both neighbor and citizen. It is at odds with our experience and the meaning we assign to neighbors good and bad, and it is unfaithful to the terms in which we express these evaluations to one another and to ourselves.

We learn from settler, immigrant, and suburban narrative threads and from our own experience that good neighbors can provide aid and company, signal that we are safe with one another, offer gestures of recognition that enhance the quality of life—especially under exigent conditions, help repair newcomers' ignorance, "show us how to practice in the world." All are infused with the democratic ethos I have described. But *qua* neighbors we are not civic activists, agents of social justice, guardians of equal rights, or citizens committed to reform. If neighbor relations are cast as a way station to civic engagement or as exemplary citizenship, the democracy of everyday life is lost from view. Good neighbor is not the equivalent of good citizen or preparation for it, and America as the "good neighbor nation" is certainly not the whole of American democracy.

What is at stake in my theory of the distinctiveness of the democratic ethos of good neighbor and the independence of the domain of neighbor relations? I've spoken of its inestimable value for us personally and individually, in everyday life, at home, and in extreme situations. I've spoken, too, of its place in the larger picture of the moral uses of pluralism. Good neighbor has a claim on political theory, too. What is the significance of the democracy of everyday life for democracy in America?

The American story was from the start a history of neighbors. Neighbor relations and the democratic ethos I describe came first, and institutional development and articulated, legally enshrined public principles came later. [23] Reciprocity among "decent folk," self-governing neighbors speaking out, and the injunction to live and let live preceded and underwrote public life and political practices. This conforms fairly enough to Tocqueville's story. It conforms to the narrative offered up in settler, immigrant, and suburban accounts of neighbors enacting the democratic ethos outside of and apart from political institutions.

We can think of the democracy of everyday life as the substrate of American democracy. As democracy's personal, individual, human substrate—its earthy material, its environment. The democracy of everyday life is familiar and accessible to us, whether or not we articulate it. Bound up with good neighbor as a facet of moral identity, it is there when we move out into civil society and political life, and again when we come home. Its importance is not as preparation or stand-in for political participation and political institutions. To be clear: I intend no brief against political activism. I am not encouraging some overlooked exit from political engagement. I suggest nothing so absurd as neighbor relations substituting for or replacing government, law, and public policy. Rather, the democracy of everyday life alerts us to the limits of the political and to the anxieties of democracy. It provides a ground, a place to stand, when consciously organized aspects of democratic public life are fragile or broken entirely. When we are reluctant to join civic associations or have no confidence in the meaning and value of our vote and voice, when political resources are liable to be overwhelmed, weakened, or abandoned, we neighbors can sustain the democracy of everyday life. The democracy of everyday life is the enduring substrate of democracy, which we fall back on at crucial moments to maintain our democratic bearings.

So:

The democracy of everyday life, with its disregard for social and political inequalities in deference to neighbors as "decent folk," is a gauge of the profusion of sectarian identities and social and economic inequalities in public political life.

The improvised self-governing of the democracy of everyday life—and the sense of collective efficacy that comes with rallying, decision-making, and enforcement—is a gauge of our distance and felt remove from sites of political decision.

The democracy of everyday life is an index of political catastrophe. When officials set neighbors against one another or condone violence so that everyday life is horribly deranged, we recognize that democracy is diminished in a special, deeper way than exclusively political standards allow us to see.

The democracy of everyday life is a compass for maintaining our democratic bearings when organized aspects of social and political life have lost their integrity or simply do not make sense to us. When public life is unjust, or beyond our capacity to influence, or so unappealing as to provoke retreat—when the mind is at the end of its tether with government and politics and with our fellow citizens, or when mindlessness rules—the democracy of everyday life is a hardy remainder. Not a substitute for political democracy and not compensation for political disaster, but a saving remnant.

That was Thoreau's provocative conclusion: treating one another as neighbors is available to us even when our government and we as citizens have fallen into evil or just fallen off the rails.

We can understand it this way. Though good neighbor is imperfectly realized, neighbors are the last (as they were the first) station of the democratic ethos, a bulwark against its disappearance rooted deeper even than a public culture of rights. And the quotidian disposition to see neighbors as "decent folk," speaking out, and live and let live are ethical bulwarks against our own worst impulses and against the demons of cruelty and despotism, large and small, unleashed where we live.

The democracy of everyday life is ground for maintaining our democratic bearings just because it arises outside the bounds of public, political life—because it grows out of experiences of sociability that are not fastened to particular institutions and do not usher in prescriptions for repairing political dysfunction. It is a form of democratic excellence. One that is known, accessible, contained already in our day-to-day encounters.[24]

Constancy, intimacy, and love are for friends. Good works are for great souls. Justice is for citizens. I've set out what good neighbor promises and demands of us. I've portrayed it as a deeply etched facet of personal moral identity and as the substrate of democracy in America.

# ACKNOWLEDGMENTS

My initial debt is to my neighbors at the Payne Project in Cambridge and at Shearwater in Truro, Massachusetts, whose kindnesses and offenses inspired this work. My second debt is to colleagues, family, and friends who shared their stories and joined in puzzling through the ethic of neighborliness.

Harvard University provided me with a sabbatical leave. The Straus Institute at New York University Law School provided a venue for sharing early versions of this work with a wonderful, neighborly group of fellows. I am grateful to Rick Pildes and Sam Issacharoff for inviting me to join their yearlong program on democracy in 2012–13, and for acknowledging a place for "the democracy of everyday life."

Two anonymous reviewers for Princeton University Press gave me invaluable advice; I have tried to respond to their sharp queries and generous suggestions. Readers like these provide the gift of articulating just what the author has tried to say, and why it has value. My editor of many years, Rob Tempio, offered encouragement and advice, not least that less is sometimes more and that titles matter.

In seminars and lectures, colleagues and graduate students helped me sift through material and sharpen arguments. I am grateful to colleagues who read and discussed pieces of this project and whose suggestions I have incorporated, sometimes verbatim: Jeffrey Abramson, Eric Beerbohm, Bruce Cain, Joshua Cherniss, John Ferejohn, Cary Franklin, Lee Ann Fujii, Bryan Garsten, Jeffrey Green, Harry Hirsch, Christopher Kutz, Charles Lesch, Jacob Levy, Russell Muirhead, Kalypso Nikolaidis, Anna Rosenblum Palmer, Sabeel Rahman, Andrew Rehfield, Rob Reich, Samuel Scheffler, Lucas Swaine, Dennis Thompson, Jeremy Waldron, and Alan Wertheimer.

# NOTES

## Introduction: Good Neighbor Nation

1. Judith Shklar, *Ordinary Vices* (Cambridge, MA: Harvard University Press, 1984).
2. Willa Cather, *My Mortal Enemy* (New York: Vintage Classics, 1990), p. 56.
3. Aesop's Fables, 83, "Jupiter, Neptune, Minerva, and Momus"; Henry D. Thoreau, "Walden," in *Walden, Civil Disobedience and Other Writings* (New York: Norton, 2008), p. 26.
4. Cited in Emily Cockayne, *Cheek by Jowl: A History of Neighbors* (London: Bodley Head, 2012), p. 48.
5. Isaiah Berlin, "Two Concepts of Liberty," in *Four Essays on Liberty* (Oxford: Oxford University Press, 1969), p. 129.
6. Thoreau, "Walden," pp. 31, 34.
7. Robert Frost, "The Constant Symbol," in *Selected Prose* (New York: Collier Books, 1968), p. 24.
8. Doris Lessing, *The Diaries of Jane Somers: The Diary of a Good Neighbor* (New York: Vintage Books, 1983), pp. 8–9.
9. "Between neighbors this hostility is so common that it can seem to be the human condition," see Jonathan Glover, *Humanity: A Moral History of the Twentieth Century* (New Haven: Yale University Press, 2000), p. 119.
10. Vasily Grossman, "The Old Teacher," in *The Road*, trans. Robert and Elizabeth Chandler (London: MacLehose, 2010), pp. 112, 114.
11. Thoreau, *Walden*, p. 65.
12. I have substituted neighborliness for friendship in Danielle Allen's sentence in *Talking to Strangers: Anxieties of Citizenship since Brown v. Board of Education* (Chicago: University of Chicago Press, 2004), pp. 136–37, xxi, 120.
13. Soren Kierkegaard, *Works of Love* (Princeton: Princeton University Press, 1995), p. 52.
14. Mark 12:31.
15. Mary Parker Follett, *The New State: Group Organization the Solution of Popular Government* (University Park, PA: Pennsylvania State University Press, 1998), p. 193.
16. This policy with respect to Latin America was designed to mark a break from the imperialist past. On the relation between settler nation and the dynamic of oppression and exclusion/republicanism, see Aziz Rana, *The*

*Two Faces of American Freedom* (Cambridge, MA: Harvard University Press, 2010).

17. Sigmund Freud, *Civilization and Its Discontents* (New York: W. W. Norton, 1961), p. 63; "occasion for enmity" at p. 66.

18. Robert C. Ellickson, *Order without Law: How Neighbors Settle Disputes* (Cambridge, MA: Harvard University Press, 1991), pp. 184–85.

19. Michel de Certeau, *The Practice of Everyday Life*, trans. Timothy J. Tomasik (Minneapolis: University of Minnesota Press, 1998), vol 2, p. xxi.

20. I write against the backbground of feminist thought, which has effectively pointed out that the public/private boundary, conceived in legal and political terms, has operated to preserve patriarchy. That the private is revealed to be political, and may have to be more deliberately politicized in order to mitigate domination and enforce standards of equality in the family, above all, is one enduring contribution of feminism. (Though where to draw this line between public and private is an ongoing problem in law and politics, and for political theory.) But this project should not eclipse the experience and personal meaningfulness of the private and sociable domain around home and the regulative ideal of good neighbor.

21. The idea of the present narrator is from Vivian Gornick, *The Situation and the Story* (New York: Farrar, Straus and Giroux, 2001).

22. Harry Eckstein, *The Natural History of Congruence Theory* (Denver, CO: University of Denver, 1980), p. xiii.

23. Certeau, *The Practice of Everyday Life*, vol. 2, p. xiv.

24. Robert J. Sampson, *Great American City: Chicago and the Enduring Neighborhood Effect* (Chicago: University of Chicago Press, 2012), p. 6.

25. "Mr. Roger's Neighborhood" had two: the "real TV neighborhood" and the neighborhood of make-believe. The prevalence of this setting is understandable; the people next door and down the block are the child's first world outside home. The message that people living nearby are friendly, accessible, and safe is driven home.

26. Joan Didion, *Slouching towards Bethlehem* (New York: Washington Square Press, 1961), p. 94.

27. Charles Taylor, "Interpretation and the Science of Man," *Review of Metaphysics* 25, no. 1 (September 1971): 3–51 at 16.

28. Cited in Greil Marcus, *Mystery Train* (New York: Penguin Books, 1975), p. 50.

29. Taylor, "Interpretation and the Science of Man," p. 4.

## Chapter 1: Who Is My Neighbor?

1. Erving Goffman cited in Suzanne B. Kurth, "Friendships and Friendly Relations," in *Friendship as a Social Institution* (New Brunswick, NJ: Transaction Publishers, 2011 [1970]), pp. 141–42.

2. Emily Cockayne, *Cheek by Jowl: A History of Neighbors* (London: The Bodley Head, 2012), p. 6.

3. Pierre Mayol, in *The Practice of Everyday Life* (Minneapolis: University of Minnesota Press, 1998), vol. 2, p. 9.

4. Michael Walzer, *Spheres of Justice: A Defense of Pluralism and Equality* (New York: Basic Books, 1983), p. 32.

5. F. Scott Fitzgerald, *The Great Gatsby* (New York: Collier, 1991), p. 189.

6. Harper Lee, *To Kill a Mockingbird* (New York: Grand Central Publishing, 1960), pp. 6, 175.

7. "Community: Frequently Asked Questions," Second Life, accessed November 10, 2015, http://secondlife.com/community/faq/

8. Cites are from Sherry Turkle, *Alone Together: Why We Expect More from Technology and Less from Each Other* (New York: Basic Books, 2011).

9. Sampson, *Great American City*, p. 372.

10. Adam Smith cited in Alan Silver, "Friendship and Trust as Moral Ideals: An Historical Approach," *European Journal of Sociology* 30, no. 2 (1989): 274–97 at 290.

11. Lee, *To Kill a Mockingbird*, p. 373.

12. Thoreau, "Walden," p. 95.

13. Kierkegaard, *Works of Love*, pp. 18–19.

14. W. H. Auden, "Robert Frost," *Prose, Vol. I 1926–1938*, ed. Edward Mendelson (London: Faber and Faber, 1996), pp. 139–40.

15. Thoreau, *Walden*, p. 34.

16. OED Online. Quotation from A. Porson, *Notes on Quaint Words and Sayings in the Dialect of South Worcestershire* (Oxford: Parker, 1875), p. 23. This point evokes Georg Simmel, "The Stranger" in *The Sociology of Georg Simmel*, ed. Kurt Wolff (Glencoe, IL: Free Press, 1950), pp. 402–8.

17. Georg Wilhelm Friedrich Hegel, *Philosophy of History*, trans. J. Sibree (New York: Colonial Press, 1900), p. 253.

18. Henry Goldschmidt, *Race and Religion among the Chosen Peoples of Crown Heights* (New Brunswick, NJ: Rutgers University Press, 2006), pp. 109–10.

19. Ibid., pp. 18, 95.

20. For Caribbean immigrants, Crown Heights was the center of West Indian life in the United States. Other African American residents interpreted the lay of the land through historical legacies of segregation and discrimination. "In a neighborhood populated by chosen peoples in exile—by descendants of immigrants, refugees, and slaves." Ibid., pp. 89, 76–77, 204, 14.

21. Thoreau, *Walden*, p. 192.

22. Ibid., p. 173.

23. Stanley Milgram, "Cities as Social Representation," in Robert M. Farr and Sergo Moscovic, *Social Representations* (Cambridge: Editions de la Mai-

son des Science de l'Homme, 1984), pp. 289–309, esp. p. 305. Stanley Milgram, "The Idea of Neighborhood," *Science* 178 (1972): 494–95; *The Individual in a Social World: Essays and Experiments* (Reading, MA: Addison-Wesley, 1977), p. 48; "A Psychological Map of New York City," ch. 5, pp. 54–65.

24. In *Talking to Strangers*, Danielle Allen gives an example of the geographical bounds of "political friendship" whose core is the University of Chicago with extensions encompassing more and more neighborhoods and (following Aristotle) totaling the 99,999 members of her polis, p. 173.

25. "Democratic citizenship is as much a matter of how strangers interact in public spaces as of institutions." Allen, *Talking to Strangers*, p. 23.

26. Robert D. Putnam, "E Pluribus Unum: Diversity and Community in the Twenty-First Century. The 2006 Johan Skytte Prize Lecture," *Scandinavian Political Studies* 30, no. 2 (2007): 137–74 at 156.

27. Douglas S. Massey and Nancy A. Denton, *American Apartheid* (Cambridge, MA: Harvard University Press, 1993), pp. 11, 111. "Most blacks prefer to live in racially integrated neighborhoods," but suffer dignitary harms at the hands of hostile neighbors and are deterred from seeking housing in overwhelmingly white neighborhoods. The motive for both groups on this account is "ethnocentrism" or in-group affinity, not racial prejudice. Elizabeth Anderson, *The Imperative of Integration* (Princeton: Princeton University Press, 2010), p. 5, asks how the mere presence of members of diverse racial groups poses an obstacle to in-group affiliation, p. 73. One response is that the emotional predominance of home and the pressing presence of near neighbors is more than "mere presence."

28. Thomas C. Schelling, "Models of Segregation," *American Economic Review* 59, no. 2 (May 1969): 488–93 at 490.

29. Thoreau, *Walden*, p. 91.

30. Willa Cather, *My Antonia* (New York: Barnes and Noble, 2003), p. 11.

31. Thoreau, *Walden,* p. 52.

32. Silver, "Friendship and Trust as Moral Ideals," p. 275.

33. Aristotle, *Nichomachean Ethics*, bk. 9, sec. 4: "We define a friend as one who wishes and does what is good or seems so, for the sake of his friend," http://classics.mit.edu/Aristotle/nicomachaen.9.ix.html

34. Mayol, in *The Practice of Everyday Life,* p. 20.

35. *Nichomachean Ethics*, bk. 9, sec. 4; bk. 9, sec 1. Bryan Garsten finds in Aristotle "the key ingredient of friendship"—the separateness of friends in "Rhetoric and Human Separateness," *Polis* 30, no. 2 (2013): 210–27.

36. Ralph Waldo Emerson, "Friendship," in *The Collected Works of Ralph Waldo Emerson*, vol. 2, *Essays: First Series*, ed. Joseph Slater, Alfred R. Ferguson, and Jean Ferguson Carr (Cambridge: Harvard University Press, 1979), p. 123.

## Chapter 2: Narrative Threads

1. Andrew Delbanco, *The Real American Dream: A Meditation on Hope* (Cambridge, MA: Harvard University Press, 1999), pp. 107, 114.
2. Gornick, *The Situation and the Story*, p. 33.
3. Norman Mailer quoted in Andrew Delbanco, *The Real American Dream*, p. 6.
4. Annie Dillard, *Living by Fiction* (New York: Harper and Row, 1982).
5. Willa Cather, *My Antonia*, p. 16.
6. Didion, *Slouching towards Bethlehem*, p. 94.
7. Vivien Gornick, "Radiant Poison: Saul Bellow, Philip Roth, and the End of the Jew as Metaphor," *Harper's* (September 2008), p. 74. http://harpers.org /archive/2008/09/radiant-poison/
8. Fitzgerald, *The Great Gatsby*, p. 189.
9. For a critique of Charles Tibout's economic theory of markets and localities for assuming ease of individual movement and insensitive to constraints on mobility, see Richard Briffault, "Our Localism: Part II—Localism and Legal Theory," 90 *Columbia L. Rev.* 346 (1990) at pp. 399ff., 415, 420, 421.
10. Nicholas Lemann, "Get Out of Town: Has the Celebration of Cities Gone Too Far?," *New Yorker*, June 27, 2011, pp. 76–80, esp. p. 80.
11. Cited in Joan Didion, *Where I Was From* (New York: Random House, 2003), p. 28.
12. Philip Abrams, *Neighbours: The Work of Philip Abrams* (Cambridge: Cambridge University Press, 1986), p. 41.
13. Hester Kaplan, "Companion Animal," *Ploughshares* 29, no. 1 (Spring 2003): 131.
14. W. H. Auden, "Robert Frost," in Auden, *Prose, Vol. IV: 1956–62*, ed. Edward Mendelson (Princeton: Princeton University Press, 2010), p. 700.
15. Kai Erikson, *Wayward Puritans: A Study in the Sociology of Deviance* (Boston: Pearson, 2005), p. 51.
16. Steffens, *Autobiography*, cited in Didion, *Where I Was From*, p. 203.
17. Gornick, "Radiant Poison," p. 71.
18. Jeremy Waldron, "Secularism and the Limits of Community," (working paper no. 10–88, New York University School of Law Public Law and Legal Theory Research Paper Series, December 2013), p. 10.
19. John Pipkin, *Woodsburner* (New York: Anchor Books, 2010), pp. 64–65.
20. Delbanco, *The Real American Dream*, p. 69.
21. Rana, *The Two Faces of American Freedom*, p. 9.
22. Cather, *My Antonia*, p. 11.
23. Robert Frost, "American Poetry," cited in Auden, "Robert Frost," *Prose, Vol. IV*, p. 701.
24. Cather, *My Antonia*, p. 11.

25. Laura Ingalls Wilder, *On the Banks of Plum Creek* (New York: HarperTrophy, 1965), pp. 275, 1.
26. Cather, *My Antonia*, p. 38.
27. Thoreau, *Walden*, p. 105.
28. Didion, *Where I Was From,* pp. 8, 7, 29.
29. Thoreau, *Walden*, p. 65.
30. Didion, *Where I Was From,* pp. 23–24.
31. In 1950, forty percent of Americans lived in rural places and by 2000 that portion of the population had declined to twenty-three percent. J. E. Oliver, *Democracy in Suburbia* (Princeton: Princeton University Press, 2001), p. 136, gives the figure of nearly one in four Americans.
32. Didion, *Where I Was From,* pp. 30–31.
33. Fitzgerald, *The Great Gatsby,* p. 8.
34. Jonathan Franzen, "Good Neighbors," *New Yorker*, June 8, 2009: http://www.newyorker.com/magazine/2009/06/08/good-neighbors
35. Saul Bellow, *Adventures of Augie March* (New York: Penguin, 1953), p. 39.
36. Kate Simon, *Bronx Primitive* (New York: Penguin, 1997), pp. 53, 99.
37. Anzia Yezierska, *Hungy Hearts* (New York: Penguin Books, 1997), p. 171.
38. Ibid., pp. 107, 168, 13.
39. Bellow, *Adventures of Augie March,* p. 154.
40. Ibid., pp. 71, 4, 10, 23, 34.
41. Ibid., pp. 203, 432, 159.
42. Ibid., p. 12.
43. The phrase is from Judith Shklar, *Ordinary Vices*, p. 77.
44. Immigrants can be "acculturated," as sociologists put it, yet still experience "stalled mobility." Edward Telles, Mark Q. Sawyer, and Gaspar Rivera-Salgado, eds., *Just Neighbors?: Research on African American and Latino Relations in the United States* (New York: Russell Sage Foundation, 2011), p. 5.
45. Gornick, "Radiant Poison," p. 76.
46. "In 2005, it is estimated that 4.4 million immigrants went to suburbs and 2.8 million to cities." Alan Ehrenhalt, *The Great Inversion and the Future of the American City* (New York: Knopf, 2012), p. 101.
47. Douglas S. Massey, ed., *New Faces in New Places: The Changing Geography of American Immigration* (New York: Russell Sage, 2008).
48. Jhumpa Lahiri, "Mrs. Sen's," *Interpreter of Maladies* (New York: Houghton Mifflin, 1999), p. 116.
49. Chang-rae Lee, *A Gesture Life* (New York: Riverhead Books, 2000), p. 1.
50. Lahiri, "The Third and Final Continent," *Interpreter of Maladies*, p. 198.
51. A helpful definition is "that part of a metropolis not within the *political boundaries* of the central city." Oliver, *Democracy in Suburbia*, p. 35.
52. Briffault, "Our Localism: Part II," p. 348.
53. "A good chunk of us—65 percent—live in large metro areas of over one-

half million people, and 45 percent of the U.S. population resides in the suburbs of large metro areas," William H. Frey, "Population Growth in Metro American since 1980: Putting the Volatile 2000s in Perspective" (Washington, DC: Brookings Institution, 2012), http://www.brookings .edu/~/media/research/files/papers/2012/3/20%20population%20frey/0320 _population_frey.pdf. According to a report on the 2010 Census by the Population Reference Bureau: eighty-four percent of the US population lived in metropolitan areas, with thirty-three percent in "central cities" and fifty-one percent in the suburbs. Mark Mather, Kelvin Pollard, and Linda A. Jacobsen, *Reports on America: First Results from the 2010 Census* (Washington, DC: Population Reference Bureau, 2011), http://www.prb .org/pdf11/reports-on-america-2010-census.pdf. Comparative statisics are difficult to sort out.

54. Herbert J. Gans, *The Levittowners: Ways of Life and Politics in a New Suburban Community* (New York: Pantheon Books, 1967), p. 36.

55. Donald Waldie, *Holy Land*, cited in Didion, *Where I Was From*, p. 106.

56. "The late 20th century was the age of poor inner cities and wealthy suburbs; the 21st century is emerging as an age of affluent inner neighborhoods and immigrants settling on the outside," Alan Ehrenhalt, *The Great Inversion and the Future of the American City*, cited in Fred Siegel, *New York Times Book Review*, August 12, 2012.

57. Gans, *Levittowners*, pp. 271, 37.

58. Peter Lovenheim, *In the Neighborhood: The Search for Community on an American Street, One Sleepover at a Time* (New York: Perigree Books, 2010), p. 68.

59. Lewis Mumford, *The Culture of Cities* (New York: Harcourt, Brace and Company, 1938), p. 215.

60. As sometimes happens. Cf. the mass shooting at San Bernardino in 2015: "Behind a Façade of Suburban Normality, Couple Hid Arsenal," *New York Times*, December 4, 2015, http://www.nytimes.com/2015/12/04/us /san-bernardino-shooting-syed-rizwan-farook.html

61. Famous critiques from the 1950s and '60s remain reference points: Vance Packard's 1959 *The Status Seekers*, for example, which disparaged "the creation of many hundreds of one-class communities unparalleled in the history of America." Cited in Lizabeth Cohen, *A Consumer's Republic: The Politics of Mass Consumption in Postwar America* (New York: Vintage Books, 2004), p. 212.

62. Gans, *Levittown*, p. 174.

63. Delbanco, *The Real American Dream,* p. 105.

64. Oliver, *Democracy in Suburbia,* p. 143.

65. Ehrenhalt, *The Great Inversion,* p. 217.

66. Oliver, *Democracy in Suburbia,* p. 138. Studies fail to confirm any differ-

ence in loneliness or alienation among residents of urban, suburban, or rural areas.

67. Criticism cited but not endorsed by Lemann, "Get Out of Town," p. 76. On "dignity," Nicholas Lemann, private communication, November 7, 2011, on file with the author.

68. Richard Ford, *Let Me Be Frank with You* (New York: Ecco, 2014), p. 79.

69. Ehrenhalt, *The Great Inversion*, p. 230. The result of many factors including the de-industrialization of cities—epitomized by the first conversions of SoHo lofts in lower Manhattan.

70. Marshall Berman cited in Allen, *Talking to Strangers,* pp. 165–66, 167.

71. Briffault, "Our Localism: Part II," p. 445. David J. Barron and Gerald E. Frug, "Defensive Localism: A View of the Field from the Field," 21 *J. L. & Policy* 261 (2005): 261–91.

72. Briffault, "Our Localism: Part II," p. 414.

73. Walzer, *Spheres of Justice*, pp. 36–37.

74. Cited in Briffault, "Our Localism: Part II," p. 441.

75. One explanation is that while the capacity for participation is present, incentives are lacking. Oliver, *Democracy in Suburbia*, p. 82; democratic politics is stimulated by conflict and diversity, which suburbs presumably lack. This thesis understates disagreement over property taxes and support for schools, low-income housing and the terms of development review, and so on. Briffault, "Our Localism: Part II," p. 439.

76. *Lionshead Lake, Inc. v. Wayne Township*, 89 A.2d 693 (N.J. 1952). Full text available at http://www.leagle.com/decision/195217510NJ165_1156.xml /LIONSHEAD%20LAKE,%20INC.%20v.%20TOWNSHIP%20OF%20 WAYNE. Also cited in several books on land use/law, e.g., J. Barry Cullingworth, *The Political Culture of Planning: American Land Use Planning in Comparative Perspective* (New York: Routledge, 1993), p. 45.

77. "The privatization of suburban public life, the class and race homogeneity . . . the parochialization of the local relationship to outsiders and the legal rules that permit . . . the insulation of suburbs . . . all breed an ideology of localism." Briffault, "Our Localism: Part II," p. 444.

78. Ibid., p. 446. In the same vein, "homevoter," and "selfish local policymaking" are staple tags. William A. Fischel, *The Homevoter Hypothesis: How Home Values Influence Local Government Taxation, School Finance and Land-Use Policies* (Cambridge, MA: Harvard University Press, 2001); Barron and Frug, "Defensive Localism," p. 216.

79. Barron and Frug, "Defensive Localism," p. 267.

80. Robert Reich cited in Nancy L. Rosenblum, *Membership and Morals: The Personal Uses of Pluralism in America* (Princeton: Princeton University Press, 2000), p. 146. Some scholars "see economic segregation as *the* driving force in the politics of suburbia." Oliver, *Democracy in Suburbia,* p. 69.

81. Ehrenhalt cites a US Census Bureau report from October 2011 that in the first decade of the new century, poverty increased by fifty-three percent in

the suburbs compared to twenty-six percent in the cities. Ehrenhalt, *The Great Inversion*, p. 12.

82. Didion, *Where I Was From,* p. 183.

83. Massey and Denton, *American Apartheid*, p. 11. Before the twentieth century whites and blacks lived in close proximity in cities and towns; even in northern cities blacks were scattered throughout white neighborhoods, p. 17. For segregated neighborhood effects, see Edward G. Goetz, *Clearing the Way: Deconcentrating the Poor in Urban American* (Washington, DC: Urban Institute Press, 2003), esp. pp. 26–27. Analysis of the 2000 census finds "promising" evidence that residential segregation is at its lowest since 1920 and that fewer African Americans live in "hypersegregated areas" (where over eighty percent of residents are black) but the level of segregation remains staggering. Edward L. Glaeser and Jacob L. Gigdor, "Racial Segregation: Promising News," in Bruce Katz and Robert E. Lang, ed., *Redefining Urban and Suburban America: Evidence from Census 2000* (Washington, DC: Brookings Institute, 2003): 155–79 at 215–16. "The urban ghetto . . . represents the key institutional arrangement ensuring the continued subordination of blacks in the United States," p. 18. It is maintained by low-income housing subsidies that permit building in segregated areas: "The End of Federally Financed Ghettos," *New York Times,* July 12, 2015, sec. 1., p. 1.

84. Ehrenhalt, *The Great Inversion,* p. 6.

85. William H. Frey, "Melting Pot Suburbs: A Study of Suburban Diversity," in Katz and Lang, ed., *Redefining Urban and Suburban America,* pp. 155, 167.

86. John Logan, "Ethnic Diversity Grows, Neighborhood Integration Lags," in Katz and Lang, ed., *Redefining Urban and Suburban America,* pp. 225–55. Hispanic segregation has increased, on one account, and Asian segregation has not decreased, pp. 242, 254.

87. In some large majority / minority cities the trend is toward "increasing residential integration of blacks and Latinos." Edward Telles, Mark Q. Sawyer, and Gaspar Rivera-Salgado, eds., *Just Neighbors*, pp. 8–9.

88. Clarissa Rile Hayward, *How Americans Make Race* (Cambridge: Cambridge University Press, 2013).

89. "Affordable Housing, Racial Isolation," Editorial, *New York Times,* June 29, 2015, on a Supreme Court ruling forbidding spending federal housing money in ways that perpetuate segregation: http://www.nytimes.com/2015 /06/29/opinion/affordable-housing-racial-isolation.html. The recent case is *Texas Dept. of Hous. & Community Affairs v. Inclusive Communities Project, Inc.*, 576 U.S. ___ (2015). On George Lucas's attempt to build and pay for affordable housing on his property in Marin County, see Elahe Izadi, "George Lucas Wants to Build Affordable Housing . . . ," *Washington Post*, April 17, 2015, http://www.washingtonpost.com/news/morning-mix/wp /2015/04/17/george-lucas-wants-to-build-affordable-housing-on-his-land -because-weve-got-enough-millionaires.

90. Black residential segregation has been compared to earlier white ethnic en-claves, but the differences are notable. Ethnic enclaves were always more diverse and ethnically diluted than sociology suggested ("in none of these 'ghettos' did the ghettoized group constitute even a bare majority of the population"). They were short lived. And unlike African Americans, resi-dents were not isolated from the rest of society. Massey and Denton, *American Apartheid*, pp. 32–33.

91. "Middle-Class Black Families, in Low-Income Neighborhoods," David Leonhardt, *New York Times*, June 24, 2015, http://www.nytimes.com/2015 /06/25/upshot/middle-class-black-families-in-low-income-neighborhoods .html?_r=0

92. "Weclome to Celebration," *Town of Celebration, Florida*, accessed Novem-ber 11, 2015, http://www.celebration.fl.us/

93. "Our Story," *Suburban Homestead*, accessed November 11, 2015, http:// www.yoursuburbanhomestead.com/sh_pages/sh_story.html

94. Urban developers resist randomness too: Hilary Stout, "The Social Build-ing," *New York Times*, September 10, 1010, http://www.nytimes.com/2010 /09/12/realestate/12cov.html?pagewanted=all.

95. Francis Fitzgerald cited in Rosenblum, *Membership and Morals*, p. 66.

96. A large proportion of home building in the US outside the northeast con-sists of these associations; in 2004, eighteen percent of the population lived in one. See Robert H. Nelson, *Private Neighborhoods and the Transforma-tion of Local Government* (Washington, DC: Urban Institute Press, 2005), p. xiv.

97. Ibid., pp. 11, 4. On conflict and litigation, see Rosenblum, *Membership and Morals*, ch. 4.

98. Didion, *Slouching towards Bethlehem*, p. 94.

99. For these descriptions of the characters, see Michael Davis, *Street Gang: The Complete History of* Sesame Street (New York: Penguin Books 2008). On 2016 changes to *Sesame Street*: http://www.nytimes.com/2016/01/13/business /media/sesame-street.

100. Cited in ibid., pp. 142, 220.

101. Ibid., pp. 184, 164.

## Chapter 3: Reciprocity among "Decent Folk"

1. Robert Cialdini and Melanie Trost, "Social Influence: Social Norms, Con-formity, and Çompliance," in Daniel Gilbert, Susan Fiske, and Gardner Lindzey, *The Handbook of Social Psychology,* vol. 2, 4th ed. (Boston: McGraw-Hill, 1998). Reciprocity implies the belief that "in the long run the mutual exchange of services will balance out," p. 170. See too Seth W. Mallios, "Reciprocity," in *International Encyclopaedia of the Social Sci-ences*, 2d ed., pp. 105–7.

2. Alvin W. Gouldner, "The Norm of Reciprocity: A Preliminary Statement," *American Sociological Review* 25, no. 2 (April 1960): 161–78.

3. Cited in ibid., p. 161.

4. Amos Oz, *How to Cure a Fanatic* (Princeton: Princeton University Press, 2002), p. 22.

5. John Rawls, *A Theory of Justice*, (Cambridge: Harvard University Press, 1971), pp. 494–95; 433; *Political Liberalism*, (New York: Columbia University Press, 1993), p. 17.

6. Russell Hardin writes: Generalized social "trust" is "nothing more than optimistic assessment of trustworthiness and willingness therefore to take small risks . . ." in "Conceptions and Explanation of Trust," in Karen S. Cook, ed., *Trust in Society* (New York: Russell Sage, 2001): 3–39 at 15.

7. This distinction has been formulated in terms of "pristine" trust and "confidence," i.e., reliance on institutional arrangements. Adam B. Seligman, *The Problem of Trust* (Princeton: Princeton University Press, 1997), p. 24.

8. Russell Hardin cited in Cook, et al., *Trust in Society,* p. 1.

9. "Once an individual has extended to another enough consideration to hear him out for a moment, some kind of bond of mutual obligation is established . . . once this new extended bond is granted, grudgingly or willingly, still further claims for social or material indulgence can be made." Erving Goffman, cited in Kurth, *Friendship as a Social Institution,* pp. 141–42.

10. The quote comes from Alan D. Schrift, ed., *The Logic of the Gift: Toward an Ethic of Generosity* (New York: Routledge, 1997), p. 10, paraphrasing Jacques Derrida from *Given Time: I. Counterfeit Money* (Chicago: University of Chicago Press, 1991).

11. Doris Lessing, *The Diaries of Jane Somers,* p. 28.

12. I am indebted to Mara Marin's discussion of commitment in her unpublished dissertation on file with the author.

13. See Lawrence Becker, "Reciprocity," in E. Craig, ed., *Routledge Encyclopedia of Philosophy* (London: Routledge, 2010) online version. https://www.rep.routledge.com/articles/reciprocity/y-1.

14. Gouldner, "The Norm of Reciprocity," p. 164.

15. Raymond Carver, *Cathedral: Stories* (New York: Vintage Books, 1989), p. 71.

16. John Skoyles, "Spite Fence," *Plume,* 2015, http://plumepoetry.com/2015/08/two-poems-45/.

17. Thomas Berger, *Neighbors* (New York: Simon and Schuster, 1980), p. 1.

18. Ibid., pp. 18, 162, 173, 169, 160.

19. Leonard Kent, ed., *The Complete Tales of Nikolai Gogol, Volume 2* (Chicago: University of Chicago Press, 1985), pp. 169–214.

20. Oz, *How to Cure a Fanatic*, p. 63.

21. Thoreau, *Walden*, pp. 83, 112.

22. From a public point of view, the provision of expert services is very costly and the provision of neighboring very cheap, but from the point of view of

the individual, the balance is reversed. Martin Bulmer, *Neighbours: The Work of Philip Abrams* (Cambridge: Cambridge University Press, 1986), p. 32.

23. A working assumption in sociology is that "neighborhood effects" of poverty and delinquency are deterrents to trust, and that "in many urban communities, strong ties among neighbors are no longer the norm." Sampson, *Great American City*, p. 184.

24. Carol Stack, *All Our Kin: Strategies of Survival in the Black Community* (New York: Harper and Row, 1974), pp. 29, 32–33; 37–38.

25. Stack, *All Our Kin,* p. 22. On Oscar Lewis's "culture of poverty" and the concept of an urban underclass, see Massey and Denton, *American Apartheid*, pp. 4, 5.

26. Stack, *All Our Kin*, p. 42.

27. Ibid., p. 40.

28. Ibid., p. 31.

29. Ibid., pp. 42, 124, 5. "Residential segregation is the principal organizational feature of American society that is responsible for the creation of the urban underclass." Massey and Denton, *American Apartheid*, p. 9. Public policies aim at getting poor families out of disadvantaged neighborhoods; see Binyamin Appelbaum, "Helping Families Move from Public Housing," *New York Times*, July 5, 2015, sec. 1, p. 1.

30. A range of individual considerations as well as fear of discrimination are at work. Goetz, *Clearing the Way,* p. 239ff.

31. Stack, *All Our Kin*, p. 36.

32. Lee, *To Kill a Mockingbird*, p. 44.

33. Thoreau, *Walden,* pp. 106, 54.

34. Shklar, *Ordinary Vices*, p. 87.

35. Barbara Herman, "Articulated Beneficence," unpublished paper on file with the author.

36. Cited in Cockayne, *Cheek by Jowl,* p. 3.

37. Chang-rae Lee, *A Gesture Life*, p. 44.

38. Hester Kaplan, "Companion Animal," in *Unravished* (New York: IG Publishing, 2014), p. 89.

39. Frost, "Build Soil, a Political Pastoral," p. 296

40. The significance of disassociation will vary depending on thick / thin community.

41. Negatively, "decent" conjures moral judgment of women and white judgments of African Americans generally and members of other "out" groups. I owe this caution to Laurie Balfour in her comments on "Good Neighbor Nation" at the Gage Colloquium, Miller Center, University of Virginia, November, 2011. The obverse is not indecent, clearly.

42. Frost, "The Ax-Helve," in *Collected Poems*, p. 174.

43. David Cannadine, *The Rise and Fall of Class in Britain* (New York: Colum-

bia University Press, 1999), designates the US as the "nonhierarchical, non-divided, overwhelmingly 'middle class' nation that remains the closest thing we in the West know to be a 'classless' society," p. 191. Identified middle-classers in the US are neither contemptuous of those below nor envious of those above, p. 124.

44. Silver, "Friendship and Trust as Moral Ideals," p. 294.

45. Anderson, *The Imperative of Integration*, p. 78.

46. "Neighbour | neighbor, v." *Oxford English Dictionary*. 2nd ed., s.v. 20 vols. (Oxford: Oxford University Press, 1989), p. 307–8

47. Tocqueveille, *Journeys to England and Ireland* (New Haven: Yale University Press, 1958), p. 68.

48. Paul Theroux, *The Kingdom by the Sea: A Journey around Great Britain* (Boston: Houghton Mifflin, 1983), p.58.

49. Stein Ringen cited in Cannadine, *The Rise and Fall of Class in Britain*, p. xi.

50. Zadie Smith, *NW* (New York: Penguin Press, 2012), p. 166, 207.

51. P. N. Furbank, cited in Cannadine, *The Rise and Fall of Class in Britain*, p. vii.

52. Delbanco, *The Real American Dream*, p. 63

53. Judith N. Shklar, *American Citizenship: The Quest for Inclusion* (Cambridge, MA: Harvard University Press, 1991), p. 3.

54. Lee, *To Kill a Mockingbird*, p. 243.

55. Ibid., p. 167.

56. Ibid., pp. 61, 6.

57. Ibid., pp. 302–3, 304.

58. Ibid., p. 373.

59. Ibid., pp. 205–6.

## Chapter 4: Taking Offense, Speaking Out

1. Kristin Kimball, *The Dirty Life: On Farming, Food, and Love* (New York: Scribner, 2010), pp. 71–72.

2. Elizabeth Barrett Browning, *Aurora Leigh* (1857), bk. 4.

3. Gilbert K. Chesterton, *The Uses of Diversity: A Book of Essays* (New York: Dodd, Mead, and Company, 1921), pp. 51–52.

4. "Neighbour | neighbor, v.," OED Online (see chap. 3, n. 44).

5. *Kline v. Shearwater Ass'n, Inc.,* 63 Mass. App. Ct. 825 (2005), http://caselaw .findlaw.com/ma-court-of-appeals/1003016.html

6. "Anti-Social Behaviour Order," *Wikipedia*, last modified October 7, 2015, http://en.wikipedia.org/wiki/Anti-Social_Behaviour_Order. The application of this act has been challenged, and in some areas rolled back.

7. Raymond Carver, "Neighbors," in *Where I'm Calling From* (New York: Vintage, 1989) pp. 86, 89.

8. Thomas Nagel, "Concealment and Exposure," in *Concealment and Exposure and Other Essays* (Oxford: Oxford University Press, 2002), p. 15.

9. Robert Frost, "Provide, Provide," in *Collected Poems,* p. 280.

10. John Locke, *Second Treatise of Government,* in *Two Treatises of Government*, ed. Peter Laslett (Cambridge: Cambridge University Press, 2004).

11. Ellickson, *Order without Law,* p. 4.

12. Thoreau, *Walden*, p. 95.

13. I owe this formulation to an anonymous reviewer for Princeton University Press.

14. See Rosenblum, *Membership and Morals*, pp. 279–80.

15. Anderson, *The Imperative of Integration*, p. 97.

16. Ibid., p. 89.

17. Analyses of the scope of racial discrimination or of "hostile environment" under sexual harassment law remind us that the line between offense and injustice is not always sharp. "Things slide and merge into other things." In that case, our response qua neighbor and qua citizen may be impossible to unravel. Conor Cruise O'Brien, *God Land: Reflections on Religion and Nationalism* (Cambridge, MA: Harvard University Press, 1988), p. 9.

18. T. M. Scanlon, "Blame," in *Moral Dimensions* (Cambridge, MA: Harvard University Press, 2008), pp. 138, 150, 131.

19. I am indebted to Mara Marin's discussion of commitment in her unpublished dissertation on file with the author.

20. Frost, "Build Soil, a Political Pastoral," p. 296.

21. Tadd Friend, "The Great Suburban Leaf War," *New Yorker*, October 25, 2010, pp. 52, 55. http://www.newyorker.com/magazine/2010/10/25/blowback

22. Jonathan Franzen, *Freedom: A Novel* (New York: Farrar, Straus, and Giroux, 2010), pp. 7–8.

## Chapter 5: What Anyone Would Do, Here

1. Fitzgerald, *Great Gatsby*, p. 45.

2. David Myers, cited in Bill Bishop, *The Big Sort: Why the Clustering of Like-Minded America Is Tearing Us Apart* (Boston: Houghton Mifflin Harcourt, 2008), p. 41.

3. Bishop, *The Big Sort*, p. 13. Political sorting is his focus.

4. Cited in ibid., p. 306.

5. Elizabeth Harman shared this quote from the sitcom "How I Met Your Mother" (season 3, episode 11).

6. Douglas S. Massey and Magaly Sanchez R., *Broken Boundaries: Creating Immigrant Identity in Anti-Immigrant Times* (New York: Russell Sage, 2010), p. 247. Noah Pickus and Peter Skerry, "Good Neighbors and Good

Citizens: Beyond the Legal-Illegal Immigration Debate," in Carol Swaine, ed., *Debating Immigration* (Cambridge: Cambridge University Press, 2007), pp. 95–113. "While the current debate asks whether immigrants can be good citizens, we argue that to many Americans the more immediately pressing question is whether immigrants can be good neighbors," pp. 100, 105.

7. Conor Cruise O'Brien, *God Land,* p. 33.

8. Chang-rae Lee, *A Gesture Life*, pp. 4, 44.

9. David Drury, "Things We Knew When the House Caught Fire," in *The Best American Nonrequired Reading 2003,* ed. Dave Eggers (Boston: Houghton Mifflin, 2003), p. 118.

10. Erikson, *Wayward Puritans*, p. 6.

11. Jumpa Lahiri, "Sexy," in *Interpreter of Maladies,* p. 95.

12. Drury, "Things We Knew When the House Caught Fire," p. 122.

13. Eudora Welty, "Curtain of Green," in *The Collected Short Stories of Eudora Welty* (New York: Harcourt Brace and Company, 1980), pp. 108, 2, 1.

14. Cited in Constance Perin, *Belonging in America* (Madison: University of Wisconsin Press, 1988), p. 63.

15. Gans, *The Levittowners*, p. 52.

16. Drury, "Things We Knew When the House Caught Fire," pp. 122–23.

17. James Q. Wilson and George L. Kelling, "Broken Windows," *Atlantic,* March 1982, p. 3. The authors speak of the informal "control mechanisms" neighbors provide. See too George L. Kelling and Catherine M. Coles, *Fixing Broken Windows* (Free Press: New York, 1996).

18. Putnam, "E Pluribus Unum," p. 138.

19. Local standards may permit public drinking or not, for example. Wilson and Kelling, "Broken Windows," pp. 2, 6, 8, 4.

20. Attention has focused on the heavy human costs of "broken windows" policing policy. "Safer Era Tests Wisdom of 'Broken Windows' Focus on Minor Crime," *New York Times,* July 25, 2014, A-21; Editorial Board, "Broken Windows, Broken Lives," *New York Times,* http://www.nytimes.com /2014/07/26/opinion/broken-windows-broken-lives.html.

21. Crime and disorder are not causally related but arise from the same conditions: Sampson, *Great American City,* p. 150.

22. Ibid., pp. 27, 146–47.

23. Ibid., citing Granovetter, pp. 150, 151. Mark Dunkelman, *The Vanishing Neighbor: The Transformation of American Community* (New York: Norton, 2014).

24. The phrase is Robert Nisbet's cited in Sampson, *Great American City,* p. 44.

25. Sampson, *Great American City,* pp. 4, 57, 56.

26. Keith Wrightson, "The 'decline of neighbourliness' revisited," p. 1. Unpublished paper on file with the author.

27. Sampson, *Great American City*, p. 4.
28. Dunkelman, *Vanishing Neighbor*, pp. xiii; xvii, 119, 152.
29. Didion, *Where I Was From*, p. 95.
30. Joan Didion painted this apocalyptic picture in the culturally turbulent 1970s, *Slouching towards Bethlehem*, p. 94.
31. Thoreau, *Walden*, p. 95.
32. Cited in Theresa M. Bejan, "The Bond of Civility': Roger Williams on Toleration and Its Limits," *History of European Ideas* 37 (2011): 409–20 at 414, 416.
33. Recent scholarship explores the King James Bible's translation. The profound "otherness" of ancient Jewish society was altered and "reassuringly familiar" English terms like "neighbor" elected to encourage the gentry families that ruled the shires and all the "good folk" of Jacobean England to aspire to modest acts of charity, assistance, and comfort. Diarmaid MacCulloch, "How Good Is It?," *London Review of Books* 33, no. 3 (2011): 20–22. Leviticus 19:18 is rendered "love thy friend," closer to the Hebrew language of amity. Naomi Tadmore, "The Social Universe of the King James Bible" discussed in Arnold Hunt, "400 Years of the King James Bible" *Times Literary Supplement*, February 9, 2011, pp. 5, i.
34. Kierkegaard, *Works of Love*, pp. 52, 89. "The neighbor is a purely spiritual specification," p. 57.
35. New England town covenants echoed Winthrop: "We whose names are hereunder written . . . promisse and bind ourselves . . . in all sincere conformity to his holy Ordinances and in mutuall love. . . ." The Charlestown-Boston compact, cited in James Morone, *Hellfire Nation* (New Haven: Yale University Press, 2003), pp. 40, 43.
36. We can set Leviticus alongside other moral codes. In Deuteronomy, obligation is rooted in familial relationship, and the object of assistance is most commonly "your brother." The command is a strong one. [15:7–8] The community of Israelites was the scene of "a wide open hand." Michael Walzer, *In God's Shadow* (New Haven: Yale University Press, 2012), p. 155.
37. Wrightson, "The 'Decline of Neighbourliness' Revisited," p. 12.
38. Governor John Winthrop, "A Model of Christian Charity." http://history .hanover.edu/texts/winthmod.html
39. O'Brien, *God Land*, p. 41.
40. Shklar, *Ordinary Vices*, pp. 49, 50.
41. Instructional letter to his neighbours, Nehemiah Wallington, London, 1640; cited in Cockayne, *Cheek by Jowl*, p. 21.
42. O'Brien distinguishes "in ascending order of arrogance and destructiveness" "chosen people," "holy nation," and "deified nation," *God Land,* p. 41. Tocqueville's "first Puritan" is cited on p. 43.

43. Frances Fitzgerald, *Cities on a Hill: A Journey through Contemporary American Cultures* (New York: Simon and Schuster, 1986).

44. J. S. Mill, "On Liberty," in *Mill: Texts and Commentaries*, ed. Alan Ryan (New York: Norton, 1997), pp. 104, 50.

45. Ibid., p. 99.

46. Roger Williams cited in Bejan, "The Bond of Civility," p. 419.

47. Thoreau, *Walden,* p. 57.

48. Oz, *How to Cure a Fanatic*, pp. 57–58.

49. Daniel M. Hausman and Brynn Welch, "Debate: To Nudge or Not to Nudge," *The Journal of Political Philosophy* 18, no. 1 (2010): 123–36.

50. I follow James L. Kugel's exegesis, *In Potiphar's House: The Interpretive Life of Biblical Texts* (Cambridge, MA: Harvard University Press, 1990), "Hatred and Revenge": 215–46.

51. Ibid., p. 217.

52. Ibid., p. 18.

53. Freud, *Civilization and Its Discontents*, p. 63.

54. Kierkegaard, *Works of Love*, pp. 29, 27.

55. The cautions are in Shklar, *Ordinary Vices*.

56. On forms of racial discrimination, see Anderson, *The Imperative of Integration*, p. 45ff.

57. Bishop, *The Big Sort,* p. 3.

58. Anderson, *The Imperative of Integration,* p. 2. Racial segregation is a principal cause of stigmatization, p. 63.

59. Sampson, *Great American City*, p. 55.

60. Russell Hardin, *Trust and Trustworthiness* (New York: Russell Sage Foundation, 2003), p. 23, 3. Putnam, "E Pluribus Unum" on the positive relationship between trust and racial and ethnic homogeneity, p. 147. Other studies find that racial diversity has declined as a predictor of mistrust. Robert J. Sampson and Corina Graif, "Neighborhood Networks and Processes of Trust," in Karen S. Cook, Margaret Levi, and Russell Hardin, ed., *Whom Can We Trust?: How Groups, Networks, and Institutions Make Trust Possible* (New York: Russell Sage, 2009), p. 209.

61. The phrase is Glenn Loury's, cited in Anderson, *The Imperative of Integration,* p. 175.

62. Ibid., p. 124.

63. Elijah Anderson, "The Code of the Streets," *Atlantic Monthly*, May, 1994, pp. 81–94.

64. Shklar, *Ordinary Vices,* pp. 115–16.

65. Philip Roth, *Patrimony: A True Story* (New York: Simon and Schuster, 1991), p. 125, cited in Bob Pepperman Taylor, "Democracy and Excess: Philip Roth's Democratic Citizen," unpublished paper on file.

66. Philip Roth, "Eli, the Fanatic," in *Goodbye, Columbus: And Five Short Stories* (Boston: Houghton Mifflin, 1989), pp. 263, 275–76, 269, 292.

## Chapter 6: Live and Let Live

1. Stephen Holmes and Cass Sunstein, *The Cost of Rights* (New York: W. W. Norton, 1999), p. 205.

2. Nathan Glaser, cited in Wilson and Kelling, "Broken Windows," p. 4.

3. Philip Roth, *American Pastoral* (New York: Vintage, 1997), p. 235.

4. Isabel Wilkerson, *The Warmth of Other Suns*, cited in "The Uprooted: Chronicling the Great Migration," review by Jill Lapore, *New Yorker*, September 6, 2010, p. 80.

5. Vaclav Havel, "An Anatomy of Reticence," *Living in Truth* (Faber and Faber: London, 1986), p. 171.

6. "Shhh, Peaceful," March 7, 2011, http://bradplumer.tumblr.com/post/3702 831859/even-rosa-parks-got-mugged-in-detroit-her

7. Robert J. Sampson, Stephen W. Raudenbush, and Felton Earls, "Neighborhoods and Violent Crime: A Multilevel Study of Collective Efficacy," *Science* 277 (August 1997): 918–24 at 919. "Even when personal ties are strong. . . . daily experiences with uncertainty, danger, and economic dependency are likely to reduce expectations for taking effective collective action." Robert J. Sampson, *Great American City,* p. 186.

8. Elijah Anderson, *Streetwise,* cited in Darryl Pinckney, "Invisible Black America," *New York Review of Books*, March 10, 2011, http://www .nybooks.com/articles/archives/2011/mar/10/invisible-black-america/

9. Paul Butler, "Control and Containment Requires Nonlethal Force Not Armed Cops," Opinion Pages, *New York Times*, August 15, 2014, http:// www.nytimes.com/roomfordebate/2014/08/14

10. "The lifetime risk of incarceration for a child born in 2001 is 1 in 3 for black males, 1 in 6 for Latino males, and 1 in 17 for white males." Darryl Pinckney, "Invisible Black America," *New York Review of Books,* March 10, 2011, p. 33.

11. Tommie Shelby, "Justice, Deviance, and the Dark Ghetto," *Philosophy and Public Affairs* 35, no. 2 (2007): 126–60 at 136, 145.

12. "The existence of the dark ghetto—with its combination of social stigma, extreme poverty, racial segregation . . . and shocking incarceration rates—is simply incompatible with any meaningful form of reciprocity among free and equal citizens." Shelby, "Justice, Deviance, and the Black Ghetto," pp. 142, 150.

13. Here and throughout, my focus is informal neighbor relations outside of political institutions and activity. Of course, as citizens faced with injustice, we demonstrate, protest, organize, advocate, vote, and more. My aim is to illuminate the domain of the informal democracy of everyday life around home.

14. Grossman, "The Old Teacher," in *The Road*, pp. 112, 114.

15. Goldschmidt, *Race and Religion*, pp. 50, 103.

16. Ibid., pp. 67, 52. Edward S. Shapiro, *Crown Heights: Blacks, Jews, and the 1991 Brooklyn Riot* (Waltham, MA: Brandeis University Press, 2006).

17. Jan Feldman, *Lubavitchers as Citizens* (Ithaca, NY: Cornell University Press, 2003), p. 58.

18. Anna Deveare Smith, interview with Roslyn Malamud, *Fires in the Mirror: Crown Heights, Brooklyn and Other Identities* (Dramatists Play Services, Inc., 1998).

19. Goldschmidt, *Race and Religion,* pp. 18, 95.

20. Ibid., pp. 193–94.

21. Cited in ibid., pp. 193, 194, 119.

22. Michael Walzer interpreting Martin Buber in *The Company of Critics* (New York: Basic Books, 2002), p. 68.

23. "If I see in my lifetime the State of Israel and the State of Palestine living next door to each other as decent neighbors . . . I will be satisfied even if love does not prevail." Oz, *How to Cure a Fanatic*, p. 14.

24. Ibid., p. 66.

25. Allen, *Talking to Strangers*, pp. 156, 167.

26. Except for violent crime, I have not tried to define the class of acts that neighbors should be willing or reluctant to report. My concern is the phenomenology of reticence.

27. Bob Pepperman, private conversation, University of Vermont, 2011.

28. Reluctance to inform on a colleague has some of the same elements with this difference: exposure at work is incidental and unlikely to be a regular feature of interactions. Personal interactions are not the ground of relations among colleagues as they are for neighbors, either. Clinching the difference is the unique connection to private life at home.

29. Undocumented immigrants are not an isolated group "living in the shadows"; they have driver's licenses, pay taxes, join unions in significant numbers, and ten percent are estimated to be homeowners. Pickus and Skerry, "Good Neighbors and Good Citizens," pp. 100–101.

30. Mary Jane Freeman, "How to Report Illegal Immigration," *eHow.com,* last modified December 8, 2014, http://www.ehow.com/how_4448030_report -illegal-immigration.html. At this writing, federal policy on deportation is in flux.

31. That is, undocumented immigration, which used to be a civil misdemeanor, has been criminalized. There may be civil penalties for anyone who "conspires to or takes any action designed to prevent or hamper the alien's departure pursuant to the order of removal." 8 U.S.C. § 1324D. In some states failure to report felonies is a misdemeanor. http://www.law.cornell.edu /uscode/text/8/1324d. Adam Goodman, "A Nation of (Deported) Immigrants" *Dissent*, Spring 2011, https://www.dissentmagazine.org/article/a -nation-of-deported-immigrants

32. Judith Resnik on continuities among war tribunals, military commissions,

detainee review procedures, and administrative decisions in prisons and for immigrants in "Detention, the War on Terror, and the Federal Court," 110 *Colum. L. Rev.* 579 (2010).

33. Some cities have instructed law enforcement and city employees not to cooperate with the federal government and "sanctuary cities" bar police from inquiring into legal status. The analogy to the fugitive slave law that provoked Thoreau's "resistance to civil government" bears mention, and to neighbors in the "dark ghetto" who refuse to report crimes because they believe that offenders will not be afforded equal (or reasonable) legal protection.

34. David Cole, "Are Foreign Nationals Entitled to the Same Constitutional Rights as Citizens?" 25 *T. Jefferson L. Rev.* 367 (2002–03), p. 380.

35. I am grateful to Samuel Scheffler for instructive conversation on this point, and others in this section.

36. Samuel Scheffler, *Boundaries and Allegiances: Problems of Justice and Responsibility in Liberal Thought* (Oxford: Oxford University Press, 2001), p. 96.

37. Avishai Margalit, *The Ethics of Memory* (Cambridge, MA: Harvard University Press, 2002).

38. Scheffler, *Boundaries and Allegiances,* pp. 100, 6.

39. Ibid., p. 98.

40. Niko Kolodny, "Which Relationships Justify Partiality? General Considerations and Problem Cases," in Brian Feltham and John Cottingham, eds., *Partiality and Impartiality: Morality, Special Relationships and the Wider World* (Oxford: Oxford University Press, 2010), pp. 183, 185.

41. OED definition of betrayal, cited in Shklar, *Ordinary Vices,* p. 139.

42. Steve Hindle, "Without the Cry of Any Neighbor: A Cumbrian Family and the Poor Law Authorities, c. 1690–1730," in *The Family in Early Modern England,* ed. Helen Berry and Elizabeth Foyster (Cambridge: Cambridge University Press, 2007), p. 126.

43. Cited in Alan Ehrenhalt, *The Great Inversion,* p. 23.

44. Raymond Geuss, *Public Goods, Private Goods* (Princeton: Princeton University Press, 2001), p. 86

45. Cited in Cockayne, *Cheek by Jowl,* p. 3.

46. Geuss, *Public Goods,* p. 88.

47. Disclosing our neighbor's business is not by definition an invasion of something that is ontologically private (the example Raymond Geuss uses is our spiritual state). Geuss, *Public Goods,* p. 110.

48. Berlin, *Four Essays on Liberty,* p. 129.

49. Thoreau, *Walden,* p. 98.

50. I add the modifier "liberal" here to underscore a point implicit thoughout this study: democracy in America, and the democracy of everyday life entail respect for privacy and personal freedom in contrast to majoritarianism without constitutional or legal limits.

51. See, for example, Geuss, *Public Goods,* pp. 88–90.
52. "The liberal idea, in society and culture as in politics, is that no more should be subjected to the demands of public response than is necessary for the requirements of collective life," Nagel, *Concealment and Escape,* p. 13.
53. I am mindful of feminist thought and the reasons for challenging public/private boundaries. But this ongoing project should not eclipse the value and personal meaningfulness of the domain around home and the reasons for live and let live as an element of good neighbor.
54. Harvey A. Silverglate, *Three Felonies a Day: How the Feds Target the Innocent* (New York: Encounter Books, 2009), p. xxx.
55. Cockayne, *Cheek by Jowl,* pp. 209, 136.

## Chapter 7: Betrayal

1. Ibid., p. 332.
2. Paul Betts, *Within Walls: Private Life in the German Democratic Republic* (Oxford: Oxford University Press, 2010), pp. 28–29.
3. Svetlana Boym, *Common Places: Mythologies of Everyday Life in Russia* (Cambridge, MA: Harvard University Press, 1995), p. 123.
4. Ibid., p. 145.
5. Timothy Garten Ash, *The File* (London: Atlantic Books: 1997), pp. 55, 17. For figures on the numbers of unofficial informants, see p. 74; an estimated 1/5 of the adult population had a direct connection to the secret police.
6. Orlando Fige's *The Whisperers: Private Life in Stalin's Russia*, cited in Betts, *Within Walls,* pp. 8–9.
7. Boym, *Common Places*, p. 129.
8. Kalyvas *Logic of Violence,* p. 337.
9. Cited in ibid., p. 361.
10. Garton Ash, *The File*, p. 102.
11. Boym, *Common Places*, p. 143.
12. Betts, *Within Walls,* p. 32.
13. Garton Ash, *The File*, pp. 109, 223.
14. Adam Michnik, *Letters from Prison and Other Essays,* trans. Maya Latynski (Berkeley: University of California Press, 1985), p. 8.
15. Grossman, "The Old Man," in *The Road*, p. 85.
16. Grossman, writing on Poland under the Nazi occupation in "The Old Teacher," in *The Road*, p. 97.
17. Berlin, *Four Essays on Liberty*, p. 165.
18. Betts, *Within Walls*, p. 3.
19. Louis Fiset, *Camp Harmony* (Urbana: University of Illinois Press, 2009), p. 39.
20. Edward Shills, 1956, cited in Victor Navasky, "Naming Names: The Social Costs of McCarthyism," Modern American Poetry, accessed November 10,

2015, http://www.english.illinois.edu/maps/mccarthy/navasky.htm. Eric L. Muller, *American Inquisition: The Hunt for Japanese American Disloyalty in World War II* (Chapel Hill: University of North Carolina Press, 2007), p. 136.

21. The term "betrayal" was applied to some witnesses' testimony as well. Morton Grodzins, *The Loyal and the Disloyal* (Chicago: University of Chicago Press: 1956), p. 232.

22. Muller, *American Inquisition* p. 1.

23. Federal Loyalty-Security Program, Bontecou, cited in Muller, *American Inquisition*, p. 137. The 1950 Internal Security Act took Japanese incarceration as its model and had a "concentration camp" clause that would have permitted mass detention without charges. Allan Wesley Austin, "Loyalty and Concentration Camps in America: The Japanese American Precedent and the Internal Security Act of 1950," in Erica Harth, ed., *Last Witnesses: Reflections on the Wartime Internment of Japanese Americans* (New York: Palgrave, 2001): 253–70.

24. "The Truth about American Muslims," *New York Times,* April 1, 2011, http://www.nytimes.com/2011/04/02/opinion/02sat2.html

25. Paul Howard Takemoto, *Nisei Memories: My Parents Talk about the War Years* (Seattle: University of Washington Press, 2006), p. 200.

26. Yuri Tateishi, cited in Lawson Fusao Inada, ed., *Only What We Could Carry: The Japanese Internment Experience* (Berkeley: California Civil Liberties Project, Heyday Books, 2000), p. 62.

27. Inada introduction to Hiroshi Kashiwagi's "The Betrayal," in Inada, ed., *Only What We Could Carry,* p. 270.

28. Fiset, *Camp Harmony*, pp. 26, 32, 45. For a first-hand report of dealing with the Enemy Control Unit and its "standards," see Minoru Yasui, in John Tateishi, *And Justice for All: An Oral History of the Japanese American Detention Camps* (New York: Random House, 1984), pp. 62–93.

29. Morton Grodzins, *Americans Betrayed* (Chicago: University of Chicago Press, 1949), p. 2.

30. *Personal Justice Denied: Report of the Commission on Wartime Relocation and Internment of Civilians* (Seattle: University of Washington Press, 2011), p. 94.

31. Page Smith, *Democracy on Trial: The Japanese American Evacuation and Relocation in World War II* (New York: Simon and Schuster, 1995), p. 250.

32. Every intelligence service agreed that the indiscriminate focus on ethnic Japanese was unnecessary and wrong; none successfully challenged the Army and the interest groups that had lined up for mass evacuation. *Personal Justice Denied,* ch. 2. Scholars agree that the two men responsible for the policies, Milton Eisenhower and Dillon Myer, were "nonbelievers." Smith, *Democracy on Trial,* p. 219.

33. "Formulaic expressions of 'blood-will-tell racism'" were unconstrained in

the press. John W. Dower, *War without Mercy: Race and Power in the Pacific War* (New York: Pantheon, 1986), p. 80.

34. Cited in ibid., p. 78.
35. General John L. DeWitt, head of the Western Command, cited in *Personal Justice Denied*, p. 66.
36. Cited in Dower, *War without Mercy*, p. 81.
37. *Personal Justice Denied*, p. 27.
38. Mitsuye Yamada, "Legacy of Silence (1)" in Harth, *Last Witnesses*, p. 40.
39. Yoshito Wayne Osaki, in Brian Komei Dempster, ed., *Making Home from War: Stories of Japanese Exile and Resettlement* (Berkeley: Heyday, 2010) p. 103.
40. Julie Otsuka, *When the Emperor Was Divine* (New York: Anchor, 2003), p. 143.
41. Quoted in Valerie Nao Yoshimura, "The Legacy of the Battle of Bruyeres," p. 239.
42. Smith, *Democracy on Trial*, p. 146.
43. Tateishi, *And Justice for All*, pp. 190–91.
44. Fiset, *Camp Harmony* pp. 33, 36.
45. Harth, *Last Witnesses*, p. 285.
46. Otsuka, *When the Emperor Was Divine,* p. 3.
47. Takemoto, *Nisei Memories*, p. 80.
48. Tateishi, *And Justice for All,* p. xix.
49. Patrick S. Hayashi, "Pictures from Camp," in Harth, *Last Witnesses*, p. 141.
50. Families were forced to sell personal property and to agree to any terms. Property stored by the government was often lost or destroyed. Businesses were taken over. Farmers were forced to sell their land, or it was auctioned. Japanese-owned land, which the Farm Security Administration was commissioned to lease on "fair and equitable terms," was neglected, equipment ruined or stolen, tenant operators refused to leave the farms after the war. Morton Grodzins attends to the organized economic interests that benefited from the evacuation and were a force behind the policy in state legislatures and Congress, *Loyal and Disloyal* (Chicago: University of Chicago, 1956), cf. pp. 27ff., 58ff.
51. Otsuka, *When the Emperor Was Divine*, p. 115.
52. Maya Angelou, "I Know Why the Caged Bird Sings," in Inada, ed., *Only What We Could Carry*, pp. 53–54.
53. Smith, *Democracy on Trial*, p. 159; Mary Tsukamoto, p. 9, and Yuri Tateishi, p. 23, in Tateishi, *And Justice for All*.
54. Otsuka, *When the Emperor Was Divine*, pp. 3, 115, 121.
55. Marnie Mueller, "A Daughter's Need to Know," in Harth, *Last Witnesses*, p. 108.
56. Ibid.
57. Otsuka, *When the Emperor Was Divine*, p. 70.

58. All quotes are from Yoshiko Uchida, *Desert Exile: The Uprooting of a Japanese American Family* (Seattle: University of Washington Press, 1982), pp. 76, 96, 133, 75, 123.

59. Otsuka, *When the Emperor Was Divine*, p. 99.

60. Smith, *Democracy on Trial*, p. 162.

61. Havel, "The Power of the Powerless," *Living in Truth*, pp. 54, 42.

62. On organized resistance to the draft at Heart Mountain, see Stephen S. Fugita and Marilyn Fernandez, *Altered Lives, Enduring Community: Japanese Americans Remember Their World War II Incarceration* (Seattle: University of Washington Press, 2004), pp. 92ff.

63. Tateishi, p. 115.

64. Grodzins, *Loyal and Disloyal*, p. 120.

65. Morgan Yamanaka, p. 115, and Harry Ueno, p. 197, in Tateishi, *And Justice for All*.

66. Yohito Wayne Osaki, in *Making Home from War*, pp. 105, 107. The ripest site of conflict was Tule Lake, the segregation center designated for "traditionalists" or those with "national sympathies" for Japan, those who renounced their American citizenship (sometimes in protest or under pressure from fellow internees—"resegregationists"), those who requested repatriation, and those whose answers to the loyalty questionnaire were suspect. Fugita and Fernandez, *Altered Lives,* pp. 56, 57.

67. George F. Brown from his father's papers in "Return to Gila River," in Harth, *Last Witnesses*, p. 118ff.

68. This is a case for puzzling out the moral contours of professional responsibility in wartime. On camp social scientists and the work of Margaret Mead, Gregory Bateson, and others supplying clinical diagnoses, see Dower, *War without Mercy,* p. 130ff.

69. Smith, *Democracy on Trial*, p. 247

70. Otsuka, *When the Emperor Was Divine*, p. 61.

71. Takemoto, *Nisei Memories*, p. 171.

72. Fugita and Fernandez, *Altered Lives*. "Sometimes an indescribably longing for freedom comes over me," he wrote in his memoir. Robert J. Maeda, "Isamu Noguchi: 5–7-A, Poston, Arizona," in Harth, *Last Witnesses*, pp. 153–66. Noguchi, *Isamu Noguchi: A Sculptor's World* (New York: Harper and Row, 1968).

73. Harth, *Last Witnesses*, pp. 195, 197.

74. Muller, *American Inquisition*, p. 145. In prosecuting activist George Ochikubo, evidence consisted of casual comments accumulated and slanted by authorities and by other internees, and in one instance appears to have been wholly manufactured. Pp. 115ff, 130ff. *Ochikubo v. Bonesteel*, 60 F. Supp. 916 (S.D. Cal. 1945), http://law.justia.com/cases/federal/district-courts/FSupp/60/916/1968886/

75. Cited in Uchida, *Desert Exile*, p. 62.

76. Fugita and Fernandez, *Altered Lives,* pp. 10, 108.
77. Florence Ohmura Dobashi, *Making Home from War*, p. 7.
78. Greg Robinson, Forward, to *Making Home from War*, p. ix.
79. Reported in Sato Hashizume, *Making Home from War*, p. 33.
80. Smith, *Democracy on Trial*, p. 399.
81. Otsuka, *When the Emperor Was Divine*, pp. 54, 66, 123, 115.
82. Roth, *American Pastoral*, p. 256.
83. Otsuka, *When the Emperor Was Divine*, p. 134.
84. "Bob Fletcher . . ." Obituary, *New York Times*, June 7, 2013.
85. Hayashi, "Pictures from Camp," in Harth, *Last Witnesses*, p. 151.
86. Chizu Omori, in Harth, *Last Witnesses*, p. 215.
87. Takemoto, *Nisei Memories*, p. 156–57.
88. Ibid., p. 219.
89. Chizu Omori, in Harth, *Last Witnesses*, p. 215.
90. In *Making Home from War*, p. 50.
91. Cited in Fugita and Fernandez, *Altered Lives,* p. 47.
92. The Commission on Wartime Relocation and Internment of Civilians, which issued its 1983 report *Personal Justice Denied*, held twenty days of hearings and took testimony from Japanese Americans as well as officials and others. Introduction, p. 3.
93. Stewart David Ikeda, "Mixing Stories," in Harth, *Last Witnesses*, p. 87.
94. Roth, *American Pastoral*, p. 72.
95. Garton Ash, *The File,* p. 103.
96. Otsuka, *When the Emperor Was Divine*, p. 120.
97. Reported in Martha Minow, *Between Vengeance and Forgiveness: Facing History after Genocide and Mass Violence* (Boston: Beacon Press, 1998), p. 94.
98. Vaclav Havel, "The Power of the Powerless," in *Living in Truth*, p. 100.

## Chapter 8: Killing

1. Albert Camus, *The Rebel* (New York: Vintage, 1956), p. 54.
2. James Cameron, *A Time of Terror: A Survivor's Story* (Baltimore: Black Classics Press, 1982), p. 15.
3. Grossman, "The Old Teacher," in *The Road*, p. 96.
4. Cameron, *A Time of Terror*, p. 113.
5. In other explanations, economists focus on "the resource crunch." Mamdani objects, "there is no *necessary* connection between a drastic reduction in resources and deadly human conflict." Cultural explanations emphasize deeply engrained obedience to authority or a congenital culture of conformity. Mahmood Mamdani, *When Victims Become Killers: Colonialism, Nativism, and the Genocide in Rwanda* (Princeton: Princeton University Press, 2001), pp. 198, 199–200, 195.

6. Ibid., p. 14.

7. As Mamdani writes, "atrocity cannot be its own explanation. Violence cannot be allowed to speak for itself, for violence is not its own meaning," pp. 228–29. *In Killing Neighbors: Webs of Violence in Rwanda* (Ithaca, NY: Cornell University Press, 2009). Lee Ann Fujii argues that in cases of "intimate mass violence" local social relations and recruitment are the propulsion to participation."Killing produced groups and groups produced killing," p. 19.

8. Antony Polonsky and Joanna B. Michlic, eds., *The Neighbors Respond: The Controversy over the Jedwabne Massacre in Poland* (Princeton: Princeton University Press, 2004), p. 412.

9. Glover, *Humanity*, p. 43.

10. Hans Magus Enzensberger, cited in Kalyvas, *The Logic of Violence,* p. 352.

11. Glover, *Humanity*, p. 119.

12. Ibid., p. 408.

13. Emanuel Ringelblum, cited in Polonsky and Michlic, *The Neighbors Respond,* Introduction, p. 4.

14. Glover, *Humanity*, p. 151.

15. Cited in Philip Dray, *At the Hands of Persons Unknown: The Lynching of Black America* (New York: Random House, 2002) p. 17. "Peculiarly American" is W. Fitzhugh Brundage, *Lynching in the New South: Georgia and Virginia, 1880–1930* (Urbana: University of Illinois Press, 1993), p. 3.

16. Orlando Patterson, *Rituals of Blood* (Washington, DC: Civitas Counterpoint, 1998), p. 169.

17. "Crystallizaion," in Cameron, *A Time of Terror,* p. 115. On Cameron's testimony, authorship, and later life as a crusader, see Cynthia Carr, *Our Town: A Heartland Lynching, a Haunted Town, and the Hidden History of White America* (New York: Crown Publishers, 2006), pp. 23, 29, 15. On the authority of Cameron's account: "A lot of [black] people think his book is a lie," p. 345; Carr confirms Cameron's basic story.

18. "Blacks were 'in some cases allowed to police and punish their own.'" Crystal N. Feimster, *Southern Horrors: Women and the Politics of Rape and Lynching* (Cambridge, MA: Harvard University Press, 2009), pp. 102–3.

19. On lynching outside the South, see John D. Bessler, *Legacy of Violence: Lynch Mobs and Executions in Minnesota* (Minneapolis: University of Minnesota Press, 2003). James H. Madison, *A Lynching in the Heartland* (New York: Palgrave, 2001) on Muncie, Indiana.

20. Michael J. Pfeifer, *Rough Justice: Lynching and American Society 1874–1947* (Urbana: University of Illinois Press, 2004), p. 13.

21. The chief data source is the archive of Tuskegee Institute: 4,743 persons were lynched between the earliest date on record, 1882 and 1968; of these, over seventy-two percent were black. Cited in Stephen J. Whitfield, *A Death in the Delta: The Story of Emmett Till* (New York: Free Press, 1988),

p. 5. Tuskegee records showed 3,417 lynchings of blacks and 1,291 of whites through 1944. Dray, *At the Hands of Persons Unknown,* pp. viii, 406, 49. Tuskegee, the NAACP, and the Association of Southern Women for the Prevention of Lynching all collected data since 1882 but the groups had difficulty agreeing on a definition. Marvin Dunn, *The Beast of Florida: A History of Anti-Black Violence* (Gainesville: University Press of Florida, 2013), p. 34. For a recent estimate and project to build markers at lynching sites, see "Lynching as Racial Terrorism," Editorial Board, *New York Times,* February 11, 2015, http://nyti.ms/1AkywZq.

22. "Some of us had shotguns . . . laying under the bushes for several days." Carr, *Our Town,* pp. 46, 123. On the hundreds of "disappeared" African Americans between 1920–1960, see Margaret A. Burnham and Margaret M. Russell, "The Cold Cases of the Jim Crow Era," *New York Times,* August 28, 2015, A-21.

23. On lynching to frighten black voters from the polls, see Bruce E. Baker, "Up Beat Down South: The Death of Emma Hartsell," *Southern Cultures* 9, no. 1 (Spring 2003): 82–91 at 83. On antirepublicanism, see Eric Foner, *Reconstruction: American's Unfinished Revolution 1863–1877* (New York: Harper and Row, 1988): "In effect, the Klan was a military force serving the interests of the Democratic party, the planter class, and all those who desired the restoration of white supremacy," p. 41.

24. Cited in Dray, *At the Hands of Persons Unknown,* p. 5.

25. On the antimodern thesis, see Amy Louise Wood, *Lynching and Spectacles: Witnessing Racial Violence in America 1890–1940* (Chapel Hill: University of North Carolina Press, 2009). This list is not exhaustive.

26. Freed African Americans were cast as the "domestic enemy" of society. Patterson, *Rituals of Blood,* p. 192. On racism, see the great contemporaneous work of Ida Wells-Barnett, *On Lynching* (New York: Humanity Books, 2002).

27. Foner, *Reconstruction,* p. 41.

28. Dray, *At the Hands of Persons Unknown,* pp. 43, 80.

29. Wells-Barnett, *On Lynching,* p. 48.

30. On political insurrection by slaves, Eugene D. Genovese, *Roll, Jordan, Roll: The World the Slaves Made* (New York: Vintage, 1974).

31. Anthony E. Kaye, *Joining Places: Slave Neighborhoods in the Old South* (Chapel Hill: University of North Carolina Press, 2007), p. 119.

32. Brundage, *Lynching in the New South,* p. 34.

33. For categories and examples see ibid., p. 18 ff.; on classical lynching, p. 37.

34. Wells-Barnett, *On Lynching,* pp. 58, 60.

35. Cited in Dray, *At the Hands of Persons Unknown,* p. xi.

36. James R. McGovern, *Anatomy of the Lynching: The Killing of Claude Neal* (Baton Rouge: Louisiana State University Press, 1982), p. 6.

37. Richard Wright cited in Whitfield, *A Death in the Delta,* p. 8.

38. Richard Wright, "Between the World and Me," http://www.americanlynch ing.com/literary-old.html

39. Kalyvas, *Logic of Violence,* p. 332. Just as "asking what causes a civil war is not the same as asking what causes violence within a civil war," ibid., p. 392, asking what causes lynching is not the same as asking what causes the selection of this black boy for lynching.

40. Tuskegee Institute statistics cite the proportions by accusation: over forty-one percent assault, roughly twenty-six percent rape and attempted rape, and in much smaller proportions robbery, theft, and insult to a white person. The twenty-three percent "other" category included disputing with a white man, unpopularity, testifying against a white man, registering to vote, and peeping in a window. Robert A. Gibson, "The Negro Holocaust: Lynching and Race Riots in the United States, 1880–1950": http://www .yale.edu/ynhti/curriculum/units/1979/2/79.02.04.x.html

41. Mary Turner lynched for "unwise remarks," Julie Bucker Armstrong, *Mary Turner and the Memory of Lynching* (Athens: University of Georgia Press, 2011).

42. Slave laws made offensiveness, sauciness, and disobedience grounds for punishment. In *Ex Parte Boylston* in 1847: "Insolence of a slave towards a white person is, in this State, an offence for which he may be tried and punished." Language and deportment of a slave towards a white person, which is inconsistent with the relation between them, and which we denominate insolence, cannot, however, be supposed to have been overlooked . . ." *Ex Parte Boylston*, 2 Strobhart 41 (1847). I am grateful to John Harpham for this citation.

43. Nicholas Lemann, *The Promised Land: The Great Migration and How It Changed America* (New York: Vintage, 1991), p. 36.

44. Lee Ann Fujii observes that members of the same family could behave entirely differently towards neighbors; the wife might steal while the husband helped the family, giving them food. For all we know, she observes, the wife was jealous of the husband's kindness toward them. Personal communication, December 3, 2014.

45. Sharecropping "comprised a system of race relations that was, in its way, just as much a thing apart from the mainstream of American life as slavery had been." Lemann, *The Promised Land,* p. 15.

46. Brundage, *Lynching in the New South,* p. 25.

47. Lemann, *The Promised Land,* pp. 36, 54.

48. Dray, cited in Carr, *Our Town,* p. 52.

49. Cited in Whitfield, *A Death in the Delta,* p. 2. "Political, economic and social equality took on a sexual connotation because of the association of equality with sexual license." Feimster, *Southern Horrors,* p. 49.

50. Feimster, *Southern Horrors,* p. 149.

51. Lemann, *The Promised Land,* p. 27.

52. Martha Gelhorn, "Justice at Night," in *The View from the Ground* (New York: Atlantic Monthly Press, 1988), pp. 5–6.

53. Baker, *This Mob Will Surely Take My Life,* p. 143.

54. See the discussion in Kalyvas, *Logic of Violence,* 142ff.

55. Referring to Israeli soldiers and Palestinians at checkpoints in the West Bank in Oded Na'aman, "The Checkpoint," *Boston Review* (July/August 2012), http://bostonreview.net/world/checkpoint-oded-naaman.

56. Carr citing Cameron, *A Time of Terror,* p. 16.

57. Cameron, *A Time of Terror,* pp. 9, 54, 47.

58. Foner, *Reconstruction,* p. 432.

59. Kalyvas, *Logic of Violence,* p. 132.

60. Cameron, *A Time of Terror,* p. 98.

61. The phrase is Patterson's, *Rituals of Blood,* p. 169.

62. Dray, *At the Hands of Persons Unknown,* p. 12.

63. Armstrong, "Appendix Six: Memorandum for Governor Dorsey from Walter F. White," *Mary Turner,* pp. 212–15.

64. Cameron, *A Time of Terror,* p. 60.

65. Ibid., p. 18.

66. John Cumming, *The Lynching at Corunna* (Mt. Pleasant, MI: Private Press of John Cumming, 1980) p. 35.

67. Brundage, *Lynching in the New South,* p. 43.

68. From "Strange Fruit," Lewis Allan (Abel Meeropol).

69. Glover, *Humanity,* p. 48.

70. Wood suggests that photographs of lynching were collected by African Americans "as tokens of mourning and memory" of particular victims, *Lynching and Spectacles,* p. 208.

71. Wells-Barnett, *On Lynching,* p. 49.

72. Armstrong, "Appendix Six," *Mary Turner,* pp. 212–15.

73. Cumming, *Lynching at Corunna,* pp. 41, 45. Cameron recalls: "Inside the jail . . . the mobsters saw police officers armed with submachine guns, revolvers, shotguns, repeating rifles, and tear gas. Not one piece of this equipment was used . . . Sheriff Campbell had not rescinded his order 'Don't shoot! There are women and children out there.' No officer did." Cameron, *A Time of Terror,* p. 59.

74. Foner, *Reconstruction,* p. 434.

75. Dray, *At the Hands of Persons Unknown,* p. 119.

76. After the lynching of Emmett Till in the 1950s this dialogue is reported between the murderer, acting now as enforcer, and a black witness: "Before leaving, Milam asked Wright if he knew him. Wright said no. Milam then asked his age, and when Wright replied 'sixty-four,' Milam advised him that if he ever did recognize him, he 'wouldn't live to be sixty-five.'" Dray, *At the Hands of Persons Unknown,* p. 424. Despite warnings not to take the stand, Wright did. Reporting for the *New York Post,* Murray Kempton de-

scribed the testimony as "the hardest half hour in the hardest life possible for a human being in these United States." Cited in Whitfield, *A Death in the Delta,* p. 39.

77. Ralph Ellison, "The Birthmark," in *The New Masses,* July 2, 1940, pp. 16–17, http://www.unz.org/Pub/NewMasses-1940jul02–00016

78. Nadezhda Mandelstam, cited in Glover, *Humanity*, p. 274.

79. Hugh Gusterson, "Not All Secrets Are Alike," *Bulletin of Atomic Scientists*, July 23, 2013, http://thebulletin.org/not-all-secrets-are-alike

80. Dray, *At the Hands of Persons Unknown,* p. 42.

81. Ibid., p. 227.

82. Brundage, *Lynching in the New South,* p. 245ff. Public spectacle murders were replaced by "private lynchings," Baker, *This Mob Will Surely Take My Life,* p. 165ff. For example, Dunn, *The Beast of Florida,* on the lynching of Claude Neal in 1934, Reuben Stacey in 1935, and Willie James Howard in 1944, p. 139ff.

83. Wood, *Lynching and Spectacles,* pp. 202, 204, 216.

84. Whitfield, *A Death in the Delta,* p. 27.

85. Ibid., pp. 142–43.

86. Alan Tate, "The Swimmers," http://www.americanlynching.com/literary-old.html

87. Wood draws a connection to the tradition of public executions in which spectators were "central to the rituals of retributive justice," making lynching respectable, *Lynching and Spectacles,* pp. 24, 43.

88. On studying people who did not kill in the Rwanda genocide, Lee Ann Fujii, "Genocide and the Psychology of Perpetrators, Bystanders, and Victims: A Discussion of Ethics in an Age of Terror and Genocide: Identity and Moral Choice," *Perspectives on Politics* 10, no. 2 (June 2012): 415–424 at 417.

89. White women were active in the crowd: they fired at the hanging bodies, kicked, and spit. Feimster, *Southern Horrors*, p. 146.

90. Cameron, *A Time of Terror,* p. 10.

91. Carr, *Our Town,* p. 25.

92. "Administrators, typists, drivers, workmen. . . . who did not kill people but provided necessary back-up. . . . [They] kept their consciences quiet with the thought that their own role was harmless," Glover, *Humanity*, p. 379. The same belief in harmlessness likely applies to lynching.

93. "Thus has lynching become an almost integral part of our national folkways." Cited in Carr, *Our Town,* p. 53. The black press especially represented lynchings as festive events. Feimster, *Southern Horrors*, p. 153.

94. Dray, *At the Hands of Persons Unknown,* pp. 17–18.

95. Gelhorn, "Justice at Night," p. 8.

96. W. H. Auden, "The Shield of Achilles," in *Collected Poems*, ed. Edward Mendelson (London: Faber and Faber, 2007), p. 595.

97. Wood, *Lynching and Spectacles*, p. 4.

98. Carr, *Our Town*, p. 121.

99. Gelhorn, "Justice at Night," p 9.

100. Fujii, "Genocide and the Psychology of Perpetrators, Bystanders, and Victims," p. 417.

101. Mark Twain, "The United States of Lyncherdom," pp. 35–36. http://people .virginia.edu/~sfr/enam482e/lyncherdom.html

102. "Numbing" and "doubling" in Robert Jay Lifton, *The Nazi Doctors: Medical Killing and the Psychology of Genocide* (New York: Basic Books, 1988).

103. Twain, "The United States of Lyncherdom," p. 5.

104. Cameron, *A Time of Terror*, pp. 74–75.

105. Dunn, *The Beast of Florida*, pp. 139–41. In contrast, the Governor, forewarned of the lynching, stayed out of reach, p. 141.

106. Lemann, *The Promised Land*, p. 37.

107. Carr, *Our Town*, pp. 117–18. Lee Ann Fujii observes that apart from the group, on their own, Hutus saved Tutsis where they could and reverted to ordinary ties with their Tutsi neighbors, *Killing Neighbors* (Ithaca, NY: Cornell University Press, 2011), p. 178

108. Lee, *To Kill a Mockingbird* , pp. 204–6

109. Dunn, *The Beast of Florida*, p. 148.

110. On the significance of black neighborhoods for slave rebellion, see Anthony E. Kaye, "Neighborhoods and Nat Turner," *Journal of the Early Republic*, 27 (Winter 2007): 705–20 at 706. Runaway slaves, debtors, and fugitive strangers did not enjoy the solidarity of the neighborhood; they cast suspicion over everyone. See too Genovese, *Roll, Jordan, Roll*, p. 649ff.

111. Feimster, *Southern Horrors*, p. 45. These neighborhoods were also, briefly during Reconstruction, the site of Republican electoral politics. As they were earlier for slave rebellion: "The challenge of slave rebellion was to build on neighborhood solidarities." Kaye, *Joining Places*, p. 217.

112. Lemann, *The Promised Land*, p. 7. Between 1910 and 1970, six and a half million African Americans moved from the South, p. 6.

113. Cameron, *A Time of Terror*, p. 106. I accept that these sentiments seem genuine—not the "etiquette of race relations" under slavery that made "courtesy and self-protective dissembling inseparable," Genovese, *Roll, Jordan, Roll*, p. 610.

114. In 1994 Florida paid reparations to survivors of the Rosewood massacre, Dunn, *The Beast of Florida*, p. 121. On apologies for lynching, see Baker, *This Mob Will Surely Take My Life*, p. 138ff.

115. Quoted in Feimster, *Southern Horrors*, p. 233.

116. Timothy Snyder, *Bloodlands: Europe Between Hitler and Stalin* (New York: Basic Books, 2012).

117. Grossman, "The Hell of Treblinka," in *The Road*, p. 179.

118. Jan T. Gross, *Neighbors* (Princeton: Princeton University Press 2001), pp. 37–38.

119. Marta Kurkowska-Budzan, "My Jedwabne," in Polonsky and Michlic, *The Neighbors Respond*, pp. 202–3. "In personal memories Poles are always in the foreground. The Nazis are the obvious context," p. 204.

120. German authorities permitted the slaughter but did not initiate it; their role was limited to taking pictures. Commentary attributes anti-Semitism in the town to the recent Soviet occupation, and the harm Jews presumably did to Poles by cooperating with the Bolsheviks. "For the Jews, the Soviets were the lesser evil," Polonsky and Michlic, *The Neighbors Respond*, pp. 153, 214.

121. Cited in Maxine D. Jones, "The Rosewood Massacre and the Women Who Survived It," *The Florida Historical Quarterly* 76, no. 2 (Fall 1997): 192–208 at 199.

122. Gross, *Neighbors*, p. 121.

123. Just about every fact and assessment in Gross's account has been examined including the part played by the Germans. The critical literature ranges from Polish apologists to careful historical reconstructions, see Polonsky and Michlic, *The Neighbors Respond*. One report is that German officers tried to save craftsmen, carpenters, and others whose labor was needed; reports are that the Germans "looked with disdain upon the overt bestiality of the Poles," Andrezej Kaczynski, "Burnt Offering" in Polonsky and Michlic, *The Neighbors Respond*, pp. 54–55.

124. Dariusz Stola, "Jedwabne: How was it Possible" in Polonsky and Michlic, *The Neighbors Respond* p. 396

125. Kaczynski in Polonsky and Michlic, *The Neighbors Respond*, p. 52.

126. Maria Kaczynska, "In Memory and Admonition," in Polonsky and Michlic, *The Neighbors Respond*, p. 65.

127. Gross, *Neighbors*, p. 9.

128. Yehuda Bauer, *The Death of the Shtetl* (New Haven: Yale University Press, 2009), pp. 12, 138, 120.

129. Anna Bikont, "We of Jedwabne," in Polonsky and Michlic, *The Neighbors Respond*, p. 276.

130. Gross, *Neighbor*, pp. 84, 37–38, 68, 121, 9. In the Oliner's account, the reason why many rescuers remained silent was to avoid painful confrontations with friends, neighbors, and family; "for most, the reason was their greater concern with the resumption of normalcy," Samuel P. Oliner and Pearl M. Oliner, *The Altrustic Personality: Rescuers of Jews in Nazi Europe* (New York: The Free Press, 1988), pp. 225–26.

131. Miep Gies and Alison Leslie Gold, *Anne Frank Remembered: The Story of*

*the Woman Who Helped to Hide the Frank Family* (New York: Simon and Schuster, 1987), p. 88.

132. More than resonance, the Oliners' study shows that one attribute of the majority of rescuers of Jews was that they lived among them, p. 115.

133. "People look to philosophy for the knockdown argument ... but ethics, being bound up with people, cannot escape soft-edged psychology, all dispositions and tendencies rather than hard universal laws," Glover, *Humanity*, p. 27.

134. Interviews in Kristen Renwick Monroe, *The Heart of Altruism: Perceptions of a Common Humanity* (Princeton: Princeton University Press, 1996), pp. 124, 92.

135. The "human responses" are sympathy and respect, Glover, *Humanity*, p. 22. "Someone decent to other people merely out of self-interested calculation, with no independent inclination towards respect or sympathy, could be said to lack humanity," p. 25.

136. This is what Glover calls the moral resource of "moral identity," p. 27. Joshua Cherniss, "Neither Angel nor Maggot: Adam Michnik on the Ethics of Resistance," paper presented at the Canadian Political Science Association, Montreal, June 2010, on file with the author.

137. Lee Ann Fujii in *Killing Neighbors* interviews some few who refused to be "joiners" in the slaughter of Rwandan Tutsis: "Gustav and Frederic drew firm lines between what they were willing to do and what they were not willing to do. Both had a clear sense of what was right or wrong under any circumstances and both abided by that sense ... even under threat of harm. ... situational exigencies did not override their own personal, moral compass." In an interview Gustave speaks in terms of "no choice": "When I notice someone has bad ways I cannot go near them. Even today, I cannot be friends with people who think like that," p. 169.

138. Monroe, *The Heart of Altruism*, p. 220.

139. Cited in ibid., pp. 158, 117.

140. Cited in ibid., p. 104.

141. Ibid., p. 108.

142. Gies's account opens with the disclaimer, "I am not a hero. I stand at the end of the long, long line of good Dutch people who did what I did or more." P. 11.

143. Monroe, *The Heart of Altruism*, p. 197.

144. Glover, *Humanity*, p. 408.

145. Martin Amis, *The Zone of Interest* (New York: Knopf, 2014), p. 136.

146. Grossman, "The Old Teacher," in *The Road,* p. 112.

147. Albert Camus, *The Plague* (New York: Vintage, 1948), p. 308.

148. The expression is Vivian Gornick's in *Emma Goldman* (New Haven: Yale University Press, 2011), p. 3.

## Chapter 9: Disasters

1. Adam Michnik, "Why You Are Not Signing . . . ," in *Letters from Prison,* trans. Maya Latynski (Berkeley: University of California Press, 1985), p. 8.
2. "Disasters occur when there is a coincidence between natural hazards and conditions of vulnerability." *Perspectives on Social Vulnerability*, ed. Koko Warner, Selected Papers from the First Summer Academy on Social Vulnerability, July 22–28, 2006, Hohenkammer, Germany, p. 74. Kai Erikson classifies an event as disaster if it brings about traumatic reactions (e.g., numbness of spirit, susceptibility to anxiety and rage and depression, a sense of helplessness, and more) in *A New Species of Trouble* (New York: Norton, 1989), pp. 20–21.
3. Rebecca Solnit, *A Paradise Built in Hell: The Extraordinary Communities that Arise in Disaster* (New York: Penguin, 2009), p. 2.
4. William Langewiesche, *American Ground* (New York: Farrar, Straus, and Giroux, 2002), p. 6.
5. Ibid., p. 7.
6. Joseph E. Trainor, Silliam Donner, and Manuel R. Torres, "There for the Storm: Warning, Response, and Rescue among Nonevacuees," in *Learning from Catastrophe: Quick Response Research in the Wake of Hurricane Katrina*, Natural Hazards Center Special Publication #40 (Boulder: Institute for Behavioral Science, University of Colorado at Boulder, 2006), p. 308.
7. Timothy Brezina and Joanne M. Kaufman, "What Really Happened in New Orleans? Estimating the Threat of Violence during the Hurricane Katrina Disaster," *Justice Quarterly* 25, no. 4 (2008): 701–22 at 718.
8. Halvidan Rodriguez, Joseph Trainor, and Enrico L. Quarantelli, "Rising to the Challenge of a Catastrophe: The Emergent and Prosocial Behavior Following Hurricane Katrina," *Annals of the American Academy of Political and Social Sciences*, vol. 604, *Shelter from the Storm: Repairing National Emergency Management System after Hurricane Katrina* (March 2006), pp. 82–101.
9. Erikson, *New Species of Trouble*, pp. 130, 238.
10. Lux Saturnine, in Rebeca Antoine, ed., *Voices Rising: Stories from the Katrina Narrative Project* (New Orleans: UNO Press, 2008), p. 51.
11. Jordan Flaherty, *Floodlines: Community and Resistance from Katrina to the Jena Six* (Chicago: Haymarket Books, 2010), p. 42.
12. Barb Johnson, "Introduction," Rebecca Antoine, ed., *Voices Rising II: More Stories from the Katrina Narrative Project* (New Orleans: UNO Press, 2010), p. 20.
13. Eric Klinenberg, *Heat Wave: A Social Autopsy of Disaster in Chicago* (Chicago: University of Chicago Press, 2002), p. 17.
14. Elaine Scarry, *Thinking in an Emergency* (New York: Norton, 2011), pp. 51ff, 82,

15. Ibid., p. xv.

16. Cited in Trainor et al., "There for the Storm," p. 315.

17. Bryan Realon: Spanish-speaking residents informally organizing evacuation in "Hard Decisions in the Big Easy: Social Capital and Evacuation of New Orleans Area Hispanic Community during Hurricane Katrina," in Koko Warner, ed., *Perspectives on Social Vulnerability*, pp. 72–83.

18. Cited in Brezina and Kaufman, "What Really Happened in New Orleans?," p. 718.

19. Holly Gee, in *Voices Rising II*, p. 37.

20. Lora Crayon and Sabrina Avalos, in *Voices Rising*, pp. 113–14.

21. Solnit, *A Paradise Built in Hell*, p. 237.

22. Stephanie Skinner, in *Voices Rising II*, p. 187.

23. Solnit, *A Paradise Built in Hell,* p. 233.

24. "I knew that something was out of the ordinary when the animals that I have upstairs, the exotics that would be more pure of nature, went into hiding two days before. My big iguana hid in the cabinet in the bathroom . . . It gave you this idea that something very, very serious was going to happen." John T. Martin, in *Voices Rising,* p. 64.

25. Michael Ward Prevost, in *Voices Rising,* p. 237.

26. Glen Kirkland, in *Voices Rising II*, p. 64.

27. Stephanie Skinner, in *Voices Rising II*, p. 187.

28. William James, "On Some Mental Effects of the Earthquake," first published in *Youth's Companion*, June 7, 2006, reprinted from *William James: Writings* (New York: Library of America, 1987): 1215–22 at 1220.

29. Quoted in Solnit, *A Paradise Built in Hell*, p. 4.

30. Cited in Kathleen Koch, *Rising from Katrina: How My Mississippi Town Lost It All and Found What Mattered* (Winston-Salem, NC: John F. Blair: 2010), p. 53.

31. Keith Wagner, in *Voices Rising*, p. 41.

32. James, "On Some Mental Effects of the Earthquake," pp. 1221–22.

33. Solnit, *A Paradise Built in Hell*, p. 209.

34. Erikson, *A New Species of Trouble*, p. 235.

35. Koch, pp. 36–37 .

36. James, "On Some Mental Effects of the Earthquake," p. 1219.

37. Solnit, *A Paradise Built in Hell*, p. 56.

38. Ibid., 55.

39. James, "On Some Mental Effects of the Earthquake," p. 1220.

40. Michael Ward Prevost, *Voices Rising II*, p. 241.

41. Rodriguez et al., p. 91. Uptown, white neighbors organized themselves into a heavily armed group to protect against rumored invading gangs of young black men, p. 92.

42. Margie Stoughton-Pyburn, *Voices Rising II*, p. 312.

43. Scarry, *Thinking in an Emergency,* pp. 7–8, 11–12, 14.

44. Langewiesche, *American Ground*, p. 12.
45. Ibid., p. 94.
46. Pat Evans and Sarah Lewis, "A Reciprocity of Tears," in Amy Koritz and George J. Sanchez, ed., *Civic Engagement in the Wake of Katrina* (Ann Arbor: University of Michigan Press, 2009), p. 55.
47. Koch, p. 60.
48. On the revisionist literature, see Brezina and Kaufman, "What Really Happened in New Orleans?," p. 702.
49. Rodriguez et al., p. 83.
50. Both quotations in Solnit, *A Paradise Built in Hell*, p. 236.
51. Quoted in ibid., p. 242.
52. Scarry, *Thinking in an Emergency*, p. 12.
53. Timothy Garten Ash, "It Always Lies Below," *Guardian,* September 7, 2005, www.guardian.co.uk/world/2005/sep/08/hurricanekatrina.usa6.
54. Robert Jay Lifton, *Death in Life* (Chapel Hill: University of North Carolina Press, 1991), p. 525.
55. Barb Johnson, Introduction, *Voices Rising II*, p. 22.
56. Solnit, *A Paradise Built in Hell*, p. 2.
57. Ibid., p. 305.
58. Ibid., p. 286.
59. Ibid., p. 7.
60. Holly Gee, *Voices Rising*, p. 31.
61. Erikson is emphatic on this point, *A New Species of Trouble*, p. 237.
62. Langewiesche, *American Ground*, p. 10.
63. Donovan Livaccati, *Voices Rising*, p. 96.
64. Julie Otsuka, *When the Emperor Was Divine* (New York: Anchor, 2003), p. 120.
65. Lawrence N. Powell quoted in Koritz and Sanchez, *Civic Engagement in the Wake of Katrina*, p. 11.
66. Glen Kirkland, *Voices Rising*, p. 71.
67. Cited in Solnit, *A Paradise Built in Hell*, p. 195.
68. Philip Abrams on organized care in Britain discusses "Good Neighbours" projects covering a few thousand households, each street with its own "warden" trained in health and welfare services in *Neighbours: The Work of Philip Abrams*, p. 13.
69. This is the thrust of Barbara Herman's "Articulated Beneficence," on file with the author. She uses the example of neighbors: "I'm not that close to my neighbor, but when her house flooded, we all worked pretty hard to save her furniture. On the other hand, I didn't feel called on by neighborliness to buy her a new sofa."
70. Robert Putnam and David Campbell, *American Grace* (New York: Simon and Schuster, 2010), p. 444.
71. "From the perspective of the state, the benefits produced by a nonprofit

puppet theater are as valuable as those produced by a soup kitchen," and "the opportunity cost of virtue falls as one moves up the income scale." B. Weisbrod, "The Pitfalls of Profits," cited in Rob Reich, "A Failure of Philanthropy," *Stanford Social Innovation Review* (Winter 2005): 24–33 at 28–29. Reich proposes tax advantages for programs redressing poverty specifically, p. 33.

72. For some groups political engagement is an unanticipated consequence of their defining activities: nonpolitical associations take up specific political issues and nudge them into public consciousness and onto political agendas. Others are formed from the start as pressure groups, advocacy groups, self-styled public interest groups. Rosenblum, *Membership and Morals.*

73. Charles Lesch and Nancy Rosenblum, "Civil Society and Government," in *The Oxford Handbook of Civil Society* (Oxford: Oxford University Press, 2011).

74. Council on Civil Society, *A Call to Civil Society* (New York: Institute for American Values, 1998), 14. Nancy Burns, Kay Lehman Schlozman, and Sidney Verba, *The Private Roots of Public Action* (Cambridge, MA: Harvard University Press, 2001).

75. Michael Walzer, "The Idea of Civil Society: A Path to Social Reconstruction," *Dissent* 39, no. 2 (Spring 1991): 293–304 at 298.

76. Follett, *The New State,* p. 179.

77. See essays in Koritz and Sanchez, *Civic Engagement in the Wake of Katrina.*

## Chapter 10: Thoreau's Neighbors

1. W. H. Auden, "Thanksgiving for a Habitat."

2. Frost, "Build Soil, a Political Pastoral," p. 297.

3. Berger, *Neighbors,* p. 169.

4. All quotes are from John Cheever, "The Enormous Radio," *New Yorker,* May 17, 1947, p. 28, http://www.newyorker.com/magazine/1947/05/17/the-enormous-radio

5. Philip Roth, "Eli, the Fanatic," in *Goodbye, Columbus and Five Short Stories* (Boston: Houghton Mifflin, 1959): 261–313 at 275–76.

6. Stanley Cavell, *The Senses of Walden* (Chicago: University of Chicago Press, 1981). "This writer is writing a sacred text," p. 14.

7. Thoreau, "Resistance to Civil Government" [retitled "Civil Disobedience"], in *Thoreau: Political Writings,* ed. Nancy L. Rosenblum (Cambridge: Cambridge University Press, 1996), p. 21.

8. Thoreau, *Walden,* p. 92.

9. Ibid., p. 94.

10. Ibid.

11. Ibid., p. 95.

12. Ibid., p. 98.

13. Emerson, "Friendship," Essays 6, in *Essays: First Series* (1841), http://www
    .emersoncentral.com/friendship.htm
14. Thoreau, *Walden*, p. 214.
15. Alexander Nehamas, *The Art of Living* (Berkeley: University of California
    Press, 2000), p. 179.
16. Thoreau, letter to Harrison Blake on August 9, 1850, in *The Writings of
    Henry David Thoreau*, vol. 6, ed. F. B. Sanborn (Boston: Houghton Mifflin,
    1906), pp. 186, 216.
17. Thoreau, *Walden*, p. 219. I leave aside the philosophical question whether
    "be what he was made" is a matter of discovery of some essential "nature"
    or a creative act of self-making.
18. Ibid., p. 14. Compare Montaigne, cited in Nehamas, *Art of Living*: "the peo-
    ple round about" who act well and nobly without ever having learned how,
    p. 115.
19. Alexander Nehamas discusses Socrates, Montaigne, Nietzsche, and Fou-
    cault in *The Art of Living*. Thoreau writes that "economy of living" is syn-
    onymous with philosophy, p. 47.
20. Thoreau, *Walden*, p. 118.
21. Ibid., pp. 16–17.
22. Ibid., p. 89.
23. Ibid., p. 90.
24. See Cavell, *The Senses of Walden*, p. 108, on "nextness," neighboring one-
    self; Charles Anderson, *The Magic Circle of Walden* (New York: Holt,
    Rinehart, and Winston, 1968).
25. Thoreau, *Walden*, p. 94
26. Republic, bk 4, sec. 443d. In Allan Bloom, *The Republic of Plato* (New
    York: Basic Books, 1991), p. 123. "He doesn't let each part in him mind
    other people's business or the three classes in the soul meddle with each
    other, but really sets his own house in good order and rules himself; he ar-
    ranges himself, becomes his own friend, and harmonizes the three parts,
    exactly like three notes in a harmonic scale, lowest, highest and middle."
27. Thoreau, *Walden*, pp. 52–53.
28. Ibid., p. 53.
29. Ibid., p. 55
30. Ibid., p. 54
31. Ibid., p.10.
32. Ibid., p. 53.
33. Ibid., p. 8.
34. Ibid., p. 56.
35. Ibid., p. 94.
36. Ibid., p. 53.
37. Ibid., pp. 53–55.

38. "Plea for Captain John Brown," in *Thoreau*, p. 51.

39. Thoreau, *Walden*, p. 179.

40. For discussion of Thoreau's "socialization of solitude" meant to combat his audience's dread of loneliness, see Greg Conti, "Spectatorial Thinking and Thoreau's Ethic of Solitude," 2009 Critical BA Honors Project, University of Chicago, on file with the author.

41. Thoreau, *Walden*, p. 92. There is no more gory account of war than his "battle of the ants."

42. Ibid., p. 95.

43. "Plea for Captain John Brown," p. 51.

44. Thoreau, *Walden*, p. 10.

45. "All association must be a compromise, and what is worst, the very flower and aroma of the flower of each of the beautiful natures disappears as they approach each other." Emerson, "Friendship."

46. Thoreau, *Walden*, p. 10.

47. Ibid., p. 142.

48. Ralph Ellison, *Invisible Man*, cited in Allen, *Talking to Strangers*, p. 102.

49. Thoreau, *Walden*, p. 65.

50. Ibid., p. 141.

51. Ibid., p. 52.

52. Ibid., p.181.

53. Ibid., p. 165.

54. Ibid., p. 33.

55. Ibid., p. 94.

56. Ibid., p. 217.

57. Ibid., p. 5.

58. Ibid., p. 214

59. This is a theme of Nancy L. Rosenblum, *Another Liberalism: Romanticism and the Reconstruction of Liberal Thought* (Cambridge, MA: Harvard University Press, 1987).

60. Nancy L. Rosenblum, "The Inhibitions of Democracy on Romantic Political Thought: Thoreau's Democratic Individualism," in Thomas Pfau and Robert Gleckner, eds., *The Lessons of Romanticism: A Critical Companion* (Durham: Duke University Press: 1998).

61. *Thoreau,* in Rosenblum, ed., p. 21.

62. Ibid.

63. For analysis of Thoreau on citizenship, see Rosenblum, *Another Liberalism* and Rosenblum, ed., *Thoreau.*

64. *Thoreau,* Rosenblum, ed., p. 1

65. Ibid., p. 13.

66. Ibid., p. 18.

67. Thoreau, *Walden,* p. 219.

## Conclusion

1. Max Weber, *Vocation Lectures*, "Science As a Vocation," "Politics As a Vocation," ed. David S. Owen, Tracy B. Strong, and Rodney Livingstone, (Indianapolis: Hackett, 2004), p. 93. Thanks to Jeffrey Green for bringing this citation to my attention.
2. Ellickson, *Order without Law*, p. 185.
3. This general perspective owes to Michael Walzer, *Spheres of Justice*.
4. The complex elements of moral identity and the often counterintuitive "personal uses of pluralism" are my subject in *Membership and Morals: The Personal Uses of Pluralism in America*. Incongruent associations—hierarchical, authoritarian, sectarian, ruled by the law of the heart not due process of law—are ineradicable and often psychologically and morally valuable.
5. Thoreau, *Walden,* p. 217.
6. Pluralism with respect to a sphere of personal liberty and privacy can be categorized as liberal: my theme in *Another Liberalism.* But prominent elements to "good neighbor": the "we" of self-governing neighbors and reciprocity among "decent folk" cast the die for democratic.
7. Harry Frankfurt proposed this at my Moffett Lecture, Princeton University, March 7, 2013. It has also been suggested that the ethic of neighborliness is on a continuum with the commands of a sort of "weak friendship," a distinction I explore in Chapter 1.
8. See, for example, Harry Boyte, *The Backyard Revolution: Understanding the New Citizen Movement* (Philadelphia: Temple University Press, 1980) and Gerald Frug, "The City as a Legal Concept," 93 *Harv. L. Rev.* 6 (1980): 1057–154.
9. For a critical assessment of this aspiration, see Ilya Somin, "Democracy and Political Ignorance," *Critical Review* 22, nos. 2–3 (2010): 253–79.
10. Charles Sabel, "Dewey, Democracy and Democratic Experimentalism," August 2012, p. 6, paper on file with the author.
11. Follett, *The New State*, pp. 222, 201.
12. Ibid., p. 192.
13. Ibid., p. 217.
14. Ibid., p. 201.
15. Ibid., p. 196.
16. Kay Lehman Schlozman, Sidney Verba, and Henry E. Brady, *The Unheavenly Chorus: Unequal Political Voice and the Broken Promise of American Democracy* (Princeton: Princeton University Press, 2012). We know, too, that neighbors play a part in stimulating voting in particular. Experimental studies suggest that the likelihood of voting increases when subjects are informed that their neighbors voted, or when they are led to believe that

their failure to turn out will be publicized. A sort of shaming appears to be at work. Alan S. Gerber, Donald P. Green, and Christopher W. Larimer, "Social Pressure and Voter Turnout: Evidence from a Large-Scale Field Experiment," *American Political Science Review* 102, no. 1 (2008): 33–48.

17. For a discussion, see Jeffrey Green, "Why Plebeianism," on file with the author.

18. Harry Eckstein provided the early groundwork in social science when he moved away from accounts of the general socioeconomic conditions for democracy and assigned particular weight to congruent authority structures. *The Natural History of Congruence Theory.* Eckstein adds as a reason for congruence, avoiding "role strain." Democratic theorists disagree about where to draw the line between legally mandated and voluntary congruence in civil society or the family, as contests over accommodation of religious practices show.

19. I have paraphrased Elizabeth Anderson, *The Imperative of Integration,* pp. 93, 189.

20. Delbanco, *The Real American Dream,* p. 83.

21. "That is inseparable from 'the human sciences,'" Charles Taylor, "Interpretation and the Science of Man," p. 16.

22. The suggestion has been made that a survey of American attitudes could allow for the falsification of my claims. Better would be in-depth interviews. I appeal here to the evidence of literature and to personal experience.

23. That historical order is part of the interest my quarrel with the logic of congruence thesis holds for political scientists studying contemporary democratic transitions. Whether the democracy of everyday life is a cause or necessary precondition for democratic political development overall is an empirical question outside my scope, as is whether the democracy of everyday life can exist under antidemocratic government.

24. Jonathan Lear, *Radical Hope: Ethics in the Face of Cultural Devastation* (Cambridge, MA: Harvard University Press, 2006), p. 77.

# INDEX